Policy Forum Series – 34

Reforming the Canadian Financial Sector:

Canada in Global Perspective

Editors

Thomas J. Courchene and Edwin H. Neave

JOHN DEUTSCH INSTITUTE FOR
THE STUDY OF ECONOMIC POLICY

ISBN: 0-88911-768-3 (bound)   ISBN: 0-88911-688-1 (pbk.)
© John Deutsch Institute for the Study of Economic Policy
Queen's University, Kingston, Ontario K7L 3N6
Telephone: (613) 545-2294   FAX: (613) 545-6025
Printed and bound in Canada

Canadian Cataloguing in Publication Data

Main entry under title:

Reforming the Canadian financial sector : Canada in
    global perspective

(Policy forum series ; 34)
Proceedings of a conference held at Queen's University,
June 20-21, 1996.
Includes bibliographical references.
ISBN 0-88911-768-3 (bound)   ISBN: 0-88911-688-1 (pbk.)

1. Finance - Canada - Congresses. I. Courchene, Thomas J.,
1940-   . II. Neave, Edwin H. III. John Deutsch Institute
for the Study of Economic Policy. IV. Series.

HG185.C3R43 1997   332'.0971   C97-930078-9

ACKNOWLEDGEMENT

This John Deutsch Policy Forum *Reforming the Canadian Financial Sector: Canada in Global Perspective* is based on a conference which took place in Kingston in June of 1996. The conference was jointly sponsored by the Research Program in Risk Management (Queen's School of Business) and the John Deutsch Institute.

On behalf of Ted Neave (who initially conceived of this conference and volume) and myself, our first debt of gratitude is to the authors who cooperated magnificently in converting their conference speaking notes into formal papers. Very special thanks go also to Sharon Sullivan of the JDI who not only handled the organization of the conference but also orchestrated the production of the final volume.

As is usual for JDI publications, we appreciate the editing of Marilyn Banting and the technical support of the School of Policy Studies Publications Unit. Finally, we gratefully acknowledge the financial support from the SSHRCC (Strategic Research Grants 804-92-0004 and 804-93-0004).

Thomas J. Courchene
Jarislowsky-Deutsch Professor
  of Economic and Financial Policy
and
Director, John Deutsch Institute
March 1997

TABLE OF CONTENTS

Acknowledgement   . . .   iii

Introduction   . . .   1

Session I: New Directions in Canadian Financial Policy

John F. Chant
New Directions in Canadian Financial Policy   . . .   13

Martine Doyon
Reflections on the Federal White Paper   . . .   43

Mark R. Daniels
Comment: An Insurance Perspective   . . .   48

Douglas W. Melville
Comment: A Banking Perspective   . . .   51

Roger Ware
Comment   . . .   56

Session II: Are Capital Markets Internationally Integrated?

Maurice D. Levi
Are Capital Markets Internationally Integrated?   . . .   63

Session III: Financial Regulation in the Global Economy

Randall Morck and Bernard Yeung
Financial Regulation in the Global Economy as Property Rights   . . .   87

Session IV: Canadian Regulatory Challenges

Nick Le Pan
Regulatory Issues: A Look Forward . . . 123

C. Freedman and C. Goodlet
*Large-Value Clearing and Settlement Systems and
Systemic Risk* . . . 133

Session V: Industrial Organization and the Canadian Financial Sector

Harry Hassanwalia
*Financial Sector Industrial Organization — Is Bank
Concentration Anti-Competitive?* . . . 151

John L. Evans
Mergers, Ownership and the Ten Percent Rule: Comments . . . 175

Session VI: A National Securities Commission

Jeffrey G. MacIntosh
A National Securities Commission for Canada? . . . 185

Session VII: Wrap Up

Stephen S. Poloz
Rapporteur's Remarks . . . 243

Annex 1 . . . 249

Annex 2 . . . 275

Contributors

List of Publications

INTRODUCTION

Thomas J. Courchene and Edwin H. Neave

In the annals of Canadian financial-institution regulation, 1997 may well be a watershed. This is the year that the comprehensive 1992 reforms of the Bank Act, the Trust and Loan Companies Act, the Insurance Companies Act and the Cooperative Credit Association Act sunset. To provide guidance for this legislative review, the federal government indicated that it intended to issue a White Paper early in 1996.

This was the backdrop to the June 1996 conference at Queen's and the present volume *Reforming the Canadian Financial Sector: Canada in Global Perspective.* At one level, the role of the conference was to subject the White Paper to constructive evaluation. At a broader level, however, the conference was intended to be a launching pad for some more in-depth analyses of emerging issues in the financial services arena. Thus, the intention was to devote a full evening to assessing the federal White Paper and, on the following day, to direct attention to policy and regulatory challenges in the financial area that need to be addressed as we march towards the millennium.

The only problem with this strategy was that the federal White Paper took a very long time to surface — indeed, it was made public on June 19, 1996, the day before the conference. As a result, two changes were necessary. Most obvious, the focus on the White Paper had to be curtailed. In the event, this was not a major problem since the White Paper itself backed away from most of the emerging issues. Nonetheless, we wish to thank Martine Doyon from the Department of Finance for agreeing, at such short notice, to elaborate on aspects of the White Paper as part of the opening session of the conference and volume. We have also included the core of the White Paper (except for the

1

technical amendments) as an Annex to the volume. This is an appropriate occasion to note that we have also appended Ted Neave's recent C.D. Howe Commentary, *Canadian Financial Regulation: A System in Transition*. This paper served as part of the background material for the conference and represents a complementary approach and analysis to the range of issues addressed by contributions to this volume.

The second change was much more important to the conference and the volume. In recognition of the fact that the White Paper might not appear prior to the conference, John Chant accepted our request to covert his contribution from a commentary on the White Paper to a full-fledged White Paper in its own right. (Actually, Chant refers to his contribution as a "Green Paper".) In any event, we are enormously grateful to John for his signal contribution to the conference and volume.

One final introductory comment. The role of this introduction is to provide a capsule summary of the various contributions. The more challenging task of undertaking an overall integration and assessment of the paper is left in the hands of our competent rapporteur, Steve Poloz.

SESSION I: NEW DIRECTIONS FOR FINANCIAL POLICY

In addition to the earlier-noted elaboration by Martine Doyon of the federal White Paper, the opening session included the impressive *New Directions ...* paper by John Chant and brief commentaries by representatives of the insurers' (Mark Daniels) and bankers' (Douglas Melville) industry associations and by Roger Ware of Queen's Department of Economics. Underpinning Chant's approach to regulation are the following two beliefs: (i) that financial markets have huge potential for innovation and (ii) that it is beyond the capacity of financial regulators to react effectively to this innovation in real time. This leads Chant to argue that we should "avoid a system that relies on intricate regulation, detailed inspection and watchful supervision to be effective". Instead, we should "choose a system that does not make strong demands on the capacity of regulators for its success". This then leads Chant to argue for regulation by "function" rather than for regulation by "institution". In tandem, this perspective provides the backdrop for Chant's proposal for "narrow banks" (which could only hold government securities) not only as an overall approach to financial-institution regulation but as well as a way of cutting through the complications relating to deposit insurance and access to the payments system. The insights from this way to approach financial regulation are valuable even if the narrow-bank approach itself does not see the light of legislative day.

In the second half of this overview paper, Chant focuses on several emerging issues. These are not the typical "headline grabbers" like bank entry into insurance or bank entry into leasing, but rather issues such as access to the payments system, approaches to depositor protection, and ownership rules and the competitiveness of Canadian banks. In each of these areas, Chant offers, as his title indicates, "new directions".

Mark Daniels, head of the CLHIA, is largely supportive of the ideas in Chant's paper. Moreover, Daniels gives reasonably high marks to the process that led to the federal White Paper. In particular, the open and participatory nature of the process has influenced the content of the debate, so much so that the issues on the table now are not the ones that were in the limelight as recently as a year ago.

Doug Melville of the CBA directs most of his comments to consumer's interests and in this context focuses on three looming issues — ownership, rules for financial institutions, delivery channels for services and the need for codes of conduct to evolve as the financial system itself evolves. Underpinning Melville's analysis is the conception (highlighted by anecdotal evidence) of a rapidly evolving financial system and the recognition that in the final analysis it is the consumers of financial products and services, not the institutions or the regulators, that will drive the future.

Roger Ware comes at the future of the financial sector from an industrial organization and competition policy perspective. His comments range across a wide swath of issues: deposit insurance impairs the functioning of competition in terms of weeding out poor-quality institutions; while we worry about not having competing electronic funds networks, the U.S. funds networks are also highly concentrated at the regional level, which means that these electronic funds networks are probably natural monopolies; the regulation of dynamic networks are fraught with challenge because regulators will always be at least one product development behind (which, in turn, supports the two-fold set of regulatory assumptions underlying Chant's paper).

All in all, this session provided an excellent platform both for new ideas and for frameworks to re-examine some of the old chestnuts.

SESSION II: ARE CAPITAL MARKETS INTERNATIONALLY INTEGRATED?

Maurice Levi's contribution "Are Capital Markets Internationally Integrated?" can easily lay claim to be the most analytical paper in the volume. Yet it is also among the most policy relevant, since the implications arising from a world where there is perfect capital mobility is dramatically different from a world of unintegrated capital markets. Levi's starting point contrasts the *assumption* on the part of Robert Mundell in the 1960s that capital mobility was perfect with the *evidence* provided by Martin Feldstein and Charles Horioka that capital markets are not fully integrated. He then addresses the question of why this issue matters for areas such as the efficient global allocation of capital, the ability to reduce risk and the operations of fiscal and monetary policy. In ways that will certainly appeal to those of us who have to pass this information on to students Levi then focuses on the analytics and empirics of the various approaches to testing the degree of capital market integration. His conclusion is that "the evidence on savings-investment correlations, home-country bias, MNC returns, asset price connections to domestic markets, and policy effects on real interest rates make it difficult to believe that capital markets are internationally integrated". Levi then goes on to add two important caveats. First, this is probably what we should expect to find (e.g., any convergence would apply only at the margins, not to the averages). The second is that perhaps we should be glad that integration is imperfect, since it is the existence of "frictions" that lend stability to systems.

SESSION III: FINANCIAL REGULATION IN THE GLOBAL ECONOMY

Randall Morck and Bernard Yeung use the implications of globalization for financial regulation to develop a theoretical framework for the financial sector. Their starting point is that both banking regulation and corporate governance were originally ways "to let trustworthy insiders show themselves to be trustworthy". Over the years this role has been lost sight of and the appearance of the White Paper represents a timely opportunity to restore this focus.

Towards this "back-to-the-basics" end, Morck and Yeung trace aspects of the history of corporate governance, financial regulation and the related roles of property rights and the development of trust. Carried over to the emerging global environment, among the implications they derive and/or recommend are: enhanced and transparent disclosure which will serve both corporate governance and investors' trust; streamlined bankruptcy laws (such as a scheme that would give the firm's creditors common shares on the day bankruptcy was declared and then let them either sell the shares for cash or remain as owners of the firm); an end to ownership restrictions designed to prevent takeovers; boards of directors that are dominated by outside directions, and so on. Provisions such as these will contribute to the underlying goals of financial regulation, which are the fostering of investors' trust in financial investments and making corporate insiders behave in ways that justify this trust.

SESSION IV: REGULATORY CHALLENGES

Session IV was devoted to emerging regulatory issues with OSFI's Nick Le Pan focusing on the regulatory challenges arising from technology along with Bank of Canada's Chuck Freedman and Clive Goodlet addressing recent developments in the areas of large-value clearing and settlement.

Le Pan addresses six looming issues — the necessary shift from quantitative to qualitative regulation or, more generally, the shift from external to internal control structures; how to manage the trade-off between the desire for greater disclosure and the implications of making public negative information with respect to certain institutions; the tricky issues of which jurisdiction regulates various activities in multinational institutions; living with the implications of institutional closure; the perennial issue of "who does what" in the financial arena and, underpinning much of the above, the interaction between technology and the regulator/supervisory function.

Le Pan devotes most of his paper to elaborating upon this technology challenge. Not infrequently, the issues that preoccupy regulators never concern us as consumers. For example, we now have access to smart cards that "contain" cash and can be "filled up" when the existing cash is depleted. For the regulators, however, these cards raise the following issues, among others:

- Are these equivalent to deposits? If so, should the issuing institutions be so regulated?
- Is the cash on these cards "insured"? If so, should the issuing institutions assets be monitored?
- Relatedly, what disclosure rules are necessary and what is the liability of the issuer in the case of failure?

Le Pan concludes his comments with reference to an intriguing notion — implicit "negative disclosure", namely that OSFI could use its web site to list all the regulated and deposit-insured institutions in Canada. If consumers want to deal with anyone else — well, go ahead, but you are on your own hook, as it were.

The paper by Freedman and Goodlet, while closely resembling the actual conference paper presented by Freedman, is reproduced from the *North American Journal of Economics and Finance*. The authors begin by briefly describing the risks that can arise in clearing and settlement systems. Their analysis then turns to the public policy objectives of controlling risk, particularly systemic risk, in clearing and settlement systems as well as alternative proposals to risk containment. The remainder of the paper deals with the manner in which Canada approaches clearing and settlement for large-value payments, for securities and for foreign exchange transactions. In the last section of their paper, Freedman and Goodlet examine the role of the Bank of Canada as the regulator of large-value clearing and settlement systems.

This is not only a major contribution to this volume, it is an important addition to our understanding of the evolving institutional environment of the Canadian and international financial sectors. It is also comforting to realize that the Bank of Canada is in the forefront of addressing these issues, both domestically and at the international level.

SESSION V: INDUSTRIAL ORGANIZATION AND THE FINANCIAL SECTOR

Despite the pretentiousness of the title of session V, the issue addressed by the Royal Bank's Harry Hassanwalia was straightforward: Are banks too big? or in Hassanwalia's terms, is bank concentration anti-competitive? The paper addresses four questions. The first is whether banks are increasing their concentration. Based on a series of tables and charts, Hassanwalia's answer is that concentration is actually decreasing, although the banks have increased their dominance in certain pockets of the financial industry (residential mortgages, consumer credit and securities). The second issue is whether there is a link between bank concentration and lack of competition. Again, Hassanwalia's answer is "no". Indeed, in terms of the above three areas where concentration has increased, this was followed by increased volumes, by improved access for consumers and new product information while at the same time prices generally remained flat or actually declined.

Likewise, Hassanwalia provides evidence to generate a negative response to the third (Do Canadian banks earn excess profits?) and fourth (Are spreads and fees out of line?) questions. Perhaps the most intriguing piece of evidence presented is the fact that smaller countries have more concentrated banking systems. Hassanwalia interprets this as evidence that "there is a gravitation towards some kind of universal size of bank". Phrased differently, if economies of scale require banks to be large, smaller countries will have to have fewer banks with a larger degree of concentration.

John Evans' comment begins by noting, first, that the banks (or some of them) appear to have reversed themselves on the issue of the desirability of the 10% rule and, second, that this conversion is related to the fact that a 10% rule will likely create barriers to potential bank mergers. (And Evans views the Hassanwalia paper as providing an excellent set of arguments for why banks are neither too big nor too concentrated and, therefore, a set of *implicit* arguments for mergers). Evans then devotes the rest of his paper to detailing the problems that the banks will have if they attempt to merge with each other. In effect, they will become so big that they will run the risk of falling into the "public utility" category in terms of government regulation and interference.

SESSION VI: A NATIONAL SECURITIES COMMISSION

Jeffrey MacIntosh provides a comprehensive and timely analysis of the pros and cons relating to the ongoing pressures to transfer provincial securities regulation to a National Securities Commission. While it is fair to say that MacIntosh views a National Securities Commission as an institution whose time has clearly arrived, it is important to note that "National" need not mean federal: it could also mean federal-provincial or interprovincial. MacIntosh documents the chronology of this oft-appearing issue, replete with the complex politics that would accompany any agreement on a national regulator. The paper reviews the potential constitutional bases for both federal and provincial control over securities regulation. MacIntosh then gets to the core of the paper — the pros and cons of a National Securities Commission and the pluses and minuses of alternative ways of constituting such a commission. While, as already noted, the balance of evidence comes down on the side of a National Securities Commission, MacIntosh approaches all of this in an even-handed way, even to the point of noting some of the likely costs that would arise from transferring regulatory authority from the provinces to a National Securities Commission.

As with other contributions to the volume, this paper will be a valuable input to the recently constituted *Task Force on the Future of the Canadian Financial Services Sector.*

SESSION VII: RAPPORTEUR'S COMMENTS

Stephen Poloz performs admirably as the conference rapporteur. He is refreshingly candid in his assessments of the various issues raised by the conference participants. Most readers would probably benefit by reading Poloz prior to tackling the other papers.

By way of concluding this introduction, we cannot do better than fall back on Stephen Poloz's concluding paragraph:

> Indeed, it seems to me that financial institutions' ability to adapt to a changing world is being constrained by the existing regulatory framework, and we are all paying a price for that constraint. Change is the constant that we must shoulder, whether we are consumers, providers or regulators of financial

services. And that suggests the following guiding principle in moving forward: If we are going to invest another four or five years in its development, let us make our next piece of financial services legislation sufficiently dynamic that we do not need a sunset clause.

All will agree that this is a goal that is worthy of our collective endeavours.

Session One
NEW DIRECTIONS IN CANADIAN FINANCIAL POLICY

NEW DIRECTIONS IN CANADIAN FINANCIAL POLICY

John F. Chant, Simon Fraser University

I. SOME FUNDAMENTALS

Before presenting the proposals for my own version of a financial "Green Paper", I will set out my beliefs and understanding of the financial services industry. This will be a motley list, but it will develop the rationale for my proposals. I offer it because it may be more constructive to argue about the beliefs and understanding, rather than the proposals themselves. A change in the list, of course, would produce a different set of proposals.

The Case for Prudential Regulation

Dewatrapont and Tirole (1994) in their recent, thoughtful book, *The Prudential Regulation of Banks* observe that the regulation of financial institutions has been justified in a number of different ways: their participation in the payments system, their high leverage and their ability to transform the quality of assets. They argue, however, that the main motive for regulation is the need to protect small depositors:

> Banks, like most financial and nonfinancial companies, are subject to substantial moral hazard and adverse selection. Investors must therefore perform a variety of monitoring functions: screening, auditing, covenant writing, intervention. Such functions are complex, expensive, and time-consuming. Furthermore their exercise is a "natural monopoly" in that their

duplication by several parties is technically wasteful. Bank debt is primarily held by small depositors. Such depositors are often unsophisticated, in that they are unable to understand the intricacies of balance and off-balance sheet activities. More fundamentally the thousands or hundreds of thousands of customers of a bank have little individual incentive to perform the various monitoring functions. This free-riding gives rise to a need for private or public representatives of depositors. We call this the *representation hypothesis.* (pp. 31-32)

While this is stated more precisely and elegantly here, there are strands of the same approach in my Bank of Canada Technical Report, *Regulation of Financial Institutions: A Functional Approach* (1987). There I called it the efficiency approach to regulation.

The *representation hypothesis* provides a general rationale for the regulation of the intermediary function of financial institutions. Different types of regulation may be appropriate for different types of intermediation. The issuing of fixed money claims such as deposits may require different regulations than the issue of variable value claims such as mutual fund shares. The issuing of claims against a portfolio of non-marketable assets requires different treatment than claims against a portfolio of liquid, marketable assets. Intermediation is not the only function of financial institutions that requires regulation. Insurance and the underwriting of securities both raise the same issues of representation. For other reasons, clearing and settlement systems associated with the supply of payments services also require regulation.

The efficiency approach provides insight into the apparent conflict for regulators between soundness and efficiency. The efficient working of the financial system requires customers to have enough faith in financial institutions that they will entrust their funds to them. There need not be any inherent conflict between soundness and efficiency. The two can be mutually supportive. This does not mean that all measures taken in the name of soundness are consistent with efficiency. Rather, some regulation directed towards soundness may be needed to assure the efficient operation of financial institutions and markets.

Appropriate Approach to Regulation

The *representation hypothesis* establishes a reason for regulation but does not by itself establish the appropriate means. The important thing about financial institutions is what they do. Thus, regulation should be based on functions that financial institutions perform and not their institutional status. Merton puts the choice very clearly:

> One perspective takes as given the existing institutional structure of financial intermediaries, and views the objective of public policy as helping institutions currently in place to survive and flourish. ... An alternative to this institutional perspective is the functional perspective that takes as given the economic functions performed by financial intermediaries, and asks what is the best institutional structure to perform these functions. In contrast to the institutional perspective, this functional perspective does not posit that existing institutions, whether operating or regulatory, will necessarily be preserved. Instead, its structure rests on two basic premises: 1) financial functions are more stable than financial institutions — that is, functions change less over time and vary less across geo-political boundaries; and 2) competition will cause the changes in institutional structure to evolve toward greater efficiency in the performance of the financial system. (1990, p. 3)

The application of functional regulation to the financial system raises two questions. First, which functions of the financial system pose problems that require regulation? Second, what types of regulation are appropriate to the needs of each function?

This approach can be compared with the expression, "a level playing field" so prominent in discussions of financial regulation in whose name many travesties have been committed. I see nothing wrong with a brain surgeon caring for his family's garden. The reverse — a gardener performing surgery — leaves me more than uncomfortable. Too often, the level playing field is interpreted to mean if you can do what I do, I should be able to do what you do.[1] A level paying field should mean that the same rules are applied to all those seeking to perform a given activity.

The Bank Act has never defined banking. From the perspective of the functional approach, it may be just as well. The functional approach views banks

---

[1]This point applies, for example, to the requirement for reciprocal treatment for the entry of foreign banks. If we are concerned about the effectiveness of our banking system, we should only ask whether a foreign bank can make a contribution. Our prime concern should not be whether the banking authorities in that country mistreat their public.

as institutions that perform a collection of activities. Some functions, such as the payments function tend to be more identified with banks than other institutions. Another function, the transformation of risky non-marketable claims into fixed value deposits, also is identified closely with banking. But these functions are also carried on by institutions other than banks. Moreover, innovation and technical change gives no assurance that banks will continue to be the dominant suppliers of these services.

The bank lending function differs from institutions that hold marketable securities. Banks and other institutions that perform this type of lending must devote resources to assessment, monitoring and supervision to shape the risks of non-marketable securities whose value is difficult to determine. Information is the stock-in-trade for this type of active intermediation.

The Limits to Regulation[2]

The regulators of financial institutions face an inherent dilemma. Banks and other financial institutions specialize in the collection, interpretation and assessment of information. It is their efficiency in this activity that allows them to collect funds from one group and direct these funds to use by others. But the information advantages of financial institutions creates a problem for their supervision and regulation. To judge the condition of a financial institution, any regulator must duplicate to some degree the institution's own efforts in interpreting and assessing the information.[3] Unless they do so, regulators will have less information than the management of the institutions they regulate.[4]

---

[2]This section draws on my statement to the Senate Committee on Banking, Trade and Commerce (1995b) and my *Policy Options* paper (1995a).

[3]John Palmer, Superintendent of Financial Institutions, makes much the same point in a speech to the Canadian and Empire Clubs, stating that the only way that a Barings-like derivatives disaster "can't happen here is to post teams of derivatives experts on a 24-hour basis in every trading room of every Canadian financial institution." Address to the Joint Meeting of the Canadian Club and the Empire Club, April 7, 1995 (www.osfi-bsif.gc.ca/empire.htm).

[4]The problems at Barings and Daiwa suggest that even that amount of information would not be sufficient for effective regulation.

The continual failures through the 1980s have been interpreted to imply that the existing supervisory and inspection procedures were inadequate for identifying troubled institutions sufficiently early that their failure could be forestalled or the losses limited to just the shareholders and uninsured creditors. A move towards more comprehensive regulation becomes understandable in light of these failures. Many believe that more and better information could give early warnings of problems and allow greater scope for overcoming them and turning troubled institutions around.

Expanding the information available to the regulator and enhancing its powers is one path for protecting against future failures. Experience elsewhere with more comprehensive regulation is not encouraging. U.S. authorities historically have intervened more in their approach to the regulation of their financial institutions than we have in Canada. Their experience suggests that greater emphasis on inspection and supervision failed to prevent regulators from being caught off-guard by crises in financial institutions. Indeed, the collapse of the saving and loan industry dwarfs anything that we have experienced in Canada. Similarly, the losses suffered by the CDIC in the past should caution us about depending on closer surveillance through inspection and supervision to provide us with an effective "early warning" system. Too frequently the failures, and the magnitude of the eventual losses, appear to have taken both the financial community and the regulators by surprise.

I draw a lesson with respect to the approach that should be taken to regulation. We should avoid a system that relies on intricate regulation, detailed inspection and watchful supervision to be effective. Rather we should choose a system that does not make strong demands on the capacity of regulators for its success.

One final observation about regulation. Regulation deals with risk, but with a particular type of risk that is difficult to assess. It deals with the infrequent event. As Merton's (1977) approach to the pricing of deposit insurance showed, financial regulation deals with the tail of the distribution. Normal experience provides little guide to the knowledge needed for regulation. This provides another reason for not being complacent about the absence of failures in the recent past. It may be a reflection of our strengthened system of oversight. It may also be a consequence of the relative stability of our economy over the past three or four years.

The Success of Different Types of Financial Systems

Financial systems differ. Not only are there substantial differences between financial systems in market economies and controlled economies, but the differences that exist between the systems in market economies are just as great. Perhaps the most significant differences can be found in the relationship between the financial and commercial sectors — Germany and Japan both have close ties between commerce and finance.

It is an interesting academic question as to which type of system performs better. It may also be unanswerable. But it is not a practical question, at least for countries such as Canada that have long established financial traditions and institutions. We may have had the choice of different financial systems at one time. The transition from one type of financial system to another involves more complicated issues than the initial choice of a system. These issues go well beyond the questions of regulation to those of the workings of the whole system of corporate governance and management. A system where close links exist between the banking and commercial sector requires a completely different form of regulation than our system. If changes were made in these dimensions, many other aspects of Canada's financial market policy would need to be reconsidered and modified.

The adaptation of the regulatory system to such a different approach would not be easy. The required changes will make those needed to deal with deposit insurance seem trivial. The Economic Council of Canada (1976, p. 60) spelled out the problems of moral hazard of deposit insurance as early as 1975. It took costly failures to change the system incrementally, and indeed some of the changes went the wrong way.[5] I am pessimistic about our ability to introduce in a timely way the changes that would be required to our system of regulation if we changed our approach to the financial system.

The Problems of a Small Country

The problems of a small country and the solutions to these problems will be very different from those of a large country. This is amply illustrated by the

---

[5]For example, deposit-insurance coverage was raised from $20,000 to $60,000 in response to the wave of failures in the early 1980s.

Canadian payments system. Here an institution excluded from the system has no alternative means for offering payments services to its members. A payments network dominated by a handful of large banks would be less a problem in the United States since the Americans already have a number of different payments networks. A financial institution excluded from any particular network still has a choice among others.

The size of the market and the structure of the financial system means that Canadians have to be more concerned about the concentration of power than many other countries.[6] This concern magnifies if we continue to hold that a Canadian presence, indeed a majority presence, remains an objective of policy. A concentrated, bank-dominated financial system will shape the workings of the rest of our economic system.[7]

Many argue that these concerns over market power are unfounded and can be allayed by the evidence of empirical studies such as those by Shaffer (1993), and Nathan and Neave (1989) that suggest that the Canadian banking system behaves competitively. These studies should be commended for tackling difficult issues. Nevertheless, between them they have problems. They focus on institutions rather than markets, they may not be properly specified, they embody questionable results on key relationships, and may imply unsustainable behaviour.[8]

II. AN IDEAL SYSTEM OF REGULATION

My ideal system comes from two beliefs. First, financial markets have huge potential for innovation which changes the form of financial activity in

---

[6]Saunders and Walter (1994) discuss the problem of concentration of political power in relation to universal banks. As a counter argument, they suggest that the root of the problem may lie in the political process itself. Though this may be true, it may be easier to prevent the problem from growing than to remedy the political problem.

[7]See Roe (1994) for a discussion of this point.

[8]See Booth (1996, pp. 43-44) for criticisms of these studies.

innovative ways. Second, it is beyond the capacity of financial regulators to react effectively to innovation and other changes in financial markets. This makes it beside the point whether all, most or some financial innovation contributes to the efficiency of markets. My ideal prescription is based more on my pessimism with respect to the contribution of regulation than on my optimism about market forces in financial markets.

An ideal system of financial regulation must meet a number of standards. First, following the representation approach to regulation, the system must have a safe asset for those depositors for whom the monitoring and scrutiny of financial institutions is too costly. Second, government should not guarantee risks that it cannot control. Third, as much as possible, government's role in regulation should be limited to assuring high levels of disclosure and the veracity of this disclosure.

Government's role should be restricted to creating a framework within which financial institutions operate. The ideal system will have government involvement in some way in all banking, insurance, underwriting and trading. I will discuss only the elements for banking as follows:

- narrow banks that have government guarantees;
- intermediary banks that face minimal regulation;
- government participation in clearing and settlement systems.

Narrow Banks

A central element of my ideal system is a type of narrow bank that provides the safe asset in the system. Its deposits are the only financial instrument that will have a government guarantee. The narrow banks hold only government securities that match the maturity of its claims. By holding such a portfolio, narrow banks face neither market risk nor credit risk. The composition of narrow banks' assets, of course, makes the government guarantee redundant.

The narrow-bank proposal overcomes one of the shortcomings of the present system of deposit insurance. People wishing to hold safe assets should not expect to receive returns comparable to those on risky assets. Unlike the present system of deposit insurance, the narrow-bank proposal confronts depositors with the costs of holding a safe asset.

Narrow banks can participate in the payments system, but they need not. Nor do all deposits at narrow banks need to be payments deposits. Indeed narrow banks may offer any maturity of deposit provided that the deposit is matched by government securities of the same maturity. Given the presence of indexed government bonds, the narrow banks can also offer indexed deposits.

The portfolio requirement for narrow banks reduces the need for other regulation. There is no need for ownership restrictions. Narrow banks can be owned totally by one individual or widely held. They can also be owned by other financial institutions or commercial enterprises. With their portfolio limited to specific government securities, the usual reasons for regulation of financial institutions — prudential concerns, avoidance of conflicts of interest, etc. — do not apply. Nevertheless, narrow banks must be inspected regularly to ensure that their portfolios conform to their asset-holding requirements.

Left-Over Banks[9]

In addition to the narrow banks, there would be provision for other deposit-taking intermediaries, left-over or LOB banks. Deposits at these intermediaries would not be protected by deposit insurance in any way. Indeed, the government should be explicitly prohibited from rescuing these institutions. The absence of deposit insurance would not mean the absence of a regulatory role for government. The government involvement could be restricted to assuring adequate disclosure. With respect to this type of institution, James Tobin declared that

> If there were a clear and clean line between the two kinds of intermediary activity, *caveat emptor* could apply to the uninsured and less regulated business, where banks and depository institutions would be vigorously competing with each other and other market participants. (1986, p. 39)

---

[9]I was going to use rest-of-banks as in rest-of-Canada, but had second thoughts about using the acronym ROB in the case of banks.

Payments System

The government must also set the rules for the payments system. It is important for the integrity of the payments system that participating institutions be assured that they receive the promised value for claims that they have accepted from other members. While private arrangements among payments institutions might assure this condition, there is a tension between setting necessary technical standards and excluding possible competitors.

Payments systems should be designed to assure that the failure of one institution does not impose losses on its clearing and settlement partners. All participants in the system should be required to meet a common set of standards that reflect the requirements of the payments system's integrity. This could be achieved by some arrangement of gross settlement in real time together with credit limits supported by collateral requirements. The only criteria determining whether institutions can participate in the payments system should be whether they meet these standards. It should be up to a business itself to determine whether participation in the payments system contributes to its activities.

There are several reasons for allowing institutions other than narrow banks to participate in the payments system, in contrast with other narrow-banking proposals. First, monetary history consists of a succession of episodes where new monies have challenged the primacy of existing monies. These episodes suggest that efforts to suppress the development of new monies outside the current framework will prove futile. Allowing others than narrow banks to participate in clearing and settlement arrangements will encourage the evolution to take place within the payments system. Second, history also suggests that new monies arise because they offer efficiencies in some transactions over existing monies. Attempts to suppress them are not only futile, but misguided from an efficiency standpoint.

III. THE 1997 REFORMS: BUILDING ON THE CURRENT SYSTEM

The issues for the 1997 reforms that I am going to discuss are not the ones that have grabbed the headlines such as bank entry into insurance sales and auto

22

leasing or the possibility of a national securities commission. I can understand the appeal of the headline grabbers. They have immediacy and major players have lined up on each side. In the course of events, the headline grabbers will undoubtedly have some impact. But I believe the issues I have chosen have much greater significance for the future efficiency and health of the Canadian financial system. These issues are (i) participation in the payments system, (ii) the arrangements for depositor protection, and (iii) ownership rules and the competitiveness of Canadian banks. Other issues that I would have liked to discuss but did not for lack of time include the treatment of foreign banks and the limits to investments of financial institutions in related activities, the so-called downstream ownership limits.

Payments System Issues

Reform of the payments system occupies a high place on my list of priorities. It was said at a recent conference that Canada has the most efficient paper-based payments system in the world. I was impressed. This sounds like high praise. I have now discovered that may be deceiving. As Table 1 shows, Canada has few competitors vying for this honour. It lags well behind other G-10 countries in the development of paperless payments systems.[10]

For too long, the Canadian payments system remained under the control of the Canadian Banker's Association. The association's rules prohibited banks' competitors from participating in the payments system and its governance on the same basis as the chartered banks. Transfer of the clearing system to the Canadian Payments Association created an opportunity for developing the system's technology that turned out to be frustrated. Instead, the chartered banks devoted their energies to developing the Interac system, first to link their ATMs and later to develop an EFT/POS payment system. Quite under-standably, without the commitment of the banks, the Canadian Payments Association did not succeed in its mandate for the development of the payments system. The Interac Association echoed the pre-CPA payments arrangements where the banks were in control.

---

[10]As Chuck Freedman pointed out (in conversation with the author), Canada may have been able to delay its move towards electronic payments because of the efficiency of its paper-based system.

**Table 1: Use of Paper-Based Payments Instruments
(by value of transactions)**

	%
Belgium	18.0
Canada	97.0
France	72.0
Germany	43.0
Italy	27.0
Japan	8.0
Netherlands	.4
Sweden	10.0
Switzerland	.1
United Kingdom	2.0
United States	13.0

Source: Bank for International Settlements (1993).

The payments system does not consist of a single monolithic element. Rather as Quigley (1996) has explained in a recent paper, it is made up of four distinct components:

1. instructions for the transfer of value — traditionally sent through cheques, but increasingly taking place through various types of credit and debit cards and point-of-sale and large-value electronic transfers,
2. clearing systems for the receipt and processing of these instructions for the transfer of value,
3. settlement systems through which instructions are sent for the transfer of value between settlement accounts held by individual banks at the central bank, and

4. settlement accounts at the central bank where individual clearing institutions hold the funds used to make the ultimate settlement.

Each of these components has different technical requirements for its functions to be fulfilled. All involve a large number of participants interacting with each other. This interaction requires common standards so that participants do not impose costs on other participants. The first three functions are signalling functions. In these cases, the common concern should be the quality of the signal transmitted by participants. The final function, settlement, is most crucial to the working of the process. Participants must be able to meet the claims made upon them resulting from payments made through the system by their customers. The formulation of standards for signalling and especially settlement is not an easy task. But to function at all, any system must have clearly defined standards.

Participation in the two elements of the payments system, the Canadian Payments Association and Interac, is now determined by an institution's status. Membership in the CPA is restricted to banks, trust companies and credit unions, whereas charter membership in Interac is confined, with one exception, to banks.

The issue of access to the payments system will be at the centre of the debate on the 1997 reforms. Insurance companies, investment dealers and others argue that their participation in the payments system has been unduly restricted. They also maintain that the development of the system has not kept up with changing technology and customers' needs. Though the 1992 reforms opened up one avenue of access through the establishment of a banking subsidiary, this alternative appears to be unduly costly.

The establishment of the CPA in 1980 extended direct membership in the system from banks to credit unions and trust and loan companies. The consent order in the Interac case proposes extending membership in Interac to these same institutions. At present, other institutions — investment dealers and insurance companies — are seeking to become participants in the system.

Neil Quigley (1996) argues that there is a conflict between the monopoly powers provided to the CPA and its mandate for the development of the payments system. He maintains that the incentives of the incumbents are skewed towards increasing barriers to entry rather than reducing them. Legitimate concerns about prudential standards and stability of the system can be extended to protect monopoly privileges. As a result, he worries about granting extended payments powers to institutions by legislation. He fears that it may lead to the continuation of the CPA with life insurers, or whatever the new set of entrants, added to the list.

Quigley proposes that the Bank of Canada should determine which institutions can hold settlement accounts subject to the following criteria:

- their need for access to the payments facility in order to carry on their business,
- legislative authority to undertake business that involves the transfer of value,
- the technical capacity to manage a clearing business, and
- the ability to meet minimum prudential standards.

These proposals, though in the right direction, still show an undue concern with institutional status: potential members must have legislative authority to undertake payments activities. They also give inadequate recognition to the different elements of the payments system. Some businesses may wish to participate in one or several of the activities. Quigley's standards impose requirements intended for the entire process to each of its component parts.

A functional approach seems particularly appropriate for governing access to the payments system. Rules for access should be determined for each of the components of the system. Participation in the signalling functions should require that participants be able to provide signals that meet the technical standards of the system. Participation in the settlement function requires that the participants establish arrangements for the settlement of their claims to others in the payments system. Determination of need to participate in the payments system should be left to the institution itself.

Quigley's second criterion poses a bigger problem. Should access to the payments system be available only to those who have legislative authority to undertake business that involves the transfer of value? As we know, the payments system has been characterized by many innovations and by fast changing technology. It is better not to anticipate how the technology evolves, but to provide a system that avoids unnecessary obstacles to new players. We should limit the requirements to the technical and prudential standards necessary for the integrity of the system.

I have two final comments on the payments system.

Quigley favours having the Bank of Canada determine eligibility to participate in the payments system. The Bank already has other important responsibilities. I would prefer that all aspects of the payments system — its future development and eligibility rules — be assigned to an agency with these as its sole responsibilities. This step will provide a needed accountability for the future development of the system.

Any close observer of the payments system should have a sense of déjà vu. The development of e-money — the electronic purse or the smart card — seems to be following the path of the cheque payment system under the CPA and the electronic payments system under Interac. In both cases, legitimate concerns about prudential standards and stability of the system were extended to discourage competition from outsiders.

The electronic purse exhibits the same network characteristics as the other elements of the payments system. Others must accept the e-money issued by any supplier for it to be of any use to the supplier's customers. The problem of exclusion will be potentially as great as for the CPA and Interac. This problem could be prevented by giving the new agency the mandate for developing the standards for the Canadian system of e-money.

Deposit Insurance

Reform of deposit insurance should be given high priority in the 1997 review. Despite the unexpectedly large number of failures though the 1980s, the arrangements for deposit insurance have remained virtually unchanged. Some steps have been taken to increase surveillance and control. The powers of the regulators have been enhanced and greater resources have been directed towards the supervision and inspection of financial institutions. Still, the failure to reform deposit insurance has been particularly surprising in light of the continual problems with respect to soundness. The recent lull in troubled institutions may be nothing more than the consequence of the steady performance of the economy.

The Department of Finance presented a proposal for reforming deposit insurance in 1995. It included measures to strengthen intervention policy with respect to failed institutions together with modifications to the system of deposit insurance. The intervention policy consists of three elements: (i) a legislated mandate for the Office of the Superintendent of Financial Institutions to make its intentions clear to market participants, (ii) a more transparent system of intervention, and (iii) changes in procedures for closing troubled financial institutions.

The major proposal for deposit insurance calls for the introduction of risk-based premiums.[11] While the details of the scheme have not been released, the document suggests a system similar to the one introduced in the United States in 1993 under which premiums range from 0.23% of insured deposits for a healthy, well-capitalized institution to 0.31% for a troubled, less than adequately capitalized, institution.

Variable premiums for deposit insurance would restore market pressures on financial institutions. Still, critics of risk-rated deposit insurance emphasize the difficulties in setting appropriate rates, though the inability to measure financial risks precisely has not inhibited risk-rating elsewhere. Investors and rating agencies continually judge the qualities of corporate bonds using a scaled system of assessment. Nevertheless, concerns about the basis for setting the rates for risk-rated deposit insurance are real. The setting of rates requires the same type of information that is needed under the present system of regulation to identify problem institutions. To gain this information, regulators will have to oversee institutions intensively. They will be required to differentiate among institutions, even though particular institutions will not be facing a threat of immediate failure. They will also face strong pressures to maintain a favourable premium for an institution.

I have proposed the introduction of narrow banks as part of my ideal system of financial regulation. I recognize that such a system probably cannot be introduced all at once under current circumstances. On the other hand, are there reforms that could be made that would start us towards a system with narrow banking?

---

[11]The risk-rating of deposit insurance premiums was first recommended in Canada by the Economic Council of Canada in its report *Efficiency and Regulation* (1976).

Of the two alternatives — risk-rated premiums and co-insurance — that have been proposed, co-insurance may be the more promising approach. With the initiation of co-insurance, depositors could be given the option of a fully insured deposit subject to the same requirements as a narrow-bank deposit or a degree of co-insurance on a deposit under current rules. The degree of co-insurance on deposits could be increased over time until the coverage is completely phased out. Then consumers could have two choices: fully guaranteed deposits at narrow banks and uninsured deposits at LOB banks.

To me, the proposal has one significant appeal. It provides a transition towards an ideal (or at least my ideal) system of financial regulation. It also should have an appeal to the advocates of co-insurance. The proposal overcomes the criticism that co-insurance forces depositors to assess the soundness of financial institutions, a task found daunting for regulators.

Ownership Rules and the Competitiveness of Banks

The most significant issue likely to arise in the 1997 review is one that I hoped would be left out of the White Paper, namely ownership provisions. This issue, surprisingly, was never raised before the Senate Banking Committee last year, even though participants took the opportunity to suggest items for review. Banks and others now argue that our major banks may be too small to compete effectively with international banking players.[12] Further, they suggest that the 10% ownership rules that limit any party's investment in a Schedule I bank contributes to the problem because it reduces the banks' options for raising funds. Commercial interests are ruled out as significant investors as a consequence. In addition, the limit prevents a takeover attempt from either commercial interests or foreign banks. These restrictions on equity investments lower the demand for bank shares, raising the banks' cost of capital. A higher cost of funding makes it more difficult for the Canadian banks to compete with other international banks.

Before turning to possible remedies for this problem, it is useful to consider the evidence for these claims about costs of funds and competitiveness. Do the

---

[12]See, for example, *The Globe and Mail* (1996); Cook (1996); and Royal Bank Financial Group (1996).

ownership rules impose excessive costs of finance on Canadian banks? Have the Canadian banks been unable to compete with other international players?

Cost of Funding

Do Canadian banks face a higher cost of capital than other international banks? Certainly some evidence suggests that they do. Canadian banks have both lower price-earnings (P/E) ratios and lower market-to-book value (M/B) ratios than most other large international banks. To the extent that these comparisons are valid, new equity issues would dilute the interests of existing shareholders more for Canadian banks than others, making the cost of additional capital higher for them.[13]

Another indicator of a higher cost of funds for Canadian banks could be found in their international credit ratings. A higher cost of equity finance would be expected to lead Canadian banks to rely on debt financing to a greater degree than other banks. In turn, their higher debt-equity ratios could be expected to produce lower credit ratings relative to other banks which do not face the same constraints on equity finance.

Table 2 presents the FT Composite Credit Ratings for 1995 for the 200 largest banks classified by country. This measure reflects the average quality rating assigned to a bank's debt by major credit-rating services. The measure runs from 1 (high) to 10 (low). As the table shows, the average rating for the five largest Canadian banks was 3.3 as of April 1, 1995. This compares well with the other large banks. Only 23 of the 81 banks with ratings were ranked higher

---

[13]Like most international banking comparisons, there is much ambiguity in this case because of different approaches to accounting. Some countries, for example, have accounting provisions that provide for liberal "hidden reserves". These provisions tend to understate both book value and earnings, raising both M/B and P/E ratios. Preliminary examination suggests that the countries with the highest M/B ratios and the highest P/E ratios also have the smallest net interest spreads. This finding would be consistent with the use of hidden reserves.

If taken at face value, these differences in the indicated spread for France and Japan would by themselves do much to explain the decreased relative size of Canadian banks. They suggest that French and Japanese banks were much more efficient than Canadian banks.

Table 2: FT Composite Credit Ratings of 100 Largest Banks (1995)

				Country			
FT Rating	*Canada*	*France*	*Germany*	*Japan*	*U.K.*	*U.S.*	*Other*
below 2		1	5			1	3
2 to 2.99	1			2			
3 to 3.29	1			2	3	2	4
3.3 to 3.99	3	2		4			4
4 to 4.99				8		3	5
5 to 5.99		1		6		7	2
above 6		1		8		4	3

Note: Average for largest five Canadian banks = 3.3

Source: Derived from *The Banker*, July 1995.

than the average of the five largest Canadian banks. Moreover, only 2 of 28 Japanese banks and 3 of 17 U.S. banks have higher ratings than Canadian banks.

The Competitive Position of the Canadian Banks

The ability of Canadian banks to compete with other international banks is difficult to measure directly. This study examines two types of evidence. First, it reviews the literature on economies of scale and scope for large banks. If such economies can be found to be present for the Canadian banks' size range and beyond, this finding would add support to the view that Canadian banks find it difficult to compete internationally. Second, the study follows the lead of Saunders and Walter and compares the growth rates of large banks to determine whether the largest world banks have been able to expand their business more successfully than Canadian banks.

Economies of Scope and Scale

The literature on economies of scale and scope in banking has focused mainly on the experience of U.S. banks, primarily because of the availability of suitable data. These studies, which concentrate on smaller sized banks, suggest that economies of scale are exhausted at low levels of bank assets. Only recently has attention turned to economies of scale in large international banks.

Saunders and Walter, in one of the few studies of large banks, have recently examined the costs of the world's 200 largest banks over the years 1981 to 1986. The estimated cost functions over all banks in this group found evidence of economies of scale. But when they divided the banks by type (universal banks and separated banks) and size (loans < $10 billion, $10 billion < loans < $25 billion, $25 billion < loans), they found that the economies of scale were concentrated in banks with loans below $25 billion.[14] For all banks, and for separated banks alone, their evidence suggested diseconomies of scale for banks with more than $25 billion in loans.[15] They also found evidence of scope diseconomies between interest-earning and non-interest-earning activities. They conclude "positive supply-side economies of scale appear to exist only in the middle range of big banks in the world, with diseconomies being the rule for the very largest banks" (1994, p. 82). Saunders and Walter do point out that their study deals only with cost economies and may fail to capture revenue economies.

This evidence on cost economies does not support the proposition that Canadian banks are too small to be internationally competitive. Cost economies are exhausted for banks with loans of more than $25 billion (1980 U.S. dollars), a level that corresponds to $50 billion in 1996. The big three Canadian banks have loans well in excess of this amount. The other two, Scotiabank and Toronto-Dominion are close to the margin where economies of scale cease.

---

[14]These ranges are expressed in 1980 U.S. dollars.

[15]The evidence for universal banks also suggested diseconomies of scale for this range, but was statistically insignificant.

Growth of Large Banks

A second criteria for competitiveness is the growth of different sized banks. Do larger banks grow more quickly than smaller banks? Saunders and Walter have considered this question for the world's largest banks in their study of universal banking. They state that

> Our results reject the Law of Proportionate Effect during the 1980s, representing a departure from Tschoegl's conclusions. There is strong evidence that the larger the bank, the less rapid was its growth during the period under study. The elasticity of growth with respect to size was found to be less than one in all cases. (1994, p. 79)

These results do not imply that the world's largest banks are necessarily the most competitive.

Still, the shrinking relative position of Canadian banks among large banks over the past 20 years cannot be denied. Chart 1 shows the decline of the five largest Canadian banks in *The Banker's* world ranking. Though there is some period to period fluctuation, none of the big four Canadian banks are now in the top 50, compared to as many as four in 1985.

Table 3 shows the changing position of Canadian banks from a different perspective. It compares the assets of the top three Canadian banks with those of the top three banks in 1975 from the United States, France, the United Kingdom, Japan and Germany at five-year intervals. As in the previous comparison, the pattern differs year by year. Over the entire period, Canadian banks have shrunk relative to the largest banks in all the countries except the United States. Not surprisingly, the Canadian banks lost most ground to the Japanese banks, falling from over 70% to less than 20% of their assets.

Serious concern should be attached to this decline of the Canadian banks if it has resulted from restrictive regulation. But many other factors have changed over the period. Most noticeably, as shown in Table 4, the Canadian dollar has moved substantially. Since 1975, it has appreciated only with respect to the U.K. pound and has lost over half its value relative to the mark and three-quarters of its value relative to the yen.

The significance attached to the decline in the size of the Canadian banks will differ to the degree that it results from the depreciation of the dollar. If their

Chart 1: Ranking of Major Canadian Banks Among the World's Largest Banks: 1975-1995

RANK

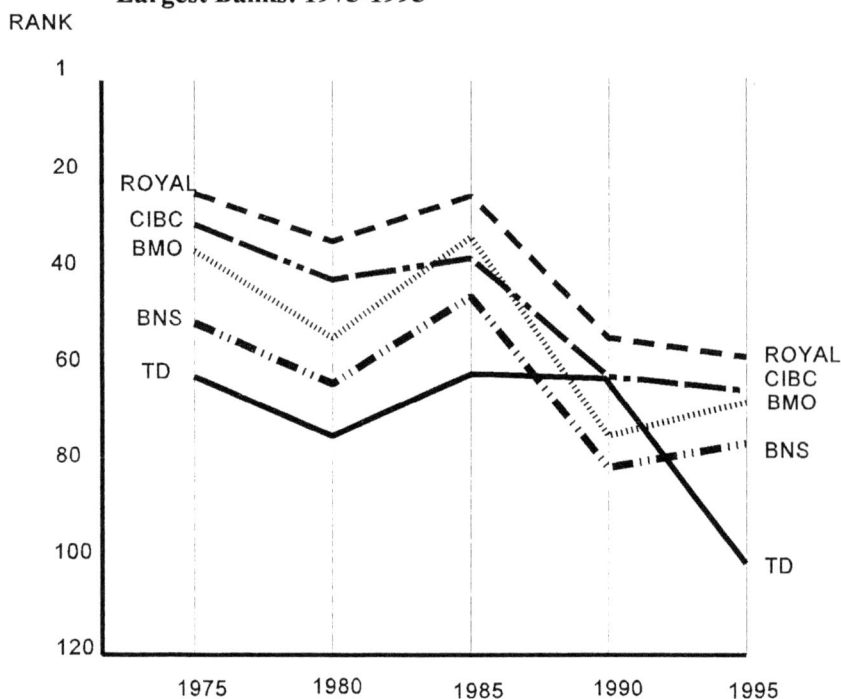

Source: *The Banker*, various issues.

Table 3: Relative Size of Assets of Three Largest Canadian Banks

	Year				
	1975	1980	1985	1990	1995
Relative to U.S. banks	36.3%	40.5%	50.1%	53.8%	56.8%
Relative to French banks	59.2%	39.6%	61.2%	37.5%	49.1%
Relative to U.K. banks	63.7%	61.5%	70.8%	47.1%	40.3%
Relative to Japanese banks	70.9%	59.0%	49.5%	20.2%	19.2%
Relative to German banks	74.0%	49.5%	100.8%	50.1%	39.1%

Note: In all cases the assets of the three largest Canadian banks as a percentage of the current assets of each country's largest three banks in 1975.

Source: Calculated from *The Banker*, various issues.

Table 4: Value of Foreign Currencies Expressed in Canadian Dollars

	Year				
	1975	1980	1985	1990	1995
U.S.$ in C$	0.988	1.17	1.32	1.16	1.388
franc in C$	0.2182	0.2878	0.139	0.1954	0.2566
pound in C$	2.302	2.574	1.567	1.853	2.165
yen in C$	0.00332	0.00487	0.00533	0.00808	0.01387
mark in C$	0.4027	0.6746	0.4356	0.6677	0.8838

Source: Cansim.

business has shrunk because of a change in the value of the currency they use for the majority of their business, this shrinkage need not reflect on their competitiveness.

Table 5 shows the size of the large Canadian banks relative to other large banks adjusted for the movements in the Canadian dollar. It exhibits a very different pattern than Table 3. It shows that Canadian banks grew relative to U.S., German and Japanese banks over the period and declined marginally against French banks. Surprisingly, Canadian banks declined substantially in size relative to U.K. banks. The data suggest that changing exchange rates have been a major contributor to the decreased relative size of Canadian banks.

Where do these two perspectives on the size and growth of Canadian banks leave us? The appropriate comparison is not clear. The significance of the adjusted data will differ according to the source of the depreciation of the dollar. If the depreciation was solely the result of higher inflation, the unadjusted data reflect better the performance of Canadian banks. The adjusted data thus need further adjustment for differential inflation. In addition, the adjustment would not be appropriate for the foreign currency business of the banks because it is insulated from the effects of the depreciation. More work needs to be done on

New Directions in Canadian Financial Policy   *35*

Table 5: Relative Size of Assets of Three Largest Canadian Banks: Adjusted

	Year				
	1975	1980	1985	1990	1995
Relative to U.S. banks	36.3%	47.3%	66.9%	63.1%	79.8%
Relative to French banks	59.2%	52.2%	39.0%	33.6%	57.8%
Relative to U.K. banks	63.7%	68.8%	48.2%	37.9%	37.9%
Relative to Japanese banks	70.9%	86.5%	79.5%	49.1%	80.0%
Relative to German banks	74.0%	82.9%	109.0%	83.1%	85.8%

Note: In all cases the assets of the three largest Canadian banks are expressed as a percentage of the current assets of each country's largest three banks in 1975 after adjustment for exchange rate changes.

Source: Calculated from *The Banker*, various issues and Cansim.

the competitive performance of the banks. The adjusted data serve only to show that conclusions based on the unadjusted data alone may be premature.[16]

The Remedies

Two remedies have been proposed for dealing with the high costs of funds and the lagging competitiveness of Canadian banks. Suggestions have been that the 10% ceiling on ownership of a Schedule I bank be removed and that a

---

[16]*The Banker* has recently published a rating of major banks according to the proportion of their business overseas. Four Canadian banks rank in the top 50 (22nd, 23rd, 42nd and 46th). This showing also is not consistent with a lack of competitiveness internationally.

permissive attitude be taken towards mergers among major banks.[17] Indeed, a newspaper report indicated that the banks would give up the 10% ceiling in exchange for permitting larger banks through mergers. The logic behind such a proposal seems curious. It is somewhat like truckers proposing to give up stop signs in return for a higher speed limit. The logic of linking the measures in this way is tenuous and each needs to be considered on its own merits.

Ownership Rules

The ownership rules assure the separation of the banking and commercial sectors that has been a cornerstone of Canadian policy towards banking. These rules allow problems such as conflict of interest and self-dealing to be avoided, not through detailed regulatory scrutiny and intricate oversight of many individual transactions, but through avoiding those situations where these problems arise. The monitoring of ownership substitutes for supervision and monitoring a whole array of other dimensions.

Ownership restrictions are an integral element of the current approach to regulation, but may not be needed for other approaches. If changes are made to ownership policy, many other aspects of Canada's financial market policy would need to be reconsidered and modified. Even those who doubt the need for the separation of banking and commerce recognize the need for other measures when banking and commerce are linked. Heurtas (1988), for example, offers as one possible set of measures a combination that includes limits on dividends, collateral requirements for loans to affiliates, enforcement of arm's-length terms in all transactions, and clear statements about deposit-insurance coverage. These restrictions, he argues, would permit regulators to confine their monitoring to banks while assuring the same degree of depositor safety as possible with unaffiliated banks.

The adoption of Heurtas's rules or any similar rules in Canada would require a substantial reorientation in the approach to regulation. Ownership rules are relatively easy to enforce because, in general, ownership is quite easy to

---

[17]Upstream ownership ceilings govern Schedule I banks and other financial institutions that surpass a given size. No party can own more than 10% of a Schedule I chartered bank. Similarly, the ownership of a large financial institution by any party cannot exceed 65% once the capital of that institution exceeds $750 million.

measure. An obligation can be placed on financial institutions to monitor their ownership and to report any significant changes. The rules needed with cross ownership are more difficult to administer. Regulation would necessarily be more intrusive because regulators need to assess many individual transactions. In addition, the application of regulation would be more discretionary than at present because regulators would be forced to rule whether specific transactions take place on arm's-length terms.

While it is clear that a regulatory regime could be constructed without the present ownership restrictions, such a regime would require a drastic change in direction for regulation. Canadian authorities would have to adopt a more intrusive, more discretionary approach to regulation. In addition, this different approach to regulation must be formulated and be ready for introduction by the time the ownership rules are removed. As I have already stated, our inability to respond to the changes created by deposit insurance gives me little optimism that we would succeed.

Mergers

The concern about the size and competitiveness of Canadian banks has led to the prescription for a relaxation of the "big shall not buy big" attitude taken by the government towards mergers among major Canadian banks.[18] Such mergers, it is argued, would create institutions of the size necessary to "stand up" to the world's largest banks. Leaving aside the effectiveness of greater size in assuring competitiveness, we should not overlook possible side effects of the remedy. What impact would one or several mergers have on the workings of the Canadian financial system?

As I have discussed earlier, we face different problems than many other countries because of the small size of our economy and the relatively large size of our banks. A merger or two among our major banks may change the competitiveness of our banking system. The recent breaking down of barriers among sectors may be some counterforce. In my testimony before the Senate

---

[18]The Bank Act already provides for amalgamations among banks (Section 223). An application must be made to the Minister of Finance. In addition, in any application involving a Schedule I bank, the successor bank must also be a Schedule I bank.

last year (1995b), I noted that independent mutual fund companies had managed to coexist with the banks entering their industry. It now appears that I may have been premature. We see an increasing tendency for the same institutions to be moving into an array of different activities, many of which used to provide competition to banking services. As already stated, I am not reassured by the studies of competition in the Canadian banking system.[19] While many of the markets in which the banks operate are clearly competitive, some may not be. For example, I am not reassured by the evidence provided by the Director of Investigation and Research of the Competition Branch. He stated

> The respondents have engaged in a practice of anti-competitive acts which has had ... the effect of preventing or lessening competition substantially in the intermediate market for Shared Electronic Network Services and in the retail market for Shared Electronic Network Services. Through their control over the governance of Interac and Interac Inc., the Respondents have restricted other interested parties from connecting directly and indirectly to the Interac network through narrow eligibility requirements, or have created financial disincentives or barriers which have achieved that result. (1995, Appendix C, p. 2)

The network may pose different problems than other aspects of banking. Still, I am sufficiently concerned about the state of competition in some banking markets that I remain apprehensive about using mergers among major Canadian banks as a remedy for their perceived lack of competitiveness.

Another option, without the same effect on concentration, would be removal of obstacles to foreign takeovers by allowing foreign banks that are broadly held to own more than 10% of Schedule I banks. This approach is consistent with the current rules for domestic ownership. Section 370(2) of the Bank Act treats a bank as widely-held even if more than 10% of its shares are held by domestic financial institutions that themselves are widely-held. This proposal would extend this treatment to foreign banks. Concerns about the need for wide ownership and the separation of banking and commerce could be met

---

[19]The much cited Shaffer (1933) study has the implausible result that the bankers' marginal cost is negative related to interest costs on deposits. This result is particularly disturbing because deposit interest accounts for 60 % of the banks' total costs.

because the privilege would be extended only to foreign banks that are themselves widely held.

This approach avoids some of the disadvantages of the alternatives. It neither breeches the separation of banking and commerce nor increases the degree of concentration. By broadening the range of potential buyers of bank stocks, it should help to overcome the problem with the cost of capital and make Canadian banks better able to compete in international markets.

On the other hand, it is not clear that such takeovers would deal with the problem of increasing Canada's international banking activity. The parent itself would likely have international business. There would be no reason to increase the international business of the Canadian subsidiary unless Canada offers a more favourable regulatory or taxation regime for this type of business.

Any option that permits foreign takeovers of Canadian banks does raise questions of extra-territoriality. Can foreign governments force the foreign-owned banks in Canada to conform with that government's interests and against its own interest or that of Canadians? There may be some risk, but it may not be significantly more than the risk at present. As recent events suggest, the widespread foreign activities of Canadian banks already makes them vulnerable to foreign pressures.

Competitiveness and Ownership Rules: A Summary

None of the remedies for the perceived restrictions on the competitiveness of the Canadian banks appears very palatable. Removal of the 10% ownership will potentially reverse the separation of banking and commerce. Domestic mergers may threaten competition in some banking markets. Many would view foreign takeovers as regrettable, threatening the strong Canadian presence in banking. As the Royal Bank proclaims

> There are not many industries, other than those based on natural resources, in which Canadian firms have a global presence and a global capacity.... As Canadian firms seek to penetrate global markets, it is natural for them to rely on Canadian banks as partners in this endeavour. A diminished capacity of the banks to offer a globally competitive service may have a negative impact on the competitiveness of Canadian firms in the global economy. (1996, p. 10)

I do not think it is necessary to choose among these remedies at this time. I am not convinced that the ownership restrictions limit the size of the Canadian banks. I am also not convinced that their size places Canadian banks at a competitive disadvantage to the larger players in the world. Finally, if I were convinced there was a problem, I would want to consider the costs and benefits of the remedy.

REFERENCES

Bank for International Settlements (1993), *Payments Systems in the Group of Ten Countries* (Basel: Bank for International Settlements).

Booth, L. (1996), "Competition and Profitability in the Financial Services Industry", in J.M. Mintz and J. Pesando (eds.), *Putting Customers First*, Policy Study 27 (Toronto: C.D. Howe Institute).

Carr, J.L., G.F. Mathewson and N.C. Quigley (1994), *Ensuring Failure: Financial Stability and Deposit Insurance in Canada*, Observer 36 (Toronto: C.D. Howe Institute).

Chant, J.F. (1987), *Regulation of Financial Institutions — A Functional Analysis*, Technical Report No. 45 (Ottawa: Bank of Canada).

_____ (1995a), "Reform and the Soundness of the Financial System", *Policy Options* (June), 11-16.

_____ (1995b), *Statement to the Standing Senate Committee on Banking, Trade and Commerce*, February 23

Cook, P. (1996), "Your Friendly Local Monster Bank", *The Globe and Mail, Report on Business*, May 20.

Dewatrapont, M. and J. Tirole (1994), *The Prudential Regulation of Banks* (Cambridge, MA: MIT Press).

Director of Investigation and Research, Competition Branch (1995), *Draft Consent Order in the Matter of an Abuse of Dominant Position in the Supply of Shared Electronic Network Services for the Consumer-Initiated Shared Electronic Financial Services*, December 14.

Economic Council of Canada (1976), *Efficiency and Regulation: A Study of Deposit Institutions* (Ottawa: Supply and Services Canada).

Globe and Mail (1996), "DBRS Says Banks Face Consolidation", *Report on Business*, April 26.

Heurtas, T.F. (1988), "Can Banking and Commerce Mix?" *The Cato Journal* (Winter), 759.

Horstmann, I.J., G.F. Mathewson and N.C. Quigley (1996), *Ensuring Competition: Bank Distribution of Insurance Products* (Toronto: C.D. Howe Institute).

Merton, R.C. (1977), "An Analytical Derivation of the Cost of Deposit Insurance and Loan Guarantees: An Application of Modern Portfolio Pricing Theory", *Journal of Banking and Finance* 1, 3-11.

_____ (1990), "The Financial System and Economic Performance", American Enterprise Institute for Public Policy Research, International Competitiveness in Financial Services Conference Paper.

_____ (1993), "Operation and Regulation in Financial Intermediation: A Functional Perspective", Harvard Business School, Working Paper WP 93-020.

Nathan, A. and E. Neave (1989), "Competition and Contestability in Canada's Financial System: Empirical Results", *Canadian Journal of Economics* 22(3), 576-594.

Quigley, N. (1996), "Public Policy and the Canadian Payments System: Risk, Regulation and Competition", paper presented to the Conference on Issues in the Reform of the Canadian Financial Services Industry.

Roe, M.J. (1994), *Strong Managers, Weak Owners: The Political Roots of American Corporate Finance* (Princeton, NJ: Princeton University Press).

Royal Bank Financial Group (1996), *Three Cs of Canadian Banking: Conduct, Competition and Concentration* (February).

Saunders, A. and I. Walter (1994), *Universal Banking in the United States: What Could We Gain? What Could We lose?* (New York: Oxford University Press).

Shaffer, S. (1993), "A Test of Competition in Canadian Banking", *Journal of Money, Credit and Banking* 25(3), 49-61.

Tobin, J. (1986), "Financial Innovation and Deregulation in Perspective", in Y. Suzuki and H. Yomo (eds.), *Financial Innovation and Monetary Policy: Asia and the West* (Tokyo: University of Tokyo Press).

REFLECTIONS ON THE FEDERAL WHITE PAPER

Martine Doyon, Department of Finance

I know that the organizers of this conference anticipated a much earlier release date for the federal White Paper, *1997 Review of Financial Sector Legislation: Proposals for Changes.* It is appropriate to begin my comments with a bit of background on the 1997 review process. The last major financial sector reform occurred in 1992, when a new framework for a competition was introduced. At that time, the government decided that instead of inserting the usual ten-year sunset clause in the legislation, given the scope of the changes made in 1992, it would probably be wise to revisit the legislation five years after its passage. The combination of the emergence of new issues and the pressures for adjustment from the various segments of the industry suggest that this five-year revisiting was probably appropriate. In addition, the 1997 revision was never envisioned to be a major overhaul of the legislation, but more of a mid-term adjustment. Thus, while Finance and the government are aware of the major issues that need to be addressed (the payments system, deposit insurance, ownership), these will not be addressed in 1997, although processes will be put in place to ensure full consideration in the future.

Turning to the issue at hand, there are three key elements to the White Paper. The first relates to a set of measures to enhance consumer protection. The second focuses on proposals to streamline and update the legislation. The third and prospectively the most important, is the announcement that the

---

Editors' Note: The White Paper was released the day before the conference. The main text is reproduced as Annex 1, pp. 249-273.

government will undertake a comprehensive review of the appropriate framework for the financial sector as we head into the 21st Century. Toward this end, a Task Force on the Future of the Canadian Financial Services Sector will be appointed.

I. CONSUMER PROTECTION

The first set of proposals relate to consumer protection. It is important to note that the federal government is not signaling a fundamental shift here. Our focus has always been on solvency regulation and this focus will remain unchanged. Nonetheless, the government recognizes that the environment is changing and that consumers are asking for better protection in their dealings with financial institutions. These changes reflect a number of considerations. One is the increased use of technology which raises concerns, for example, in the area of privacy. Thus, there are a number of proposals in the paper to enhance privacy safeguards. For example, financial institutions will be required to adopt a code of conduct regarding privacy and they will be encouraged to use the CSA model code as a minimum standard. They will also be required to establish procedures to handle privacy complaints. Some commentators have already argued that the government may not be going far enough in this area. I think that the White Paper reflects an attempt to try to strike a balance between protecting the interests of consumers on the one hand and not going ahead with very detailed rules which could be quite onerous on the institutions on the other. Ottawa clearly has the regulation-making authority so that if this approach does not work the government can always revisit the areas.

While I do not want to spend a lot of time on the other consumer-related proposals, let me mention that there are ongoing pressures on government to take action with respect to service charges, to the access to basic financial services, and to the regulation of product pricing. The government has chosen to reaffirm its position that the best approach remains one of maintaining healthy competition in the marketplace and of making sure that customers are well informed about product choices and options. What we are proposing to do in these areas is to work with the institutions to improve disclosure as opposed to stepping in and proposing some cap on service charges and other direct interventions.

Included in the White Paper are a couple of what we call "greener" proposals. One of these relates to tied selling, which was raised as an issue in our consultations. While safeguards exist in the Competition Act, in the Bank Act and in the Trust and Loan Companies Act, we are prepared to consider whether further measures are needed to protect consumers.

II. EASING THE REGULATORY BURDEN

The next set of proposals relates to the regulatory burden. One of the comments that we have heard many times — not just over the past year but since the 1992 legislation was put in place — is that with all the new powers we have bestowed on the various financial institutions, maybe there is a better way to regulate. At the very least, maybe we can achieve our regulatory objectives without imposing as much of a burden on the institutions.

There are five areas in the White Paper where the government is considering taking action in terms of easing the regulatory burden. The first relates to overlap between federal and provincial regulation. Let me just flag the three relevant areas, beginning with trust and loan company legislation. I know many people have been involved in this exercise for many years. The government is hopeful that we will get some meaningful results here in the near future. I will not deal with securities regulation here, since it will be dealt with in detail later in this volume. The last area relates to the six provincial credit union centrals regulated under federal legislation. We are proposing to end federal regulation in this area.

The second area relates to self-dealing issues. We are, in general, satisfied that the underlying philosophy is working well but have been advised (and accepted the message) that there are a number of desirable changes that should be considered. For example, we are going to refocus the role of the Conduct Review Committee, narrow the definition of "related party", and permit transactions between sister corporations.

Third, financial institutions will also be permitted to carry some activities in-house, namely information processing and specialized financing. In 1992, financial institutions were permitted to offer those services but they were required to undertake them through subsidiary operations. In part, the government opted for caution because some of these areas were new. We now have a much better understanding of the risks involved and feel comfortable giving the institutions more flexibility.

The fourth area — deposit insurance opt-out — while an important 1997 issue, is not new. It was discussed in the context of C-100. Questions have been raised as to whether it is really necessary for wholesale banks to be a member of CDIC and have to meet the CDIC reporting requirements. We do not believe that it is. So what we are proposing to do is to allow wholesale banks to opt out of CDIC coverage.

Turning finally to the foreign bank entry regime, our policy has not been reviewed in a very detailed fashion since it was adopted back in 1980. We have a number of proposals spelled out in the consultation paper to make it easier for foreign entities operating in Canada to carry on their activities.

III. FINE TUNING THE LEGISLATION

In respect of fine tuning the legislation, there are a number of proposals in the areas of corporate governance and joint ventures that need to be revisited. We are going to give more flexibility to financial institutions wishing to enter into joint-venture arrangements and there will no longer be a requirement for joint ventures to be controlled by regulated financial institutions.

Access to capital for mutual insurance companies is another area that needs fine tuning. We realize that we need to refine the measures adopted in 1992. Although there was general agreement with the principles, we did not get the implementation quite right the first time around. We have gone back to the drawing board and have put forward some proposals to deal with the concerns raised by life insurance companies.

On the payments system, I suspect that there will be disappointment that there will be no proposals in 1997. However, we realize that there are many important concerns and issues that need to be addressed. So we announced that the Department of Finance and the Bank of Canada will review payments system issues. An advisory committee will also be established to work with the Department of Finance and the Bank of Canada. Details of the work have not yet been announced, but should be made public in the near future.

IV. TASK FORCE

Finally, the government has announced that it will establish a Task Force on the Future of the Canadian Financial Services Sector. We are very mindful that there are a number of very important issues that need to be looked at. Globalization, technology and a new competitive landscape are definitely affecting the way business is being carried out and the way it is going to be carried out in the future. The government will detail the mandate and announce the composition of the task force. It is going to be a fairly small group of about half a dozen members. There will be some fairly specific questions put to the task force and that will be made public.

As for the next steps in the 1997 exercise, we are asking for comments by the end of August. Both the Senate Banking Committee and the House Finance Committee will be holding hearings. Actually, there were hearings started in June when Secretary of State Douglas Peters appeared before the House Finance Committee. We are working to have legislation tabled in the House before the end of the year and need to have new legislation in place by the end of March 1997. I think it is interesting — this is the last comment I guess I'll make on the consultation paper — that perhaps the most important driving factor in the review is that the sunset date is not very far away. In order to meet this deadline, we really have to contain the package. We felt it was better to go with perhaps a smaller package, but yet something that we could do, as opposed to trying to tackle everything and not being able to deliver in time for the expiry of the legislation.

COMMENT: An Insurance Perspective

Mark R. Daniels, Canadian Life and Health Insurance Association, Inc.

I will take this opportunity to focus on the two papers on the table, the federal government's White Paper and John Chant's "Green" paper.

With respect to John Chant's paper, I am comfortable with its clean, understandable framework. Moreover, I admit to being in almost total agreement with the content. It is a timely contribution to the important task force machinery the federal government has just announced. At the same time, in saying all this, I must apologize, John, because it is probably the kiss of death for your paper to be complimented by an insurer.

With respect to the White Paper, unlike many commentators, I do not view the process that has led to its release as having failed Canadians or the financial institutions. Admittedly, on occasion it has been a somewhat tedious process, but it has also been relatively orderly and non-traditionally open, and now the government has chosen to open it up even more. That is all very positive. In this context, my main objective today is to explain briefly the insurers' position in this debate and process.

Let me come back, for a moment, to the Chant paper. For me, the two keys to that paper lie in, essentially, two components, both of which are grounded in John's notion of the ideal system of regulation:

- First is his assertion that financial markets have huge potential for innovation, which changes the form of financial activity in innovative ways. This is a key, if not *the* key, point in this whole debate.

- Second is his assertion that it is beyond the capacity of financial regulators to react effectively to innovation and other changes in financial markets. And that is not taken as a shot at regulators at all. It is simply a recognition of the limitations of regulation.

I doubt there are any practitioners in the business — bankers, insurers, investment dealers — even regulators themselves, who would disagree with these starting points. Indeed, they account for the reason my industry colleagues and I are comfortable with the Chant paper. John's assertions do not revolve around the headline grabbers focusing on banks in insurance or auto leasing. The issues he has chosen to deal with have much greater significance for the future efficiency and health of the Canadian financial system. These issues are: (i) participation in the payments system; (ii) arrangements for depositor protection; and (iii) ownership rules and the competitiveness of Canadian banks.

These issues are at the heart of the debate as far as my industry colleagues and I are concerned. Indeed, they are the focus of the position we put forward to the Department of Finance just about a year ago to the day.

With respect to that position and our recommendations for the 1997 review of the federal financial services, essentially we said three things:

- The review should correct the policy advantages we believe the banks have enjoyed and allow other financial institutions to compete on a level playing field. And by level playing field, I do not mean we want to be bankers. I mean that, regardless of what products we are dealing with, we had better deal from the same deck. This is why we have pushed very hard for reform of the payments system, changes to the deposit insurance system, and so on.

- In the meantime, the review should not consider any measures that would further increase concentration in the financial services sector in Canada. In particular, there should be no changes to bank powers in the near term.

- As part of the review, a broadly based study should be conducted to determine what Canadians want from their financial services system. In that respect, I agree very much with my colleagues from the banks. And with respect to the payments system, the issue is now on the table.

I have watched a lot of policy development over a good many years. With respect to the current run-up to the 1997 review, far from being critical of what has gone on, I believe it has been an open and participatory process in which most of the players have had a real opportunity to air issues. There has been a wide debate, sometimes a bit silly, but a thorough debate nonetheless. And the fact is that there has been a remarkable change in the content of that debate. The issues that are on the table now are certainly not the issues that were on the table a year ago. I believe everyone who is interested in these subjects, the involved industries included, can look forward to an active and important discussion in the period to come.

In closing, I want briefly to loop back to John Chant's paper. John, you have produced a very solid analytical framework for some of the ongoing dialogue, which must follow the release of the White Paper, and I congratulate you for it. It is a useful contribution to an important national debate.

COMMENT: A Banking Perspective

Douglas W. Melville, Canadian Bankers Association

Not being an economist myself, I was in a bit of a quandary as to what approach to take to try and build on what I saw in Professor Chant's paper. I decided to take a slightly more general view of things.

On June 18, two days before this conference, I thumbed through various national daily newspapers and pulled out three items that I thought were illustrative of some of the things we will be discussing in this volume.

The first headline reads "TD Bank Unit Starts Direct Insurance Sales". Interesting, since a lot of the public policy debate going on recently is about the powers of Canadian deposit-taking institutions to retail insurance products directly to their customers through branches. Well, one bank has gone out there and is going to do it directly through other means.

The second item was in the same newspaper, "ING Group Aims to Enter Canada ... ING Group is poised to become the first foreign player to break into the hotly competitive $90 billion a year Canadian retail banking market with a virtual or electronic bank". We now face competition from a foreign player that will compete in Canada without any of the bricks and mortar and without the 125-year history and brand name recognition that the Canadian banks brought to the Canadian landscape. This is an interesting competitive challenge that we will have to face, and probably an interesting challenge for the regulators.

The third item's headline is "Levelling the Field ... Investment dealers insist on an even playing field with the banks". Well that is interesting. I do not think

I would have imagined seeing a headline like that just 10, 12 or 15 years ago. We have come a long way just in the last ten years to where the headlines on a single day in the major Canadian newspapers are painting for us a picture of just how rapidly the competitive environment is changing. The same pace of change is affecting every player in the financial services industry, both regulated and unregulated. That poses unique challenges for all of us going forward.

The release of the White Paper on Financial Services Reform marks the beginning of a very important public debate about the future of this industry. The financial sector is key to the health of the Canadian economy and this debate offers us an opportunity to examine the future of the industry at a time when truly revolutionary change is taking place, coming from the forces of globalization and technology at the same time. It is an opportunity but it is also an obligation that is on those of us who are gathered here and those that we serve. The obligation falls to every one of us who are participants in this industry, those for whom we provide services and those who regulate the providers. Government takes it upon itself to guide our behaviour, to provide for the solvency of our industries, and to regulate how we deal with individual customers. And yet it is Canadians, individual Canadians across the country, whose daily lives are the ones at stake. And we collectively have an obligation to serve their needs. We cannot let them down. So in entering into this debate we have to be very clear about one thing. This debate is not about the type of regulation that we as financial institutions would like to have, or the type of regulation that regulators would like to provide. It is more guided by an understanding that it is the consumers of financial products and services, not the institutions, and not the regulators, that are going to dictate the future shape of this industry. It is only in our ability to respond to the needs of those consumers that any one of us, regulators or providers of those services, are going to be relevant 10 or 12 years from now. So we have to be as fleet of foot as the consumers out there that we are chasing.

The question before us now is, what are the future needs of consumers? What type of regulation is required that will allow Canadian financial institutions to meet those needs in a timely and efficient manner? Because if we do not meet their needs, someone else will. And that someone else might be found among those financial institutions in other countries who are increasingly becoming world class with the scale and resources to service customers anywhere and anytime. Or it might be the unregulated "near banks" which are increasingly able to offer traditional financial services without the burden of the regulatory regimes that we currently face as financial institutions in Canada.

Perhaps such a development would not necessarily be a bad thing. But unless we address this fundamental question now, that result is going to get imposed on us rather than have it be something that we have chosen collectively as Canadians, as regulators, as providers of those services and as customers. So I would ask another even more fundamental question, do we still want a Canadian-controlled financial services industry? That objective has shaped the regulatory framework in this country for decades. But in the past, the cost of having such a priority was not so high and it was relatively easy to achieve through regulatory means. But as the price that has to be paid for that objective increases, we must ask whether it is becoming a luxury that we choose to afford going forward. I think that the task force announced in the White Paper offers us an opportunity to ask those and other fundamental questions.

So my suggestion is that that is the level of debate that has to occur right now in Canada. We invest our nation's time and energy in debating which institution will deliver what service and whose turf will be protected by the next Bank Act review. Goodness knows a number of us have spent a lot of our time over the last couple of years fighting over those less-than-fundamental issues. Much of the rest of the industrialized world is preparing their financial services industries to face the new world of a technology-driven, global financial services industry, some of the examples are those from the newspaper. We all read about the huge institutions being created in countries like Switzerland, Holland and Japan. But you have to recognize that they are not just building this type of size simply to serve their domestic customer base. That does not make sense. They are preparing to serve our customer base and the customer bases in other jurisdictions around the world.

So we no longer have the luxury of taking our financial system in Canada for granted and trying to protect what was. What was is, more than likely, gone forever. What we have to focus on is what will be there in the future. The best that we can hope for as Canadians is to focus on what will be and to try and have some say in the shape of the future before the future is imposed on us by those forces that we cannot control.

So specifically what does shaping the future mean? In my view, it means addressing three key issues, all of which focus on the consumer's interest: one is ownership, two is delivery channels and three is conduct. Under ownership we have to consider the ability of financial institutions to adapt under the current regulatory framework. Will change be required to meet the future needs of consumers and can that change be accommodated under the current restrictions? So we have to re-examine some of those fundamental concepts such as the value of domestic control and concerns over financial-commercial links to determine if the needs of consumers in the future are compatible with the current ownership constraints. It is a fundamental question. Are the assumptions we are making about the current cost-benefit analysis, the value of current ownership rules and the potential benefits from greater flexibility, compatible with what we are looking for in the future and what we expect will be our consumers' needs in the future.

Under delivery channels, the answers have to be decided by market imperatives, not by political considerations. We have to provide Canadians with products and services that they need in the future, delivered in the most timely and efficient manner possible. We owe them that and ultimately the forces of global competition will require it of us if we are to survive as financial institutions and as viable players in both the domestic and global marketplaces. That will mean providing a regulatory framework that allows for the creation of institutions with the resources to make truly massive investments in technology. They will be required to develop secure, confidential and fool-proof means of delivering financial services to individual customers. People talk about the future role of the Internet. To what extent will national boundaries and national jurisdictions' regulation be relevant if I am able to "surf the net" and source financial services? To what extent is a Canadian regulator relevant to Canadians surfing the globe trying to find where they can get a few extra basis points on a deposit-type product. Will the information necessary to make an informed decision be available to customers online already pre-sifted by someone who provides that information for a fee?

Conduct is the third element. Canadians are not likely to favour eliminating all the restrictions on the operation of financial institutions. That does not make sense. For one thing, they look to government to play that paternalistic role at times and protect them from the vagaries of individual players in the marketplace. The stability of the financial system and consumer confidence have to be maintained even in the face of revolutionary change. Therefore, regulation, or the threat of regulation, will always be necessary to ensure that consumers are treated fairly. However, concerns over market conduct will change as the relationships between consumers and their financial institutions change. Increasingly, the needs of consumers are going to be asset management and transaction-based; no longer the traditional banking services that we once provided. The old business of mortgages and consumer loans will always be there, but the traditional spread business is fast giving way to fee-based services.

So if we are to get where we must go and get there in time for it to be helpful, then we must also get the process right. I pose the question whether we and Canadians in general have been well-served by the reform process? The answer is clearly no and I think Minister Peters echoed that in his statements in the media over the last few weeks. But rather than simply complain about it, I suggest that we as institutions ask whether we failed the system, or has the system failed us. I suspect there is a combination of the two at work. So, let us back away for a moment and say that perhaps now we have an opportunity to ask some tough questions about ourselves as players in the industry; to ask some tough questions of ourselves as Canadians and to ask some tough questions of academics about what we expect to see down the line. If we do not embrace the opportunity, we will find the shape of the future is imposed on us by forces we cannot control and if we allow that to happen we will have failed in our obligations to all of us as Canadians.

COMMENT

Roger Ware, Queen's University

I should declare that I am not really a financial institutions expert but rather a student of industrial organization and competition policy. Hence, I do have an interest in the competition and industrial organization aspects of the banking and financial sector. Some of this interest was gained by a period of advising the Director of Investigation and Research in its long-running investigation of the Interac, the electronic banking network. And since that matter is tentatively still before the Tribunal I cannot offer any opinions about it except of a purely factual nature — and even then I should be careful to emphasize that my opinions of a factual nature are entirely my own and not those of the director or anybody else.

I do want to offer two comments on John's paper. I think that the paper is very interesting and very courageous because of its willingness to radically rethink the structure of the financial sector. First, John begins by stating that the rationale for regulating the banking sector is a kind of "representation hypothesis": essentially because of various kinds of market failures it is difficult for small depositors to protect their own interests. I understand the argument but I wonder how much evidence we have to support this hypothesis. How much evidence do we really have that small depositors are unable to protect themselves? And again I do not claim to have the answer to that. However, I am quite persuaded by the thesis advanced by Jack Carr, Frank Matheson and Neil Quigley that I am sure many of you are familiar with. The authors argue that deposit insurance has been very costly to Canadian banking. The argument is simply that deposit insurance encourages the entry of poor quality financial institutions who compete on an equal basis, unfortunately, with the high quality institutions. In other words, the efficient functioning of competition is frustrated and is therefore prevented from weeding out the poor quality institutions.

An argument for regulation of financial institutions is that only regulators can provide the appropriate quality and quantity of monitoring in order to protect the public. But elsewhere in the economy we expect private agencies to appear. Whenever there is a market for monitoring, private agencies set up monitoring activities and sell them in the market place. And I think the same thing would happen to the banks. I do not really see why moral hazard or adverse selection are going to be major problems among the banks themselves if we allow competition to work because we usually believe that competition tends to eliminate those problems.

The second point I wanted to make on John's paper directly is just a comment on the merger issue. Again I do not claim to have any deep knowledge about this. But I am very sceptical about the argument that there are large economies of scale in banking. And I think that the economies that exist mostly relate to various kinds of network economies; for example, those arising in shared electronic banking networks. And those economies have been internalized quite well by the creation of shared joint-venture networks. Thus, they do not support the need for increasing concentration and size in banking generally. In fact, it seems to me increasing concentration is exactly the wrong policy prescription. The policy direction most needed in Canadian banking is an increase in competition, not concentration.

I will add a couple of things not related to John's paper directly. Because it is the topic that I know most about in this area, these points concern electronic funds networks. Consider the issue of internetwork competition: for example, why don't we have competing networks for, let us say, shared cash dispensing (SCD)? But that issue, which was once debated as being the solution to the electronic funds market in Canada, is essentially dead. Canadians perhaps do not always realize that it is not just in Canada that we have a dominant shared electronic funds network. In the United States, even though there are many networks, if you look at regional concentration, almost every region is dominated by a large network. So the effective concentration in the U.S. networks is very similar to the market structure in Canada. It is not hard to see the logic of this: electronic funds networks are natural monopolies and the tendency towards increased concentration is very strong.

As a result the "policy action" in these networks has much more to do with intranetwork competition than it does to internetwork competition. And the ideas that are very important there have to do with interconnection, who can join, and with the sort of behavioural rules the network adopts in terms of exclusion, in terms of pricing, in terms of whether certain products are tied together or not, that sort of thing.

Another important challenge for regulating dynamic network industries is that the product is usually not standing still. Typically, differentiated substitute products will be appearing all the time. In the case of electronic cash dispensing there has been a striking growth of the IDP or the Interac Direct Purchase network which uses debit cards. In only two or three years both the value and volume of IDP transactions have now outstripped the value and volume of SCD transactions, or will do so this year. And it is growing so fast that we do not know where it will end up in two or three years time, but IDP will clearly be a major factor in consumer purchase behaviour. I would expect that IDP transactions will function as a substitute for cash transactions at ATM machines. They certainly do so for me already. So we are seeing ATM machines becoming slowly obsolete. And this is just one example of the problem that when you try to regulate dynamic network industries you may find that you are regulating yesterday's network but that you have not got anything to say about the network that is actually relevant today. This is a major problem in the regulatory area. To continue with my example, IDP may be the "hot" transactions medium at the moment, and smart cards may be next, but digital cash could be tomorrow's product and we do not have a regulatory framework to think about that either.

Let me return to the issue of intranetwork competition. It is important to understand how competition works between banks, financial institutions, and whoever else is on the network (for example, a network like Interac). There are many interesting issues about which we know very little. We do not know how competition really works between banks with respect to foreign fees levied on cardholders using the ATMs of other acquirer institutions. The competitive role of interchange fees is also not well understood. Further, if the consent order is approved by the Competition Tribunal then acquirers of transactions will have the ability to levy surcharges on card users. This is going to be an interesting experiment in Canada because it will probably be the largest test in the world of this kind of flexible pricing arrangement. In the United States the same thing is going on: the individual states are repealing prohibitions on those surcharges. And the tentative evidence that we have from the American experience is somewhat disturbing. What appears to happen in these industries is that consumers like using ATMs so much that they are willing to pay quite high surcharges; and even though there is a lot of competition for this business, the competition does not seem to be bringing the surcharges down or at least not very quickly. So this is an area that needs to be studied, to see how competition within a network works. And as I said, we do not really know very much about it.

To bring this back to a theme from John Chant's paper, it may not be that important to level the playing field in the sense of "if you can do this then I should be able to do it too". That is not the important issue, at least to industrial organization economists. In industrial organization we often think of two as being a number where competition starts to become quite effective. In the banking industry there seems to be a view that two is not nearly a large enough number for competition to be effective; we need five, or even more. It is not clear to me why that is. I actually see fairly vigorous competition in banking, perhaps more competition than most commentators do.

Session Two
ARE CAPITAL MARKETS
INTERNATIONALLY INTEGRATED?

ARE CAPITAL MARKETS INTERNATIONALLY INTEGRATED?

Maurice D. Levi, University of British Columbia

I. INTRODUCTION

Developments in open-economy macroeconomic theory of the 1970s and early 1980s showed the importance of the level of capital market integration, but made advances in understanding by taking the "armchair approach". Specifically, the many contributions by such macro giants as Canada's Harry Johnson and Robert Mundell, and subsequent extensions by their students Rudiger Dornbusch, Jacob Frenkel and others, proceeded by *assuming* perfect/ imperfect capital mobility and deriving the implications.[1] Therefore, conclusions concerning the effectiveness of monetary and fiscal policy under fixed versus flexible exchange rates, the dynamics of exchange rates and so on were all *conditional* conclusions. The specific recommendations on policy matters based on this research were consequently contingent on beliefs about international capital market integration. While the prevailing armchair view was one of perfect capital mobility, such a belief was based more on the general relaxation of capital controls of the postwar period than on any direct evidence.

Following Feldstein and Horioka's (1980) study of domestic savings and investment behaviour, and evidence on the "home-country bias" in typical investment portfolios, some doubt has been cast on the presumption that

---

[1]For collections of the more influential among the very many contributions of these pioneering researchers, see Frenkel and Johnson (1976), Mundell (1968) and Dornbusch (1988).

capital is perfectly mobile within a seamless, global capital market. This paper reviews the evidence on savings-investment correlations, home-country bias and other matters with implications for the degree of capital market integration/segmentation. An attempt is made to reconcile what sometimes appears as contradictory evidence as well as to identify what, if anything, might be behind any frictions in the flows of international capital. However, before reviewing the large and growing evidence on the matter, we begin with a discussion of why the issue of integration/segmentation matters at all. We engage in this discussion because, as we shall see, those coming to the integration question from different perspectives — savings/investment correlations, portfolio-composition inefficiencies, county/currency real yield differentials, macro-policy effectiveness, regulatory reform records etc. — generally have a different consequence of segmentation in mind. Furthermore, an appreciation of the different costs of segmentation and benefits of integration leads to further poorly exploited approaches to the measurement of the degree of international capital mobility.

II. WHY CAPITAL MARKET INTEGRATION MATTERS

Efficient Global Allocation of Capital

The set of investment opportunities existing in each country can be ranked from those with the highest expected returns down to those with the lowest expected returns. The resulting ordered opportunities will have different profiles in different countries depending on endowments of natural resources, the degree of economic development, the completeness and efficiency of crucial infrastructure, levels of human capital, and so on.

The extent to which any country can exploit its investment opportunities in a world of fully segmented capital markets depends on the available flow of savings within the country, with this flow itself varying from place to place. With different opportunities, and with different abilities to fund these opportunities, the expected marginal investment returns will vary. Countries with bountiful opportunities relative to their savings will enjoy high marginal returns and leave projects unfunded which offer high expected returns, but which are forgone or delayed due to shortage of funds. At the same time, countries with limited opportunities relative to their savings will pursue projects with low expected returns vis à vis expected returns elsewhere. Removal of the cause of international capital market segmentation will result in a flow of funds from the lower marginal-return country to the higher marginal-return country. Each dollar to move provides an expected gain equal to the difference between marginal returns in the two countries. Gains continue to be enjoyed until the marginal returns are equalized, with this involving a flow of funds from the country with the relative, or comparative, abundance of savings versus investment opportunities to the country with the relative abundance of investment opportunities versus savings. The overall gain depends on the sizes of these comparative advantages, just as do the gains from international trade.[2] The gain in the aggregate expected return on investment can be thought of as a first-order return, relating to the first moment of investment returns — expected returns in the different countries — not to the volatility of returns.

The Ability to Reduce Risk

Much of the recent discussion of capital market integration relates to the associated ability to reduce risk. Two different but very closely related aspects of risk reduction have received attention, one hinging on international real business cycles and the ability to borrow and lend with imperfectly synchronized cycles, and the other hinging on international asset diversification.[3]

When there is an idiosyncratic component of a country's real business cycle, integrated capital markets allow the country's residents to enjoy a higher average utility of consumption by being net borrowers during low points in the

---

[2]The appendix provides a simple graphical picture of the gain from an integrated capital market in which the distribution of gains between the countries is shown. While simple, the graphical view of the gain in global expected returns helps illustrate several points made in this paper, including the important factors influencing the deadweight loss from segmentation that go beyond unexploited risk reduction.

[3]For the work on cycles see Backus, Kehoe and Kydland (1992); Devereaux, Gregory and Smith (1992); Lewis (1996); and references contained therein. For portfolio diversification gains see Jorion (1985); Lessard (1976); Levy and Sarnat (1970); Odier and Solnik (1993) and Solnik (1974).

Are Capital Markets Internationally Integrated?   *65*

domestic business cycle, and by being net lenders during high points in the cycle; given the traditional assumption behind risk aversion, namely diminishing marginal utility of consumption, average utility is higher from a smoother consumption stream.

In an attempt to see whether countries have utilized international capital markets to smooth consumption growth rates, Brennan and Solnik (1989) compared actual volatility of growth rates in consumption of eight OECD countries, with what the volatility would have been without lending and borrowing. To compute the latter volatility, Brennan and Solnik computed what consumption would have been without capital movements by adding back net capital outflows and removing net capital inflows. The presumption that the constructed series is what consumption would have been without international capital flows involves viewing the other components of GDP, namely investment and government spending, as being invariant to the flows.[4] While Brennan and Solnik did find the constructed consumption-that-would-have-been series more volatile than actual consumption growth rates, the gain in average utility from this consumption smoothing was small: Brennan and Solnik's own calculations were challenged by Maurice Obstfeld.[5] Furthermore, as we shall explain later, the smoothing is far less than we would expect with *perfect* capital mobility, that is, complete integration.

The gain from consumption smoothing has an intertemporal element and is based on a flow, namely consumption during any given interval. A very similar but different view of risk reduction enjoyed in integrated capital markets concerns the benefit of international portfolio diversification. This relates to the value of a portfolio at a point in time, and therefore has a slightly different perspective than consumption smoothing. As we shall see, consumption smoothing and international portfolio diversification imply different ideal tests of whether capital markets are fully integrated — consumption correlations with global permanent income in the case of consumption smoothing, and the presence of home-country portfolio bias in the case of asset diversification.

---

[4]The business cycle papers by Backus, Kehoe and Kydland (1992), Devereaux, Gregory and Smith (1992) and Lewis (1996) are more general than the Brennan and Solnik approach, allowing for a wider range of components of output/spending to relate to capital flows.

[5]See Obstfeld (1992) and the reply by Brennan and Solnik (1992).

The benefit of international portfolio diversification, made possible by integrated capital markets, has received substantial attention since the early work of Grubel (1968) and Levy and Sarnat (1970). The potential to enjoy the welfare gain that Grubel articulated has been shown by forming portfolios of different stock markets, basing these on actual variance-covariance experience. Even with associated foreign exchange risk, internationally diversified portfolios have been shown by Solnik (1974), Odier and Solnik (1993) and Eun and Resnick (1988) to be substantially less volatile than domestic portfolios. The gains are particularly large when internationally diversified portfolios are compared to domestic portfolios of residents of small economies, as we would expect. When foreign exchange risks are hedged the gains are even larger.

It should be recognized that the thought experiment of forming portfolios, with or without foreign exchange-risk hedging, provides estimates only of the *potential* gain from international diversification. There is no assurance that this gain can be enjoyed, because the ability to enjoy the gain requires being able to form the portfolio suggested by the variance-covariance structure of different national stock markets. In addition, by using the within-sample variance-covariance matrix to form internationally diversified portfolios to compare portfolios, the gains from diversification are overstated. This occurs because, for example, countries with high *actual* (not expected) returns for the systematic risk they contribute carry particularly high weight within the portfolios, and vice versa. High actual returns versus risk likely contain positive shocks, and cannot be expected to be repeated in future returns. This problem of bias, and its overstatement of implied diversification gains, can be partially addressed by "shrinking" all returns towards the grand mean. Such an approach was taken by Jorion (1985) who showed that even the *potential* gains have been overstated in earlier research.

A priori, it is not clear whether the estimated potential gain from international diversification, which comes from the imperfect correlation between stock markets of different countries, is the result of countries' economies evolving differently, or the result of different industrial compositions of different stock markets. Empirically, it appears that low correlations between country indexes are almost exclusively due to country-specific factors; correlations between returns in a given industry in different countries are low, suggesting that it is countries that matter (see Heston and Rouwenhorst, 1994). This highlights the importance of barriers to capital mobility that matter for international integration of capital markets; investors need an ability to invest across borders, not industries, to gain from international diversification.

Whether we are considering intertemporal borrowing and lending or international asset diversification, the risk reduction that arises depends crucially on countries being different in their economic cycles.[6] The importance of being different to enjoy the gain from risk reduction reinforces the importance of being different for the gain from a better global allocation of capital. However, risk reduction relates to second moments of distributions while higher expected returns relate to first moments. The more countries differ, the larger the gains from integration.

The Effectiveness of Macroeconomic Policy

As we indicated in the introduction to this paper, a vast literature grew up in the 1960-80s out of concern for the implications of capital mobility, and the associated degree of integration, for the conduct of monetary and fiscal policy.[7] Monetary policy, for example, becomes blunted by market integration, at least when exchange rates are fixed. Rather, monetary expansion, which causes an incipient reduction in a country's interest rate, causes an excess supply of the country's currency. To avoid a consequent depreciation, the central bank is required to buy back the very money it created. This reduces foreign exchange reserves. Fiscal policy, on the other hand, causes an incipient increase in interest rates, an excess demand for the country's currency, and a need for the country to supply the extra money that goes with the extra money demand from an expansion in output/income. In this case foreign exchange reserves increase.

While monetary policy is ineffective and fiscal policy is effective with fixed exchange rates and internationally integrated capital markets, the reverse situation holds for flexible exchange rates. With flexible exchange rates, monetary expansion causes an incipient reduction in interest rates and a depreciation of

---

[6]The gain from asset diversification could, in principle, have been from industry differences, but as we have just stated, evidence supports the importance of country differences.

[7]See the literature in footnote 1.

the currency. This depreciation expands exports, reduces imports and causes an expenditure switching to domestic goods and consequent increase in output/income. Fiscal policy, on the other hand, causes an incipient increase in interest rates, a consequent appreciation of the country's currency, and a slowdown in output/income that offsets the fiscal expansion. Therefore, while monetary policy is effective with flexible exchange rates and perfect capital mobility, fiscal policy is not effective. Crucial to these conclusions is the mobility of capital, which in turn implies/requires that capital markets are integrated.

A further matter relating to fiscal policy concerns the crowding out that accompanies expansionary fiscal policy when the supply of loanable funds in a country is not perfectly elastic; the accompanied increase in interest rates from fiscal expansion crowds out private investment. Capital market integration prevents the crowding out by allowing the country to import capital to help fund the fiscal expansion. Indeed, the more integrated are the capital markets, the smaller is the amount of crowding out, and the smaller is the interest increase accompanying fiscal expansion. This and the preceding matters concerning policy effectiveness explain why knowledge of the integration or segmentation of capital markets matters: it is more than a matter of efficiency of capital allocation and an ability to reduce risk. In addition, awareness of the connection between integration and policy effectiveness suggests further tests of integration that have not previously been performed, such as how much influence monetary and fiscal policy have on interest rates, how much crowding out occurs from fiscal policy, and how foreign exchange reserves behave under fixed exchange rates or the exchange rates vary under flexible rates.

III. APPROACHES TO THE INTEGRATION QUESTION

Several approaches have been taken to the question of integration with the different approaches having particular relevance to the various reasons why integration matters that were discussed above. We begin with the approach that is most relevant to the question of the efficiency of the global allocation of capital.

Return Convergence and Behaviour

Return convergence takes a price — rather than quantity — perspective to the integration question. Specifically, whereas matters such as international portfolio risk reduction depend on whether there is home-country bias in amounts held in peoples' portfolios, and the savings-investment-connection depend on correlations between quantities, return convergence relates to the law-of-one price as applied to returns.

As Frankel (1993) has observed, integration is not a simple matter of convergence of different countries' real interest rates. Investors viewing return opportunities do not compare nominal returns corrected for local inflation, but rather compare nominal returns corrected for the inflation they themselves face. Since the same rate of inflation is used to adjust all countries' returns, when comparing covered bond returns investors are indifferent if

$$i - \Delta p^e = i^* + \Delta s^e - \Delta p^e \qquad (1)$$

where i and i^* are respectively domestic and foreign returns, Δp^e is the investor's relevant expected inflation, and Δs^e is the expected change in the spot rate measured as the price of foreign currency. With the common Δp^e, uncovered real interest parity reduces to

$$i = i^* + \Delta s^e \qquad (2)$$

Of course, if *ex ante* relative purchasing power parity holds — sometimes called the speculative form of PPP — then

$$\Delta s^e = \Delta p^e - \Delta p^{e^*} \qquad (3)$$

and therefore real rates using local inflation are indeed equal:[8]

---

[8]With many different investors there are many relevant inflation rates, although not the local country rates. It follows that *ex ante* relative PPP, as discussed below, is really a requirement of all forms of uncovered parity.

$$i - \Delta p^{e} = i^{*} - \Delta p^{e^{*}} \tag{4}$$

It is possible that (4) holds even if actual PPP never holds. Rational expectations as applied to *ex ante* relative PPP implies "only" that PPP holds on average, and that deviations are not predictable. Even though these conditions are less obviously violated than actual PPP — we know how poorly *ex post* absolute and even relative PPP perform — it is not a simple matter to verify *ex ante* relative PPP. Specifically, autocorrelated errors could easily be introduced in obtaining a measure of expected inflation, and in the absence of reliable survey measures, any test of (4) requires computing expected inflation: tests are a joint test of expectations formation and PPP.[9]

Uncovered interest parity is a more stringent test of integration than covered interest parity. Uncovered parity requires covered parity, and in addition the absence of any foreign exchange risk premium. Given the difficulty of obtaining inflation expectations to test uncovered interest parity, it would compound the problem to have to disentangle the risk premium from errors in measuring expectations, especially if the risk premium is time-varying. Furthermore, even if any possible violations of *ex ante* relative PPP in (4) could be confidently determined, it is difficult to move between the size of violations and the implied degree of segmentation. For example, if violations appear larger in one period than another, this could be because of larger shocks in local loanable funds suppliers and demands, or because of differences in degrees of segmentation between the periods.[10]

An alternative return-convergence view of integration that relates to equities rather than fixed income assets is to see whether securities are priced according to international or local factors. This is the approach taken by

---

[9]Lothian (1995) uses very long time series to help overcome the problem of inflation expectations versus actual inflation. His interest is the convergence of real and nominal interest rates in different exchange-rate regimes, and he finds that while nominal rate convergence varies across regimes, real rates behave similarly under the gold standard, the Bretton Woods standard and flexible exchange rates.

[10]We use loanable funds suppliers and demands rather than the components of these, namely savings and investments, to be more general than the usual Feldstein-Horioka (1980) approach. We return to this later.

Jorion and Schwartz (1986). They note that if markets are fully integrated, expected returns on securities consisting of local portfolios will depend only on systematic risk vis à vis the global-market portfolio. That is, in integrated markets expected returns depend only on β's vis à vis the global-market return. However, in completely segmented markets, expected returns depend on domestic factors, and in particular β's vis à vis the domestic market return. By isolating domestic and global factors they show that for Canadian securities domestic factors do play a role, even though there are few legal barriers. The same result applies to interlisted Canadian stocks — those listed in the United States and Canada — suggesting that segmentation is not attributable to reporting-requirement differences: Canadian companies trading on U.S. exchanges must report essentially the same information as U.S. companies.

Qualified support for segmentation has come from a different approach to interlisted stocks by Alexander, Eun and Janakiramanan (1988). They argue that if markets are segmented, the listing of a security abroad could reduce the security's expected return, and cause a jump in the security price on announcement of the listing. They find evidence of lower expected returns after listing for non-Canadian stocks, but not for Canadian stocks, implying that unlike other pairs of markets, U.S. and Canadian stock markets are integrated.

An alternative, albeit indirect way of testing for segmentation, is to see whether securities of firms that can overcome capital flow restrictions by having their "feet" in different markets, have returns related to systematic risk in international, not domestic markets. For example, if U.S. multinationals can invest abroad where ordinary U.S. citizens cannot, then U.S. multinational security returns should have β's related to international markets. Agmon and Lessard (1977) find weak evidence that U.S. MNCs can achieve something U.S. non-multinational firms cannot, but Jacquillat and Solnik (1978) disagree. A problem with comparing U.S. MNC's security pricing vis à vis the U.S. market against U.S. MNC's pricing vis à vis the international market, is that the U.S. market includes a substantial international component through overseas earnings of U.S. companies included in the U.S. market. When U.S. stock indexes are reconstructed to correct for this effect, as was done by Hughes, Logue and Sweeney (1975), the evidence for segmentation is much stronger; the pricing link of U.S. MNCs to the international market is much closer than that to the (corrected) U.S. market.

Savings and Investment Correlations

The Feldstein-Horioka (1980) view of integration/segmentation, which is based on savings-investment correlations, can be thought of as bridging two of the reasons the integration question is important. Specifically, it relates to the efficiency of global capital allocation, requiring equalization of real returns, and the intertemporal view of risk reduction, where countries can be net lenders some of the time and net borrowers at other times.

Feldstein and Horioka ran a cross-sectional regression of domestic investment and savings rates

$$(I/Y)_i = \alpha + \beta(NS/Y)_i + u_i \qquad (5)$$

where $(I/Y)_i$ is the investment rate, and $(NS/Y)_i$ is savings minus the fiscal deficit as a proportion of GDP. The finding of a β closer to 1 than zero is suggestive on first pass of evidence for segmentation: fluctuations in $(NS/Y)_i$ in an integrated market should be accompanied by capital inflows and outflows, with $(I/Y)_i$ responding to the real interest rate which would be unaffected by $(NS/Y)_i$. However, Tobin (1983) and Murphy (1984) have suggested that large countries might violate the assumption of a real rate that is unaffected by that country's (NS/Y), but since all countries would face the same real rate consequence, all countries' investment rates should respond, and the large country problem should not occur (see Frankel, 1993).

A more likely cause of bias in β estimated from (5) is omitted variables which affect both $(I/Y)_i$ and $(NS/Y)_i$. Candidates for omitted variables include global influences on investment and savings such as variations in worldwide investor/ saver confidence. The intuition is that when there is a common element in savings/investment which affects all countries, then when, for example, investment increases in one country it does so elsewhere. We then have higher interest rates and an associated increase in amounts saved along with higher investment. The bias is one of worldwide effects as described in Levi (1976), lending itself to solutions as in Levi (1973, 1977). Cyclical movements are unlikely to be a problem, at least in the Feldstein-Horioka original study, because the data are averaged over cycles to minimize this bias. Another possible cause of bias highlighted by Lewis (1996) involves non-separabilities in consumption between tradables and nontradables: perhaps the goods that can replace domestic nontradables in consumption are less than perfect substitutes.

A different perspective in the savings-investment correlation view of capital market integration which has been taken by Backus, Kehoe and Kydland (1992) involves consumption correlations across countries. As these authors and complementary work by Devereaux, Gregory and Smith (1992) point out, in a world of complete, integrated financial markets the correlation between consumption growth rates should be unity. This is because complete, integrated markets allow all risk to be avoided, with consumption smoothed according to global output/income growth. Indeed, one could think of the correlation of a country's consumption with *global* consumption as a measure of the degree of capital market integration. Then countries' correlations with global consumption can be compared with respect to how well integrated they are, something that is more difficult to do with pairwise correlations.[11] Alternatively, one country's savings could be correlated with investment in all other countries combined. If the bias in domestic investment-savings correlations is due to worldwide effects from omitting global factors, high correlations should also be found between a country's savings and investment in all other countries combined. Finding such high correlations would force us to reinterpret the high domestic investment-savings correlation.

The savings-investment and consumption-correlation approaches to testing for integration are suggested by the national income identity

$$Y \equiv C + I + G + (X - M) \qquad (6)$$

which, with $S \equiv Y - C - T$ becomes

$$S - (G - T) \equiv I + (X - M) \qquad (7)$$

---

[11]Proper ranking of the degree of capital market integration when countries differ in size would require omitting consumption of the own country, thereby removing any spurious correlation.

Then, with the fiscal deficit subtracted from S, as in Feldstein-Horioka's and subsequent authors' work, and with $X - M$ offset by net capital outflows/inflows via the balance of payments accounting identity

$$(X - M) + B_K \equiv 0,$$

we have $\{S - (G - T)\}$ differing from I by net capital flows, B_K, i.e.

$$S - (G - T) - I \equiv B_K \qquad (8)$$

A factor which the Feldstein-Horioka approach downplays is the role of money in real interest rate determination. While it is true that the *natural* interest rate as defined by Wicksell is the result of savings and investment, the *market* interest rate, at least as it is explained by the Loanable Funds Theory, is the result not only of savings and investment, but also of changes in money supply, money demand and government borrowing requirements. We can write the market clearing condition in a way that relates to the national income identity version in (7) by equating the supply of loanable funds, on the left-hand side below, with the demand for loanable funds, on the right-hand side, i.e.,

$$S + \Delta M^S + B_K = I + \Delta M^D + (G - T) \qquad (9)$$

Here, ΔM^S and ΔM^D are the changes in money supply and demand, and B_K is the supply of funds from net capital inflows (outflows if negative). The Loanable Funds view in (9) differs from the income/balance of payments identity only by the inclusion of ΔM^S and ΔM^D. This suggests a possible missing variable in the savings-versus-investment regression, at least if the money market does not clear without changes in market interest rates. Testing the relevance of this omitted variable bias would suggest going to the factors which affect ΔM^S and ΔM^D to see if they could cause bias from correlation between the regressor and error term in the Feldstein-Horioka estimation equation.

Home-Country Bias

Given the size of gains from international diversification, it has surprised numerous authors that such a high proportion of securities is held in domestic equities.[12] This propensity to hold home-country assets, which is illustrated in Table 1, is particularly surprising in view of the conclusion, first supported by Lessard (1976), that the gain from international diversification, given industrial diversification, exceeds the gain from industrial diversification, given international diversification. Even in the United States, which is 36.4% of the total market reflected in Table 1, portfolios are heavily biased towards domestic investment. While it may be argued that many of the firms in the U.S. market provide international diversification through their multinational nature, *a priori* it is difficult to believe that only 2% foreign listed firms would be enough to round out the portfolio and achieve efficient diversification.

Home-country bias relates to all the reasons we gave for caring about market integration, but mostly it relates to portfolio diversification. While a strong home-country bias is suggestive of direct or indirect barriers to cross-border capital movements, an alternative explanation of the bias is investor concern for domestic inflation. This is an aspect of work by Adler and Dumas (1983), Krugman (1981), Sercu (1980) and Stulz (1983). The relevance of this domestic-inflation argument depends crucially on departures from PPP, not *ex ante* but *ex post*, and on incomplete markets. Otherwise, the inflation risk would not exist, or it could be hedged. Could inflation hedging explain the very heavy bias towards domestic assets in typical portfolios? This is tantamount to asking whether risk aversion and PPP departures are sufficiently large, and whether state-contingent claims markets are sufficiently incomplete, for the observed home-asset preference. This question cannot properly be answered without constructing and estimating a model of asset and goods pricing and estimating this model, but it is hard to believe the numbers in Table 1 could be explained solely in terms of the hedging of domestic inflation.[13]

---

[12]See, for example, French and Poterba (1991) and Cooper and Kaplanis (1991).

[13]The model used to connect risk aversion and home-country bias, and whether the cause of PPP is endogenized in the model, can itself affect conclusions. See Uppal (1993) for a model where risk is *reduced* by holding foreign assets when shipping costs are introduced.

Table 1: The Domestic Component of Portfolios

Country	Market Capitalization (% of total)	Proportion in Domestic Equities (%)
France	2.6	64.4
Italy	1.9	91.0
Japan	43.7	86.7
Spain	1.1	94.2
Sweden	0.8	100.0
U.K.	10.3	78.5
U.S.A.	36.4	98.0
Germany	3.2	75.4

Source: Cooper and Kaplanis (1991).

Direct Observation of Institutional Barriers

Segmentation can be caused by barriers on foreign investment into a country and/or on what domestic residents can invest abroad. Inflow barriers can take various forms, such limits on the fraction of equity that can be held by foreigners, and/or restrictions on which industries in which foreigners may invest. Canada has a limited number of both types of restrictions. For example, capital outflows are limited on registered pension plans via a cap of 20% foreign content. Inflow investment in domestic air carriers is limited to 25% foreign ownership. Similarly, Japanese insurance companies and Spanish pension funds have 30% limits on the foreign content of investment portfolios. But are such restrictions binding, or can, for example, investors adjust unrestricted parts of their portfolios to offset limitations: Canadians might compensate for limited foreign content in registered pensions by having larger foreign content in their unrestricted portfolios than they might otherwise choose? Furthermore, might unrestricted flows on only some assets be sufficient to equalize expected returns on *all* assets? It is not necessary for all forms of capital to be mobile in order for capital markets to be integrated, any more than it is necessary for goods to be internationally traded for prices to be equal in different countries.

Evidence on the relevance of institutional restrictions is mixed. Studies suggesting they are relevant, thereby contributing to segmented markets, include that of Bonser-Neal, Brauer, Neal and Wheatley (1990). They find that closed-end country funds for France, Japan, Korea and Mexico trade at a premium vis à vis their net asset values. This suggests these markets are not fully integrated with the U.S. market. Hietala (1989) also supports segmentation, finding a difference between returns on Finnish assets required by residents versus foreigners. However, Gultekin, Gultekin and Penati (1989) find no evidence of segmentation between U.S. and Japanese financial markets after the removal of restrictions by enactment of the Foreign Exchange and Foreign Trade Control Law of 1980. Similarly, Fairlamb (1989) finds that the capital outflow restriction in Spain could not explain the home-country bias because the constraint was not binding: only 8% of pension funds were invested overseas, while the limit was 30%.

Policy Effectiveness and Interest Rates

An alternative view of the integration question, one that has received relatively little attention, is the effect of macroeconomic policy on interest rates and the effectiveness of the policies on output. Of course, this view relates to the policy-oriented reason presented at the beginning of this paper for being interested in the integration-segmentation question.

As we mentioned earlier, if capital markets are integrated, monetary and fixed policy should not affect real expected rates of return, and specifically real interest rates. In addition, expansionary fiscal policy would not be associated with crowding out, and expansionary monetary policy under fixed exchange rates should cause a reduction in foreign exchange reserves as the central bank buys back its currency to prevent depreciation.

While early work on the connection between fiscal policy, real interest rates, and crowding out found very little effect of budget deficits, suggestive of integrated capital markets, in the mid-1980s, when deficits exploded, evidence began to accumulate that supports market segmentation. For example, Hutchison and Pigott (1984), Hutchison and Pyle (1984), and Sinai and Rathjens (1983) all indicate some influence of fiscal deficits on interest rates, and/or the economy in ways that would not occur with complete market integration. Particularly strong evidence on fiscal deficits and interest rates indirectly supporting segmentation has been found by Tanzi (1985), although Tanzi finds that the sensitivity of interest rates to fiscal deficits has been declining. This decline in sensitivity is consistent with growing integration.

Conclusions

Even though there are alternative explanations of specific results with relevance to capital market integration, when viewed together the evidence on savings-investment correlations, home-country bias, MNC returns, asset pricing connections to domestic markets, and policy effects on real interest rates make it difficult to believe that capital markets are internationally integrated. Only the evidence on interest rates from uncovered interest parity appears consistent with market integration. Perhaps this is what we should expect to find. First, the price-oriented interest parity evidence is based on *marginal* returns, which is what we would expect to converge. Second, when the issue concerns equity investments, including direct investments, as the issue does when we consider home-country equity bias, returns on MNC that can overcome barriers etc., segmentation could arise from differential information: home-country investors are likely to know more about home investments than they do about foreign investments.[14] Indeed, in the case of foreign direct investment, not only is it necessary to have information at the time of making an investment, but in addition, it is necessary to continue to monitor and manage the investment. Furthermore, given that any asset may be sold when conditions change, steady flows of information are required.

In reality, we may never observe completely seamless, integrated markets. It is, for example, unlikely that Americans would accept 75% ownership of U.S. assets by foreigners, even if American holdings abroad matched or exceeded foreign holdings in the United States. Or how about 98% of Canadian assets

---

[14]This is the starting point of a recent paper by Brennan and Cao (1996) which derives implications which are in agreement with the segmentation evidence discussed in this paper.

Are Capital Markets Internationally Integrated?   *79*

being foreign owned? But should we feel any regret that international capital markets are not yet fully integrated and indeed may never be? Those who would like to think that domestic policymakers have influence may well be relieved to know there is some segmentation. So too might those who witnessed the crises in Mexico during the last few years, and have been troubled by the high interest rates associated with the "peso problem", where the possibility of depreciation has had long-term effects on economic growth. Economists have a predisposition towards frictionless markets, but as any engineer knows, without friction the world would be a very different place. Friction has two sides, a bad side in requiring extra energy, but a good side when it comes to acceleration/deceleration; the Second Law of Thermodynamics tells us that friction adds stability to systems. Perhaps we economists should be glad that while there is a great deal of slippage between markets, some frictions remain to help segment markets, providing policymakers with leverage, and insulating countries from adverse outside influences.

REFERENCES

Adler, M. and B. Dumas (1983), "International Portfolio Choice and Corporation Finance: A Synthesis", *Journal of Finance* (June), 1-19.

Agmon, T. and D.R. Lessard (1978), "Investor Recognition of Corporate International Diversification", *Journal of Portfolio Management* (Winter), 8-12.

Alexander, G.J., C.S. Eun and S. Janakiramanan (1988), "International Listings and Stock Returns: Some Empirical Evidence", *Journal of Financial and Quantitative Analysis* (June), 135-151.

Backus, D.K., P.J. Kehoe and F.E. Kydland (1992), "International Real Business Cycles", *Journal of Political Economy* (August), 745-775.

Bonser-Neal, C., G. Brauer, R. Neal and S. Wheatley (1990), "International Investment Restrictions and Closed-End Country Fund Prices", *Journal of Finance* (June), 523-547.

Brennan, M.J. and H.H. Cao (1996), "International Portfolio Investment Flows", Working Paper No. 3-96 (Los Angeles: University of California).

Brennan, M.J. and B. Solnik (1989), "International Risk Sharing and Capital Mobility", *Journal of International Money and Finance* (September), 359-373.

_____ (1992), "Risk Sharing and Capital Mobility: Reply", *Journal of International Money and Finance* (February), 122-123.

Cooper, I. and E. Kaplanis (1991), "What Explains the Home Bias in Portfolio Investment?" working paper, London Business School.

Devereaux, M.B., A.W. Gregory and G.W. Smith (1992), "Realistic Cross-Country Consumption Correlations in a Two-Country, Equilibrium Business Cycle Model", *Journal of International Money and Finance* (February), 3-16.

Dornbusch, R. (1988), *Open Economy Macroeconomics*, 2d ed. (New York: Basic Books).

Eun, C.S. and B.G. Resnick (1988), "Exchange Rate Uncertainty, Forward Contracts and International Portfolio Selection", *Journal of Finance* (March), 197-215.

Fairlamb, D. (1989), "The Elusive El Dorado of Spanish Pensions", *Institutional Investor* (April), 177-184.

Feldstein, M. and C. Horioka (1980), "Domestic Saving and International Capital Flows", *Economic Journal* (June), 314-329.

Frankel, J.A. (1993), "Quantifying International Capital Mobility in the 1980s", in J.A. Frankel (ed.), *On Exchange Rates* (Cambridge, MA: MIT Press), 41-69.

French, K.R. and J.M. Poterba (1991), "Investor Diversification and International Equity Returns", *American Economic Review, Papers and Proceedings* (May), 222-226.

Frenkel, J.A. and H.G. Johnson, eds. (1976), *The Monetary Approach to the Balance of Payments* (Toronto: University of Toronto Press).

Grubel, H. (1968), "Internationally Diversified Portfolios: Welfare Gain and Capital Flows", *American Economic Review* (December), 1299-1314.

Gultekin, M., N.B. Gultekin and A. Penati (1989), "Capital Controls and International Capital Market Segmentation: The Evidence from the Japanese and American Stock Markets", *Journal of Finance* (December), 849-869.

Heston, S.L. and K.G. Rouwenhorst (1994), "Does Industrial Structure Explain the Benefits of International Diversification", *Journal of Financial Economics* (August), 3-27.

Hietala, P. (1989), "Asset Pricing in Partially Segmented Markets: Evidence from the Finnish Market", *Journal of Finance* (September), 697-718.

Hughes, J.S., D.E. Logue and R.W. Sweeney (1975), "Corporate International Diversification and Market Assigned Measures of Risk and Diversification", *Journal of Financial and Quantitative Analysis* (November), 627-637.

Hutchison, M.M. and C. Pigott (1984), "Budget Deficits, Exchange Rates and the Current Account: Theory and U.S. Evidence", *Economic Review*, Federal Reserve Bank of San Francisco (Fall), 5-25.

Hutchison, M.M. and D.H. Pyle (1984), "The Real Interest Rate/Budget Deficit Link: International Evidence, 1973-1982", *Economic Review*, Federal Reserve Bank of San Francisco (Fall), 26-35.

Jacquillat, B. and B. Solnik (1978), "Multinationals are Poor Tools for Diversification", *Journal of Portfolio Management* (Winter), 8-12.

Jorion, P. (1985), "International Diversification with Estimation Risk", *Journal of Business* (July), 259-278.

Are Capital Markets Internationally Integrated?

Jorion, P. and E. Schwartz (1986), "Integration vs. Segmentation in the Canadian Stock Market", *Journal of Finance* (July), 603-616.

Krugman, P. (1981), "Consumption Preferences, Asset Demands, and Distribution Effects in International Financial Markets", *NBER* Working Paper No. 651 (Cambridge, MA: National Bureau of Economic Research).

Lessard, D.R. (1976), "World Country and Industry Relationships in Equity Returns: Implications for Risk Reduction through International Diversification", *Financial Analysts Journal* (January/February), 2-8.

Levi, M.D. (1973), "Errors in the Variables Bias in the Presence of Correctly Measured Variables", *Econometrica* (September), 985-986.

_____ (1976), "World-Wide Effects and Import Elasticities", *Journal of International Economics* (May), 203-214.

_____ (1977), "Measurement Errors and Bounded OLS Estimates", *Journal of Econometrics* (September), 165-171.

Levy, H. and M. Sarnat (1970), "International Diversification of Investment Portfolios", *American Economic Review* (September), 668-675.

Lewis, K.K. (1996), "What Can Explain the Apparent Lack of International Consumption Risk Sharing?" *Journal of Political Economy* (April), 267-297.

Lothian, J.R. (1995), "Capital Market Integration and Exchange-Rate Regimes in Historical Perspective", Fordham University, unpublished, December.

Mundell, R.A. (1968), *International Economics* (New York: MacMillan).

Murphy, R.G. (1984), "Capital Mobility and the Relationship Between Saving and Investment in OECD Countries", *Journal of International Money and Finance* (December), 327-342.

Obstfeld, M. (1992), "International Risk Sharing and Capital Mobility: Another Look", *Journal of International Money and Finance* (February), 115-121.

Odier, P. and B. Solnik (1993), "Lessons for International Asset Allocation", *Financial Analysts Journal* (March/April), 63-77.

Sercu, P. (1980), "A Generalization of the International Asset Pricing Model", *Revue de l'Association Française de Finance* (June), 91-135.

Sinai, A. and P. Rathjens (1983), "Deficits, Interest Rates and the Economy", *U.S. Review*, Data Resources (June), 1.27-1.41.

Solnik, B.H. (1974), "Why Not Diversify Internationally Rather than Domestically?" *Financial Analysts Journal* (July/August), 48-54.

Stulz, R. (1983), "The Demand for Foreign Bonds", *Journal of International Economics* (November), 225-238.

Tanzi, V. (1985), "Fiscal Deficits and Interest Rates in the United States: An Empirical Analysis, 1960-1984", *IMF Staff Papers*, 551-575.

Tobin, J. (1983), "Comment on Domestic Saving and International Capital Movements in the Long Run and the Short Run by Martin Feldstein", *European Economic Review* (March/April), 153-156.

Uppal, R. (1993), "A General Equilibrium Model of International Portfolio Choice", *Journal of Finance* (June), 529-553.

APPENDIX

Market Integration and the Efficiency of International Capital Allocation

The upper and centre panels in the figure show savings and investment in two countries, A and B. I_A and I_B show expected returns on incremental investments in the two countries as the rate of investment is expanded during any interval. Country A's expected returns are assumed to decline less rapidly as it pursues further investments than is the case for B. Savings rates are also shown for A and B, with these assumed independent of returns for simplicity of exposition.

Under autarky, or complete segmentation, returns are r^0_A and r^0_B. However, if capital markets are completely integrated returns in both countries are r_w, which is determined in the global capital market in the lower panel: here $S_A + S_B$ is the world savings supply, the horizontal sum of S_A and S_B, and $I_A + I_B$ is the world investment demand, the horizontal sum of I_A amd I_B. At r_w, B is a net lender of ΔI to A, and each dollar which flows from B to A results in a net expected return gain of the difference between the height of I_A and the height of I_B for that dollar of flow. The aggregate net gain from the capital flow from A to B is equal to the shaded area under I_A, which is the return on imported capital, minus the shaded area under I_B, which is the return foregone on exported capital. Clearly, the more different are investment opportunities versus the ability to finance opportunities, the greater is the aggregate gain from market integration.

The distribution of the higher aggregate expected returns is also shown in the figure. At r_w, country B receives area $fgjk$ from A on its lending, which equals $ebcd$ in A, which is what residents of A pay. The net return after borrowing costs in A is area aeb. The excess of earnings on capital sent from B to A over the expected return that would have been earned in B under autarky is area fgh. Of course, area $abcd$ minus area $fhjk$ equals area abe plus area fgh: the gains to A plus the gain to B equals the aggregate gain.

Figure A.1: The Allocation Gain from Integration

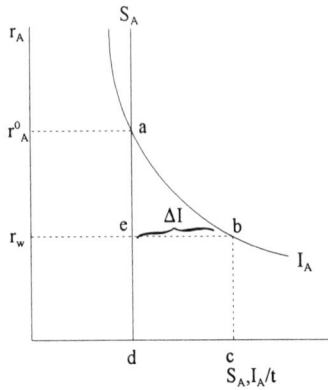

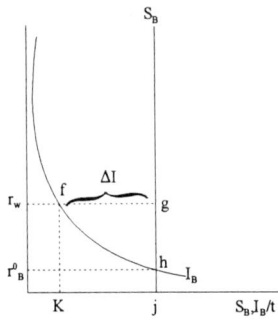

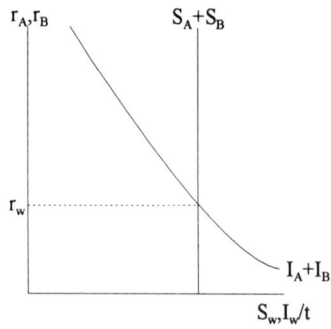

Session Three
FINANCIAL REGULATION IN
THE GLOBAL ECONOMY

FINANCIAL REGULATION IN THE GLOBAL ECONOMY AS PROPERTY RIGHTS

Randall Morck, University of Alberta
and
Bernard Yeung, University of Michigan

As pants the deer for cooling streams, so do I for regulation.
Alfred Krupp, 19th century German Industrialist

I. GOVERNMENT AND THE INNOCENCE OF ECONOMICS

People who spend their lives studying economics often develop odd attitudes towards government. Economists with a rightward perspective can become infatuated with the beauty of an untarnished free market economy — how its perfect symmetries create an astonishingly efficient information processing and action coordinating machine. To them, government is a nuisance that gums up this perfection and thereby destroys wealth, stunts progress, and harms people. Economists of a leftward persuasion see the free market economy as a soulless juggernaut, devoid of ethics or morality, that tramples human beings. They see government as a lash for taming the free market economy. By

---

This paper was completed while Bernard Yeung was visiting the Milken Institute for Job and Capital Formation.

moving a supply curve left and a demand curve up, by raising a wage level here and lowering an interest rate there, government can infuse an ethical quality into what would otherwise be a soulless monster.

These two views are quite similar: for both, government is something outside the economy. From the right, it is sand in the wheels; from the left, it is a guiding hand. But in neither case is government "inside" the economy or, in economists' jargon, "endogenous".

Our basic premise here is that this is wrong. Both views are deeply misleading in a modern market economy, and were never really right. This is because the government has the critical role of defining and enforcing property rights, and of generally fostering efficient economic exchanges. An entrepreneur must be sure his or her profits are theirs, or he/she will see little sense in launching a new business venture. An investor must be sure the money entrusted to the stewardship of business insiders, whether directly through financial markets or indirectly through financial institutions like banks, is his/her property. Without this government role, an advanced free market economy is impossible. Thus the traditional right is wrong. In the 1990s, globalization is drastically limiting governments' ability to do more than this, so the traditional left misses the point too.

In drafting new approaches to financial regulation, both traditional agendas are thus wanting. Consequently, we feel the key to sound government policy in this area is to focus on the basic purpose of financial regulations: balancing corporate insiders' and investors' property rights. We make several detailed suggestions as to how this might be done.

II. FINANCIAL MARKETS, FINANCIAL INSTITUTIONS AND CORPORATIONS

People with ideas often have little money, and people with money often have few ideas. The purpose of financial markets and institutions is to solve this imbalance. People with ideas, or entrepreneurs, get financing from people with money, or capitalists, to undertake business ventures.

People with money entrust their capital directly to entrepreneurs through financial markets, or do so indirectly via financial institutions like banks. Successful entrepreneurs pay back handsome returns to investors, who in turn give the money back to the entrepreneurs to fund further business ventures. If this cycle, illustrated in Figure 1, becomes established, an economy grows rapidly. If it does not, or if it fails, the economy fails too. This critical role for capital markets and institutions is why our economic system is called "capitalism".

Surprisingly, the magic ingredient that makes the cycle in Figure 1 work is trust. To outsiders who read of insider-trading scams and other white collar crime, this sounds strange. People who actually run businesses, however, are often surprised that anyone else is surprised. The people with money, who economists call capitalists, investors, or savers, and who include everyone from rich heiresses to Canada Savings Bond owners, must trust the financial system enough to rationally believe they will get back more money than they put in. In short, the people with money have to trust more or less the people with ideas.

The financial system that inspires this trust is both a puzzle and a thing of questionable morality to many people from post-communist countries and from traditional Third World societies. A Russian "biznesman" expressed the point succinctly to one of us recently: "Why do companies here pay dividends?" he asked. Public finance economists also often express puzzlement that companies continue to pay dividends during periods when dividends are heavily taxed. But the Russian was coming from a different direction — he thought rational corporate insiders should abscond with the investors' money, as many of his entrepreneurial countrymen actually have.

In fact, average people in the West can entrust their money to financial institutions and markets with a high probability of avoiding fraud. We shall argue that fostering their trust is the primary and critical purpose of financial regulation. From this perspective, financial regulation and corporate governance regulation are two sides of the same coin. Both are about protecting investors' property rights.

Figure 1: Financial Cycle

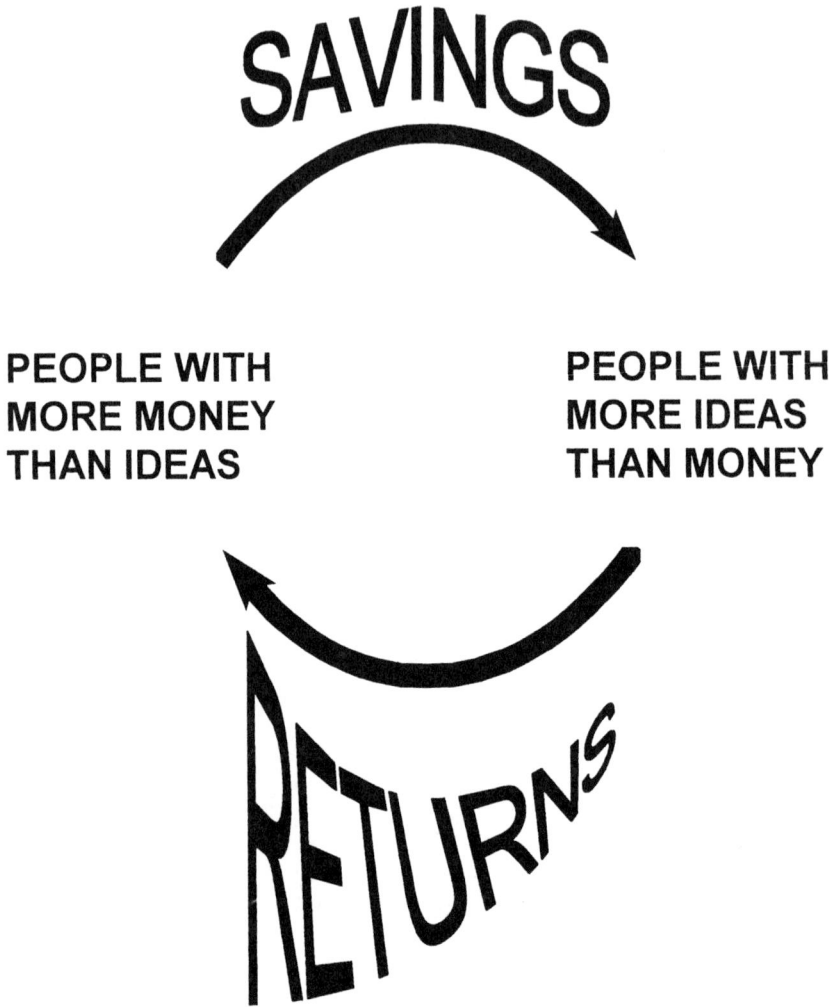

SAVINGS

PEOPLE WITH
MORE MONEY
THAN IDEAS

PEOPLE WITH
MORE IDEAS
THAN MONEY

RETURNS

Note: A Capitalist economy achieves sustained long-term growth once a cycle of this sort becomes self-sustaining. Investors entrust money to business insiders, who generate profits they share with investors, who reinvest more money. For this cycle to function, investors must have trust in the custodians of their savings.

Economists identify "property rights" protection as the weight-bearing beam that supports the superstructure of a capitalist economy.[1] If an entrepreneur's profits are not clearly his or hers, then there is little point in organizing a small business. If a consumer's goods are not clearly his or hers, then the incentives to work and save are undermined. If an investor's securities are not clearly his/hers, then the incentive to save is perverted. At a very basic level, people must trust the "system" enough to view accumulating wealth as a rational strategy. One of government's most important duties is the protection of investor's property rights over their investments.[2] Once investors can trust entrepreneurs and managers, and entrepreneurs and managers become worthy of their trust, value creating projects are financed and economic growth ensues.

Economists associated with the new "endogenous growth theory", such as Paul Romer, call diagrams like Figure 1 "positive feedback loops", and argue that they are critical in high-income economies. Positive feedback loops are systems that re-enforce themselves as they operate. We believe the property rights protection aspect of financial regulation is such a system for three reasons.

First, protecting investors' property rights encourages more investors to enter the market, which makes financial markets deeper and more liquid. This reduces investors' fears of not having access to their money when they need it, and leads to more investment, which adds further to market depth and liquidity, which ... . Second, growth in financial markets encourages some entrepreneurs to specialize in acquiring information about companies, which encourages more investors to enter the picture, which ... . This feedback system is especially strong when the information gatherer buys a relatively large block of stock. Such an investor has a clear incentive to monitor and, if necessary, challenge corporate insiders' decisions, so their presence encourages smaller investors to tag along. Third, better access to capital encourages more new firms to start up, which increases competition between firms for

---

[1]For an overview, see Shleifer and Vishny (1996).

[2]King and Levine (1993) find that a more sophisticated financial system significantly increases economic growth. Sachs and Warner (1995) report that "economic convergence", the rapid growth of poor countries as they catch up with rich countries, is only possible if the poor countries pursue free trade policies and protect property rights.

customers. Under a sufficiently honest legal system, this should encourage corporate insiders to work harder and make better use of investors' funds.

III. THE GOVERNANCE AND REGULATION OF COMPANIES AND BANKS — BACK TO THE BASICS

In 1669, Radisson and Grosselier obtained the backing of Prince Rupert, cousin to King George I of England, to establish a "Company of Adventurers to Trade into the Hudson's Bay". This, along with other just-formed companies to trade with India, the South Seas, and other newly opened markets, was one of the world's first corporations.

Until this time, business had always been a family affair. Families owned and operated stores, inns, looms, smithies, and all the other parts of a contemporary European economy. Wealthy families owned large farms, ships, or mills. But that was the scale of business. There was little that needed doing that a reasonably wealthy family could not manage. If extra money was needed, people could always turn to long-time friends and associates.

Trading into Hudson's Bay was different. It was a hugely expensive undertaking with unknown risks. If it succeeded, it also promised huge profits. Prince Rupert brought together representatives of a number of wealthy families, and obtained partial financing from each. No single family was so exposed to this risky undertaking that failure would ruin it, yet each stood to do well if fortune smiled.

Later, huge canal networks and other major investments in industrialization would have to be financed the same way. There were simply too many projects that needed doing, and with promised big returns, for the limited number of wealthy families to handle. Investors had to pool their money and entrust it to professional business managers — the people who actually handled the building and running of the canals, etc.

Hundreds, perhaps thousands of complete strangers handing over huge amounts of money to other complete strangers to build canals? It sounds like an engraved invitation to scoundrels and con artists. And it was.

The most celebrated scam of this era is the South Seas Company of England, though there were others equally colourful in other European countries. The South Seas Company was to handle trade between Britain and the southern waters of the Atlantic Ocean. Amid great hype, it raised huge amounts of money in the early eighteenth century. As far as historians know, it never got as far as even chartering a ship. In 1722, the South Seas Company and a host of copy-cat frauds were exposed, and thousands of people lost their savings — including Sir Isaac Newton. Corporate governance problems were front and centre in the first decades of modern business.

Though historians debate the true intentions of the British Parliament, it passed the Bubble Act of 1722, which made companies with traded shares illegal. Other European countries took similar measures in response to similar frauds. (The Hudson's Bay Company survived because of a grandfather clause.) Of course, this was no solution. Britain and other countries needed large pools of money for industrialization — especially to build a transportation network. Parliament was soon in the business of granting waivers of the Bubble Act, or parliamentary "charters", to such businesses. The reason our banks are called "chartered banks" is because they were established by Parliament under rules that descended from this era of British law.

When railroads and large industrial factories came of age in the nineteenth century, the Bubble Act slowly gave way. Governments in Canada and else-where retained the responsibility of granting charters to banks, perhaps because banks are more central to public trust in the financial system than are other corporations. It is no overstatement to say that the evolution of financial and corporate law over the past three centuries was very much an attempt to clear the way for more Hudson's Bay Companies while shutting out more South Seas Companies. This is the explicit purpose of corporate governance law, financial regulations, and the implicit purpose of many other aspects of business law.

IV. THE STATE AS MIDWIFE AT THE BIRTH OF CAPITALISM

The moral of the story is that capitalism depends deeply on people's ethics. Investors have to be able to turn over their money to perfect strangers with a reasonable expectation that those strangers will use their money honestly and try in good faith to pay a fair return. In a world infested with rascals, this seems a naive hope upon which to base an economic system. The South Seas fiasco convinced honest entrepreneurs, financiers, and bankers that they had to devise a credible way of convincing investors that they were, in fact, honest.

Banks and Financial Institutions

The purpose of banks was to sidestep the need for investors having to develop trust in business insiders. The investors need only trust the bankers to be sure that the business insiders deserve trust. Instead of needing information about every entrepreneur whose shares you wanted to buy, you just had to find a banker with good judgement and let him do the rest of the work. Thus developed the huge industry of financial intermediation.

Unfortunately, some bankers occasionally did not measure up. From the beginnings of modern banking in renaissance Italy to the 1930s, bank failure was a continuing spectre. Spectacular failures of huge banks decorate the panorama of European, American and Japanese history. Kindelberger (1978) argues that these repeated bank failures, as well as other crises of confidence in the financial system, triggered periodic breakdowns in the cycle of trust illustrated in Figure 1, and that these breakdowns caused the depressions that occurred every couple of decades through the eighteenth, nineteenth and early twentieth centuries.

Over the years, governments imposed increasingly strict regulations on the business of banking, usually in response to dramatic bank failures. Banking throughout Europe began along the lines now preserved in German *Discontogesellschaften*, or universal banks. Once a bank got the go-ahead from government to go into business, it could not only take in savings and make loans, but also fund business ventures, buy securities and real estate, underwrite new issues, and sell securities in-house. Some of these lines of business are highly risky uses of depositors' money, and a series of scandals and bank failures in the nineteenth and early twentieth centuries increasingly convinced most governments to enact reserve requirements of various sorts, and to restrict banking to "safe" activities like mortgages and loans. The exception was Germany, where a committee to study such reforms was dismissed by the newly elected National Socialist government in the 1930s.

Bankers themselves understood well the importance of keeping investors' trust, and so had little interest in diversifying into other lines of business. Banking was the business of guarding other peoples' money as yet other people used it. Bankers' mission was to protect their depositors' property rights while earning them as high a return as was safe.

Corporations and Financial Markets

Corporate governance is also about protecting investors' property rights. Here, the company's top managers have a fiduciary duty to act for shareholders, and are vulnerable to court action if they fail in this duty. Companies must hold meetings to inform shareholders of the companies' undertakings, and the shareholders elect boards of directors to oversee the managers. Shareholders have limited liability, so mistakes or wrongs by the stranger who managed the company cannot be blamed on an investor who knew nothing of them.

In short, all of modern corporate governance came out of a very real economic problem — honest entrepreneurs needed to be able to convince shareholders to trust them, and saw binding their actions by law as the best way to do this. Rascals would quickly be exposed, and honest entrepreneurs would be left to gather investors' money.

The Economic Importance of Trust

During this same period, businesses were coming to grips with trust problems in other dimensions too. Suppliers had to trust customers and customers suppliers. Merchants had to trust middlemen, and everyone had to trust shippers (the people with the canals and railways). In a backwater agrarian economy, people had the luxury of only dealing with friends or family. In a modern industrial economy, business with relative strangers was the order of the day. Contract law, tort law, property law and criminal law all developed to foster trust and punish betrayal in business.

The magnificent feats of a free market economy are utterly dependent on a pervasive atmosphere of trust between strangers. It is too time consuming and expensive, not to mention intrusive, for everyone to gather information themselves about the moral character of business people. The first and most essential role of government is to build and maintain a network of laws that remove untrustworthy business people from the scene. By establishing rules of good conduct, government makes a free market economy possible. The right-leaning economist who scorns government is ignorant of history. The left-leaning economist who laments the absence of ethics in business has not thought hard enough about how the economy works.

V. THE STATE AS CAPITALISM'S WET NURSE

Government is an integral and essential part of any capitalist economy. Government must establish and enforce rules of good business conduct to promote trust. This view of government is deeper and more useful than the leftist and rightist caricatures at the beginning of this paper. Government is now clearly affecting the economy, but the picture is still incomplete. Government is also affected by the free market economy.

With government making rules everywhere, business insiders and bankers quickly realized that they might be able to influence these rules to their advantage and to the detriment of their competitors. Politicians and bureaucrats, like everyone else, needed money — and businesses had lots. In countries where buying political favours with money was frowned on, there was always the possibility of favour trading — campaign contributions for favourable legislation, or job-creating investment in swing ridings for subsidies. Soon bankers were protected from foreign, or even non-local, competition; and businesses were sheltered behind other anti-competitive regulations, tariffs and quotas.

The view of government as a neutral referee that set rules, punished violators and promoted the public good in the interests of fairness alone now seems quaintly naïve. Yet this is as far as most economics textbooks, even advanced ones, go. Yes, there may be "market failures", but if the government levied this tax or changed that regulation, we could get to the economy's "optimum". The mindset that government is a neutral referee still governs much of economic theory in public finance, industrial organization, macroeconomics and other subdisciplines — and so compromises the relevance of much of the policy advice they generate.

The Nobel laureate James Buchanan developed a theory of government, called Public Choice Theory, that takes into account the pervasive favour trading and patronage that characterize government. In Buchanan's economy, corporate managers consider an expenditure on political lobbying just as they consider any other corporate investment. If lobbying promises a higher return than building a new factory, the politicians will be wined and dined, and the building site will stay vacant. The more rules and regulations there are, the higher the return to lobbying becomes, and the more funds are diverted away from economically real purposes. Public choice economists call people who lobby government for favours "political rent seekers" and the returns they gain by lobbying "political rents".

Political rent seeking can easily multiply in a chain reaction that can stifle economic activity. If politicians and bureaucrats can expect payoffs for waiving regulations, they have a strong incentive to make more regulations, and onerous ones at that. As the number of regulations grows, the return to political rent seeking rises while that to building factories falls. Many development economists believe this is what went so drastically wrong in many less developed economies in the postwar period. Entrepreneurs came to expect politicians and bureaucrats to confiscate all profits as bribes for waiving regulations, so legal private business ground to a standstill.[3]

VI. GLOBALIZATION: WEANING BUSINESS FROM THE STATE

In free market economic theory, things do not usually get out of control like that. Checks and balances usually come into play to damp down such things. You raise your prices too much and a competitor steps in to steal your customers. Only a monopoly can get away with gouging the public for long.

---

[3]The Peruvian economist H. DeSoto, in his highly influential book *The Other Path*, describes how it took his well-funded economics research institute two years and huge bribes to get permission to set up a small business in Lima. X. Klitgaard's book *Tropical Gangsters*, tells similar stories about sub-Saharan Africa.

Monopoly Government

That is precisely the problem — for most of the past century, government was a monopoly provider of economic order. If a rival firm lobbies politicians and wins favours, you could be ruined. You have no choice but to lobby harder. If you lose the lobbying war, or refuse to participate, you fund the opposition in the hope they might be different — and wait for an election. Until then, you accept Pierre Trudeau's famous one fingered salute. If there is no prospect of changing the government (as in many developing countries in most of the post-war period), you quit business and go into government.

This status gave government greater power to affect private economic decisions for good or ill than is now possible. Tools like taxes, subsidies, trade barriers and capital controls let governments affect prices throughout a national economy. For example, a government could provide subsidies to a favoured firm that would let it market its output at lower prices. This theoretically gives it an "edge" that its immediate rivals could only get from R&D to devise new low-cost technology.

In the postwar period, governments throughout the world came to view influencing corporate decision making as their legitimate responsibility. The economy was seen as too important to be left to business. Issues of social justice, fairness, regional equality and national identity required an active public sector input. Governments began to pass increasingly detailed laws affecting financial markets and institutions, and corporations' access to them. The original purpose of government in a capitalist economy, defining and enforcing property rights to make the cycle in Figure 1 work, was forgotten in a surge of social optimism.

Perhaps the most comprehensive of these intervention strategies were so-called "industrial policies", government coordinated plans to by-pass financial markets and institutions completely, and to inject money into some firms and take it away from others through systems of taxes and subsidies. (Of course, individuals' taxes also went into the pot.) Although those directly involved in formulating and implementing industrial policies often have high praise for themselves, detailed empirical studies of industrial policies come to uniformly pessimistic conclusions. Even Japan's postwar industrial policy, which for years enjoyed a mystical reputation for success, is now widely recognized as a mirage. Japan grew rapidly because of its high savings rate and rapid incorporation of foreign technology, but despite its industrial policy.[4] The Japanese government subsidized proven losers, and firms that received government money tended to perform even worse following the subsidies. Everywhere, government-subsidized corporations have attracted reputations for pork, inefficiency and corruption; and have no proven track record for stimulating overall economic activity. Even touted success stories like Airbus Industrie S.A. have less sparkle when investigated closely.[5]

Why do "industrial policies" and other forms of government intervention in the finance business not work? The answer has two parts.

First, direct government intervention itself needs to be financed. One source is taxes on individuals or on other businesses. Taxing individuals reduces their spending power and thus slows the economy.[6] Taxing other businesses slows their growth. Government borrowing, although a substitute for taxes in the short term, is just a mechanism for delaying necessary tax hikes until the government's debts come due. Governments that accumulate large debts, like Canada's and Italy's, also end up having to devote steadily larger fractions of the budget to interest payments, and face a steadily worsening tradeoff between raising taxes and cutting spending. An alternative source of funds for the government is newly printed money. This option leads to inflation, another form of tax. Countries, like Brazil, that have become politically committed to large-scale government programs but have no reliable tax base, are destined to suffer more or less permanent hyperinflation. If most subsidies go to losers, the typical industrial policy amounts to taxing winners to subsidize losers — hardly a recipe for success.

The second reason large-scale government involvement in the economy causes problems is that these well-intentioned policies erode property rights in the

---

[4]See Beason and Weinstein (1996) for a detailed statistical analysis of the assistance granted by the Japanese Ministry for International Trade and Industry.

[5]*The Economist*, February 3, 1996, p. 68 reports studies showing that Airbus fails to make enough profits to cover its subsidies.

[6]Keynesian arguments that tax and spend policies stimulate growth are now regarded as disproved. Such policies' effects are only detectable in the very short term.

private sector, and this compromises the integrity of the cycle in Figure 1. Taxes erode private property rights and subsidies give public property to private individuals. Both render vague the property rights of investors in their investments and of business insiders in their businesses. In economies with already poorly functioning legal systems, large-scale government involvement in finance leads many government officials into lives of corruption. Highly respected economists in Third World countries soberly argue that the sole purpose of most government regulations that affect business and finance is to provide opportunities for bureaucrats and politicians to accept bribes for looking away.[7] A successful business is simply subjected to more inspections, permit requirements, and fines until its profits fall to zero. Clearly, this lack of property rights protection impedes development.[8] In these countries, industrial policies or other large-scale programs of government intervention are seen as nothing more than smoke screens for establishing new bribe collection points. This cynical, but often realistic view encourages businesses to evade regulations and rules when they can, and to regard such behaviour as ethical. Clearly, this fosters an atmosphere of mistrust and makes capital difficult for entrepreneurs to obtain.

Most advanced countries do not have this form of endemic corruption, though some, like Italy, appear to come close. However, even in Canada and the United States, political economy considerations influence government decisions. In 1984 the United States established long-term trade barriers against steel imports. The steel firms that benefited from this policy were money losing, technologically retarded firms with large budgets for political influence buying.[9] In developed countries, political economy transactions are usually campaign contributions, favour trading and patronage — not outright

---

[7]See, e.g., DeSoto (1989). One should also notice that "industry policies" legitimizes entanglement between government and business and turns into sanctioned corruption and protectionism. See, e.g., the *Wall Street Journal's* October 9 article on the tainted blood scandal in Japan.

[8]Some eminent economists, notably Baumol (1990) and Murphy *et al.* (1991), argue that this is the primary reason most Third World countries remain mired in poverty.

[9]See Lenway *et al.* (1996) for an empirical study of steel protection in the United States that supports these conclusions.

corruption. Yet the result is the same. A large-scale government intervention in the economy creates numerous opportunities for crypto-corruption. If lobbying politicians brings more benefits to corporate managers than does R&D, firms will lobby more and lay off scientists.

Economists tend to associate monopolies with trouble, and monopoly government is no exception. Governments throughout the world pursued variously wrong-headed but often earnest policies aimed at miraculously curing millennia-old ills like poverty. In doing this, governments neglected or abandoned their critical role as protectors of property rights and guarantors of trust, and set up huge bureaucracies that were deeply vulnerable to rent seeking. Businesses that fundamentally disagreed with the way government supervised the economy had little choice but to wait out the bad times and give money to opposition politicians' campaigns. In this environment, lobbying and favour trading became the normal channels of government-business interaction.

Competitive Government

In early twentieth century London, private clubs proliferated. People interested in theatre joined theatre clubs, smokers joined smoking clubs, readers joined literary clubs, and misanthropes joined clubs where speaking was forbidden. James Buchanan developed a theory of government as "clubs": governments compete for citizens and their taxes just as clubs compete for members and their dues. A club with attractive rules gains members and wealth. Until recently, this was regarded as an intellectual curiosity by most public finance economists — a clever theory with little practical use. At best, the theory might describe adjacent municipalities or counties, but no application beyond that seemed plausible.

In the late twentieth century, as the reality of the global economy has become evident, Buchanan's view of government seems increasingly realistic. If people with entrepreneurial ability, money or skills dislike the rules one government establishes, they can do business under another. Government is now part of the competitive economy, not above it. If Canada's government charges more for running an efficient and orderly economy than do foreign governments, Canada loses economic activity to its competitors.[10]

A key role in transformation is a growing importance of financial markets and a declining importance of traditional financial institutions like banks that take in deposits and make loans. In part perhaps because banks were protected from competition more than financial markets were, banks have been losing business to markets steadily since the 1970s. In the United States, competition from money markets forced the repeal of the anti-competitive "regulation Q" bank deposit interest rate ceilings in 1979. A series of reforms in Japan have dismantled legislative barriers (generally believed to have been devised by the large Japanese banks) that prevented Japanese firms from issuing traded bonds. New financial institutions have developed innovative ways of "securitizing" things like mortgages and student loans so they can be traded on markets instead of handled through banks. There is a clear trend in the advanced industrial economies towards greater "disintermediation" — that is, towards sidestepping banks and using financial markets to raise money instead. Deregulation of financial markets, mainly ending anti-competitive protection of brokers, dealers and exchanges, has spurred financial markets to seize these opportunities.

Canadian banks have clearly understood these signs, and have moved to diversify out of the traditional business of deposits and loans. Canadian banks are involved in all aspects of securities transactions and in the design of new securities, and are present in financial markets around the world.

Financial markets are more footloose and free than was traditional banking. When most financial transactions were done through banks, a government could tax, regulate or supervise the banks and thereby control the transactions. With financial markets, this does not work. When John Kennedy tried to tax the foreign bond market in New York, it simply moved to London and became the Eurobond market. The more finance shifts to markets from banks, the more cosmopolitan capital becomes. In a system of global financial markets, and where markets in different countries compete for investors' funds, governments' control is minimized.

---

[10]MacIntosh (1995) independently comes to similar conclusions about financial regulation in Canada. His discussion parallels ours in many ways.

Yet globalization goes further than this. A typical Canadian toy store contains toys designed in the United States, produced in Thailand using plastic from Canada, packaged and labelled in Hong Kong, shipped by a Taiwan company, promoted and marketed by both a British and an American company, and sold in a local retail store. There are licensing and other agreements between the U.S. toy-design property-right owners and Asian manufacturers, the U.S. distributor and so on. These agreements may be designed and monitored by lawyers in the United Kingdom, Hong Kong and even China. The toy designer has collaborative agreements with the Canadian-owned film producing company whose movie characters appear on the toys — the toy designer may even be the film producing company's subsidiary. Both may hire the Irish to process their accounting data.

An immediate implication of this global economic interlinkage, and of the increasing importance of markets rather than banks for financing, is that difficult governments can be avoided. In a global market, Saudi plastic can readily replace Canadian plastic in the Thai factories if Canadian petrochemicals become more expensive. This means Canadian government policies that adversely affect Canadian petrochemicals firms can have huge and immediate consequences. And if a multinational petrochemicals firm, even a Canadian-based one, finds that Canadian government policies create unacceptable costs, it simply shifts production elsewhere — taking jobs and economic opportunities with it.

Governments throughout the world are beginning to remember the critical importance of basic economic property rights, and are adjusting their laws and institutions to reflect this. This worldwide economic liberalization has greatly increased the number of plausible locations for production facilities. Advances in communication technologies and reduced trade barriers make locating production facilities abroad more feasible than in the past. These developments make businesses increasingly impatient with government ineptness in any one country.

These same developments make firms increasingly unable to tolerate poor government policies, even should they wish to. Globalization makes companies formerly separated by geography and politics into direct competitors. A company that accepts higher costs due to poor government cannot compete against other companies that do not.

In short, globalization means governments must design and implement only sound economic policies. If they do not, their economies will suffer more than they would have in the past. This is because businesses can now choose among competing jurisdictions for the government policies that appear most attractive.

This is deeply disturbing to many with vested interests tied to rent seeking. Politicians see their power to influence business curtailed. Civil servants' freedom of action in imposing and enforcing regulations is constrained. Social reformers can no longer force wealth redistribution. Tax authorities see national revenue bases becoming increasingly fluid. Entrenched Canadian corporations, whom government has sheltered from real competition, are facing real competition for the first time. Entrenched castes of labour, who obtained government-sanctioned monopoly status as labour suppliers to whole industries, face competition from workers abroad.

VII. IMPLICATIONS FOR FINANCIAL REGULATION

The globalization of the economy places new constraints on government policies of all sorts. Tax, social, fiscal, or regulatory policies that extract too high a price have immediate effects. Financial regulation is no exception.

Footloose capital can and will leave for other jurisdictions if Canadian financial markets and institutions do not appear trustworthy. The only way to stem such an out-flow is for Canadian investments to trade at lower prices and offer higher returns. At the same time, Canada's trust fostering regulations cannot impose too heavy a burden on entrepreneurs, or they too can go elsewhere.

Canadians are used to thinking of government as able to solve any problem, and too readily conclude that government deliberately ignores them or "doesn't care" when it fails to ease the burdens of their lives. This attitude must change. Canadians must be educated to appreciate the limits of government power. Viking legends record that the Danish high king, Canute, grew weary of his ministers continual sycophantic lobbying and resolved to demonstrate the limits of royal power. He ordered his court moved to the beach, and decreed that the tide should not come in. He then had his ministers continue the normal affairs of state as the tide rose and drenched them all.

Globalization is much like King Canute's tide. It vividly highlights the limits of government power. Canada's governments have three basic options for dealing with this situation.

Option 1: Build Dykes Fast!

Canada can use taxes and investment barriers to wall off the outside world and "insulate" itself from the global economy. The essential idea is to protect the Canadian government's monopoly status as a provider of public order, and to seal off Canada's financial system from the rest of the world. This would allow Canada to implement laws detrimental to investors or entrepreneurs without an immediate flight of capital or ideas. There are several approaches to achieving this that Canada and other countries have tried.

One approach is to tax off-shore investment by residents. We feel this is unlikely to work. Multinational corporations can readily shift revenues and costs between jurisdictions to reduce their corporate taxes. Canadian individuals are becoming increasingly unwilling to tolerate higher taxes. Evasion of the GST is generally believed to be widespread, and is not regarded as unethical by a disturbingly large number of taxpayers. In short, raising the differential tax rate between foreign and Canadian investments by enough to deter foreign investment is unlikely to work, likely to stimulate further tax evasion, and would be politically unpalatable.

A second approach is to restrict off-shore investment by Canadians. Current rules on the foreign content of RRSPs and pension funds are examples of this policy. Unfortunately, an increasing number of Canadians in their 30s and 40s are convinced that government old-age pensions will not exist in a meaningful way when they reach retirement age. As this "baby boom" bulge in the population's age distribution becomes more concerned with retirement, rules that "protect" them from investing abroad are likely to be politically dangerous to any party.

Yet there appears to be considerable political sympathy for such policies in some quarters. First, some politicians and bureaucrats believe these policies help government borrow at low rates. Second, established Canadian corporations believe these policies help them to raise capital at low rates, and are grateful to politicians who help them do this.

It is doubtful that any practical market "closure" policies can actually make cheap capital available. Given the existing financial market integration in North America (e.g., cross-listing by Canadian firms, cross-border subsidiaries of financial service firms, the NAFTA) and the presence of off-shore markets, sophisticated Canadian savers should have little difficulty in by-passing capital control measures. Even if artificial market closure is successfully implemented, it gives Canadian borrowers cheap capital only if Canadian investment is less than Canadian saving. This does not seem to be the case — Canada has traditionally been a net capital importing country.

Consequently, it is improbable that such constraints actually reduce borrowers' costs of capital. They do, however, prevent investors from diversifying internationally, and thus burden Canadian investors with unnecessary risk. By limiting Canadian investors' investment alternatives, market closure regulations do ease corporate governance pressure on Canadian managers. If investors have few alternative places to put their money, they cannot punish badly run firms by selling out. Since most Canadian firms are closely-held, even large investors like pension funds can have only limited impact on management policies. (U.S. activist pension funds like the California Public Employees' Retirement system [CalPERs] explicitly invest only in widely-held U.S. firms.) This poor corporate governance reduces the values of outstanding shares held by Canadian investors, thereby reducing the returns they earn on their savings. Yet any new shares must be priced low enough to provide a competitive return, so the companies' costs of new capital are not reduced.

In short, market closure adversely affects investors but probably does nothing to reduce borrowers' costs of capital. They create unnecessary financial insecurity, and exacerbate Canada's demographic savings-investment imbalance. Since large investors like pension funds can side-step such restrictions by using derivatives to bet on changes in the values of foreign assets without actually buying the assets, such regulations also encourage the use of derivatives. Most importantly, though, we believe regulations that many Canadians would see as cynical exploitation of their retirement concerns would only encourage further unhealthy contempt for government.

Existing differential tax treatment on foreign and Canadian investments should be abolished, quantity constraints on investment by pension funds and RRSP owners should be discontinued, and no new barriers of these sorts should be contemplated. Cheap captive savings is an "advantage" of the past. Canada's financial markets and institutions should be fully exposed to foreign and domestic competition.

Option 2: Breeding an Economy of Bottom Feeders

Conservatives often argue that the global economy means government must become radically smaller. Minimal financial regulation is often seen as a part of this.

Minimal financial regulation attracts capital to countries like the Netherlands Antilles and the Channel Islands. It stimulates vibrant money laundering industries and fosters financial expertise in the evasion of other countries' taxes and other rules. To some extent Canada has pursued this strategy with the Vancouver Stock Exchange's history of lax regulation, which it is attempting to change, and the Alberta Stock Exchange's "blind pools", which remain popular.

But ultimately, as we argued above, finance is about trust! The purpose of corporations, financial institutions and financial markets is to engender trust between strangers: the insiders who run the corporation and the investors and the capitalists who fund their undertakings. A "minimalist" approach to corporate governance and financial regulation ignores a critical role of government in fostering trust.

How does Canada's current financial system stack up against other countries? This is a complex question, and a simple scale is difficult to defend. One approach for gauging outsiders' trust in insiders, suggested by the Italian financial economist Luigi Zingales, is to compare the values of corporate shares that carry voting rights (and are usually held by insiders) with otherwise identical shares that do not carry such rights (and are usually held by outsiders) (see Zingales, 1994 and 1995). If corporate insiders fulfil their fiduciary duty — to act in the interests of all shareholders equally — the difference in value should be small. If they do not, the difference should be large. Table 1 summarizes the results of several studies of this "voting premium" in different countries.

Although the studies are from different years, the changes over time in any one country's average voting premium is small relative to the difference between that in Italy, where voting shares are worth 182% of the value of otherwise equivalent non-voting shares, and the United States, where the ratio is 105.4%. Why is control worth more in some countries than others?

Zingales argues that it is because different financial systems represent different penalties to negligence, incompetence, or even larceny by crooked insiders. In short, control is worth more in Italy because the scope for theft by insiders is broader there.[11] These depressed public share prices in Italy mean firms' costs of capital are high in Italy. This sabotages the cycle of capitalist growth illustrated in Figure 1.

Investors, all else being equal, prefer to place their money with people they trust. Several recent empirical studies present evidence that the biggest impediment to growth in many countries may well be a "trust gap" caused by their legal, financial and regulatory systems (see Shleifer and Vishny, 1996; and King and Levine, 1993). Table 1 shows that Canada's system is better than Italy's by a large margin, but still might be improved. We believe there is little advantage in Canada moving towards the Italian low-level equilibrium. A minimalist regulatory strategy is neither a necessary nor a desirable implication of globalization.

Option 3: Competitive High End Government

We believe the strategy that Canada's governments should pursue is to provide "expensive government that's worth the money". Laws and regulations can be valuable to the economy if they promote trust, or investor

---

[11]Caprio and Floreanti (1995) find that the voting premium in Italy has declined markedly, to just over 18% recently, as criminal investigations have exposed corporate corruption. They also report evidence consistent with stock price manipulation as dominant shareholders sell out. Smith *et al.* (1989) report a slightly lower average premium of about 10% on superior voting shares in 1987.

Table 1: The Premium of Voting Stock over Otherwise Identical Non-Voting Stock in Various Countries

Country	Average Voting Premium %	Study
United States	5.4	Lease *et al.* (1983)
Sweden	6.7	Rydquist (1987)
United Kingdom	13.3	Megginson (1990)
Switzerland	20.0	Horner (1988)
Canada	23.3	Robinson and White (1990)
Israel	45.5	Levy (1982)
Italy	82.0	Zingales (1994)

Source: Authors' Compilation.

confidence (see also MacIntosh, 1995). We believe there are several approaches to providing such a service.

Disclosure

A central goal of corporate governance regulation should be "transparency". Failure to disclose important information must be severely punished. Self-regulation cannot punish rascals as severely as government can, so government-mandated disclosure laws are sensible. If transparency helps Canadian firms earn and keep investors' trust, investors will acknowledge the lower risk by accepting lower returns. Companies, in turn, are attracted by this legitimately cheap capital.

Government must balance transparency against compliance costs. The cost of complying with disclosure regulations is a hidden *tax*, and too high a tax could drive business elsewhere. Regulations' value must justify their cost.

Financial institutions should have to disclose their non-performing loans and their exposures to risk. In the late 1980s, Principal Trust, an Alberta-based financial institution failed and wiped out many thousands of people's savings. A scandal ensued, in which it became evident that Alberta regulators had known for several years that Principal was in trouble, but had informed the public that its finances were sound. Meanwhile, Principal undertook questionable investments to remedy its troubles. Alberta regulators testified, in essence, that they were afraid that exposing Principal's true picture would compromise public confidence, and hasten its fall.

We believe government regulators should never have been in this position. Had Principal been required to disclose its financial picture, the public would have begun demanding higher rates for bearing higher risk early on. It is at least an even bet that Principal's managers would also have been more careful custodians of other people's money if those people had known how their money was being invested.

In the case of financial markets, the important disclosure rules are those for public companies. Regulations should force the disclosure of items that well run companies should be keeping track of for internal purposes anyway. This minimizes compliance costs. We present the following "wish list" of things we would like to know about the companies we invest in, and which we think most companies already know about themselves, but which Canadian law does not require to be disclosed.

> *R&D spending*
> *Advertising costs*
> *White collar versus blue collar employees*
> *Labour costs and management costs*
> *Standardized lines of business accounting data*
> *Standardized foreign operations accounting data*
> *Pension obligations and assets at fair market values*

In some cases, corporate insiders may fear the public's reaction to disclosure, for example, of CEO paycheques. We believe the answer is not to hide CEO pay, but to convince the public they are worth the money. This has been done with sports heroes and rock stars. CEOs should be an easier sell. If a firm creates wealth, jobs, exports, etc., its CEO's pay can be placed in perspective, and public support (or at least acceptance of high CEO pay) should be forthcoming. High pay for poorly performing CEOs might receive justifiable criticism.

Low Cost Trust

Financial regulation should try to foster the most trust for the lowest cost. Our current approach does not always do this. Many of our regulatory systems grew, through historical accidents and lobbying pressure, into rather high cost/low trust creatures.

For example, consider bankruptcy laws. Under Canada's (and most other countries') bankruptcy rules, a bankruptcy is a prolonged and disruptive process that further cripples the afflicted business. Much of this complication arises because the fate of the bankrupt firm and the disposition of creditors' claims are settled as one problem. In fact, they are two separate issues, and need not be confounded.

A simple alternative would give the firm's creditors common shares on the day bankruptcy was declared, and then let them either sell their shares for cash or remain as owners of the firm.[12] At a shareholders' meeting, the new owners could decide whether or not to sack the management, restructure, or take other steps to increase firm value. Creditors who would have had different seniority rights under the old system would get different numbers of shares per $1,000 of debt under this system. The old shareholders could each be given an "out of the money call" to buy back their shares by paying off a proportion of the firm's excess debts equal to their previous fractional equity ownership. The critical point of this scheme is that it totally separates the business of what is the best way to up the firm's value from the business of who gets how much. Bankruptcy could be cheap and socially relatively painless if we wanted it to be.

---

[12]The basics of this plan were proposed by Aghion *et al.* (1992, p. 81).

Instead, our bankruptcy rules are costly and disruptive, and Canadian businesses, investors, employees and politicians rightly fear bankruptcies, especially large ones. This gives rise to a sort of "Peter Pan" approach to corporate governance. Canada is full of century-old "infant industries" that never grow up. When trouble arises, they cry out for government to wave its magic wand and bail them out. Peter Pan economics does win investors' trust, but it is a costly way of doing so.

Canadian banks made bad loans on speculative real estate ventures in the late 1980s, and the government of the day felt bank failures would destroy trust. As Figure 2 shows, chartered banks' rate spread is now much higher than it was a decade ago, the banks are posting record earnings, and government has no apparent concerns about lack of competition.[13] In the 1970s, banks got into trouble with Latin American debts, and governments assisted in resolving the problem. In the 1930s, Canadian banks were virtually all insolvent, and the government cooperatively changed the definition of solvency.

Savers are paying for "trustworthy" banks with record low rates on bread and butter bank accounts, with high spreads, and with a bevy of service charges. Is this really necessary? Bank runs in the United States in the 1930s may well have contributed to the depth of the depression by destroying public trust in the financial system. Yet there may well be easy ways to have bank failures that actually foster trust.

In principle, a bank could fail without missing a day's business. The bank's shares could become options, and the bank's creditors could receive common shares over a weekend. The bank could open under new interim management on Monday, and a shareholders' meeting a few weeks later could install a permanent new regime. Insured deposits would always be accessible. ATM machines might have to be closed the weekend of the bankruptcy.

---

[13]There is a fluctuation in rate spreads that moves with the business cycle, so this change might be due to factors other than anti-competitive behaviour. Still, the apparent lack of concern by government is of interest.

Figure 2: Canadian Commercial Bank Spreads
(Mortgage Rates Minus GIC Rates)

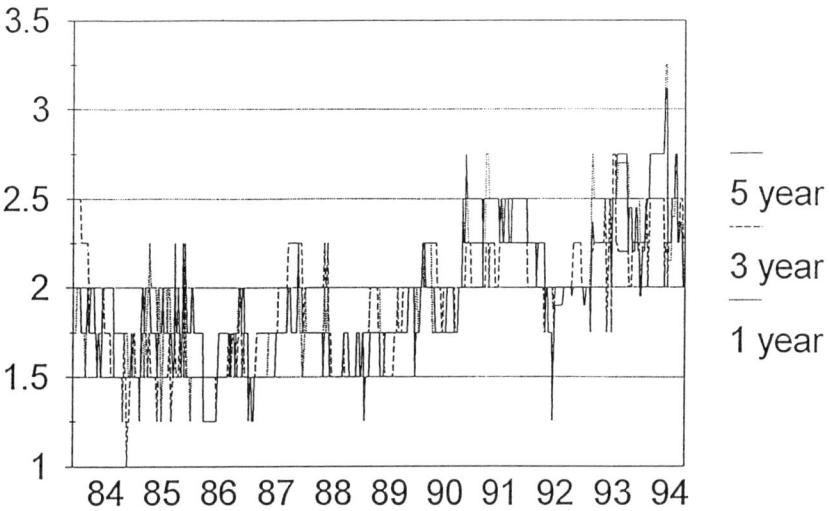

Expect Sophistication

Third, regulations should foster financial sophistication, not dumb down investors and financial institutions It is easier to trust people who know what they are doing. For example, calls to ban pension funds from using derivative securities are, we believe, misguided. Canadian financial institutions should develop the expertise to avoid poor investments, not be banned from any investments that might be poor. If they screw up, they should go under and their top executives should be disgraced. Reliance on bail-outs discourages competence.

Size

The deregulation of banking in the United States led to a wave of bank mergers, and to huge banks. It appears that there are large economies of scale in banking that justify large firms. One such economy of scale is perhaps related to trust: large banks have more expertise, more diversified portfolios, and more clout. Perhaps they are therefore more trustworthy. This may be so, but economies of scale come in different forms. If good risk assessment is the important type of expertise big banks have, then the competence and size of their risk management departments are more important than the extent of their branch systems.

Canadian chartered banks all have voting caps on their common stock. Voting caps are an early form of poison pill. They are anti-takeover devices that prevent any shareholder from voting stock in excess of a uniform fraction of outstanding shares. These not only block takeovers, but limit large outside shareholders from exercising control. Canadian banks have grown by acquiring related financial institutions like trust companies and investment firms. But to grow to the size of their new U.S. competitors, they need to merge or take each other over.

Banks' voting caps exist because Parliament put them there. What sense do they make? They do discourage market power as measured by concentration ratios, but if foreign banks have free entry into Canadian markets, this ceases to be an issue. Voting caps prevent large foreign investors from taking over Canadian banks, but foreign ownership is no longer a hot political topic. Canadians are increasingly cynical about protecting "Canadian ownership" at the expense of consumer choice. The government's recent decision to prevent Border's bookstores from doing business in Canada, apparently to protect existing Canadian book chains, was a last straw for many people. In a world where governments everywhere are increasingly unable to pressure financial markets or competitive financial institutions, foreign ownership becomes unimportant. A third reason for voting caps on banks' stocks is that they prevent Canadian elite families from controlling banks. This may be a valid concern. In prewar Japan, which allowed industrial companies to own banks, these banks were particularly prone to crashing if the parent company had problems. Yet full voting caps are unnecessary. A better solution would be to prevent any client firm or related group of client firms from owning more than, say, 3% of a bank's stock. The bank's dealings with such shareholders should also be disclosed fully and promptly. This would prevent abuse, yet leave banks open to takeovers and to pressure from large institutional investors.

We believe Canadian banks should be allowed to attain whatever size considerations of efficiency demand. Ownership restrictions that prevent bank takeovers should be discontinued.

Corporate Governance

Corporate governance is about getting the best people in charge of public companies. As markets wax in importance and banks wane, corporate governance is taking centre stage.

Good corporate governance means having trustworthy and clever managers. The voting caps that protect the managers of banks, airlines and other Canadian companies from responsibility to their shareholders are anachronisms, and should pass from the scene. Canadian banks and corporations of all types need their managers to be more irritated by shareholders. Large shareholders should be more free to communicate about corporate governance problems. Let shareholders oust top managers when the firm does poorly.

Outsiders should dominate boards of directors, and outsiders should be people with no business ties at all to the firm on whose board they sit.[14] Boards should have CEO compensation committees, CEO selection committees, and conduct committees to vet non-arm's length transactions that are all composed of true outsiders only.

Let shareholders sue top managers in class action suits if the managers fail to be trustworthy stewards of the shareholders' money. To prevent frivolous suits, managers should have a clear "prudent man" defense.

Finally, ill-run firms should be allowed to fail or be swallowed up as takeover targets. This is an uncomfortable, but essential, part of economic evolution. If Peter Pan baits a shark, he gets eaten.

Pension Funds

Pension funds are a new kind of financial institution that is having an increasingly important impact on U.S. financial markets. Multibillion dollar pension funds like the California Public Employees' Retirement system (CalPERs) are using large blocks of stock to outvote insiders at shareholder meetings and demand improved corporate governance. The long-term effects

---

[14]For empirical evidence on the importance of outsiders on boards, see Weisbach (1988); and Hermalin and Weisbach (1991).

of these interventions have yet to be studied, but the mere fact that insiders are being disturbed is good news to many investors.

Pension funds themselves are not immune to political rent seeking, favour trading and other governance problems (see, e.g. Lakonishok *et al.*, 1992; and Lakonishok *et al.*, 1991). Public pension funds run by patronage appointees and investing in politically favoured local initiative projects are unlikely to be positive long-term influences on the economy. Yet anecdotal evidence and one formal study suggest that this may be a widespread problem (see Romano, 1995). Corporate pension funds run by lap dogs of the CEO may be little better.

Pension fund managers need to be accountable to the fund's beneficiaries as directly as is possible. They should be elected by the beneficiaries and should report directly to the beneficiaries about performance.

Ideally, funds should be defined contribution plans rather than the ubiquitous defined benefit plans we now have. Defined contribution plans take an employee's contribution and matching funds from the employer, and simply invest them. The employee knows how much he or she has and where it is invested, and knows who has performed poorly if it yields a low return. In short, the advantage of defined contribution plans is that beneficiaries' property rights over their investments are clear. Defined benefit plans, in contrast, promise employees a preset retirement benefit and commit the employer to invest the annual pension contributions to reach this goal. The fund managers are appointed by the employer, and may be pressured to follow an investment strategy that benefits the employer. In principle, if the fund does poorly, the employer must make up the gap. In practice, benefits are renegotiated regularly in labour contract talks, and can be reduced if the fund does poorly or if negotiators need concessions to balance other gains. It is very unclear that defined benefit plans are safer from employees' viewpoints, and it is clear that they leave beneficiaries property rights vague and poorly protected (see Bodie *et al.*, 1985).

VIII. CONCLUSIONS

We believe financial markets are becoming more important than financial institutions like banks, and that this change is, in part, driving financial globalization. The purpose of financial regulations in any economy, but especially one in which financial markets are playing ever larger roles, is to foster investors' trust in financial investments, and to make corporate insiders behave in ways that justify this trust. This harkens back to the origins of both banking regulation and corporate governance laws: both were originally ways to let trustworthy insiders show themselves to be trustworthy. We believe financial regulation and corporate law have both lost sight of this purpose to some extent, and we outlined a series of detailed suggestions as to how this focus might be restored.

REFERENCES

Acs, Z., R. Morck and B. Yeung (1996), "Productivity Growth and Firm Size Distribution", *International Schumpeter Society 50th Anniversary Volume* (Royal Swedish Academy), forthcoming.

Aghion, P., O. Hart and J. Moore (1992), "When Firms Fail", *The Economist*, March 14, 81.

Aoki, M. (1995), "Towards an Economic Model of the Japanese Firm", *Journal of Economic Literature* 28, 1-27.

Amoaku-Adu, B. and B. Smith (1995), "Outside Financial Directors and Corporate Governance", in Daniels and Morck (eds.), *Corporate Decision Making in Canada*.

Baily, M. (1995), "Efficiency in Manufacturing and the Need for Global Competition", *Brookings Papers on Economic Activity* (Washington, DC: The Brookings Institution), 307-358.

Baumol, W. (1990), "Entrepreneurship: Productive, Unproductive and Destructive", *Journal of Political Economy* 98, 893-921.

Beason, R. and D.E. Weinstein (1996), "Growth, Economies of Scale, and Targeting in Japan (1955-1990)", *Review of Economics and Statistics* 78(2), 286-295.

Berle, A. and G. Means (1932), *The Modern Corporation and Private Property* (New York: MacMillan).

Bodie, Z., J. Light, R. Morck and R. Taggart (1985), "Corporate Pension Policy: An Empirical Investigation", *Financial Analysts Journal* (September/October).

Boycko, M, A. Shleifer and R. Vishny (1995), *Privatizing Russia* (Cambridge: MIT Press).

Caprio, L. and A. Floreanti (1995), "Transfer of Control of Listed Companies in Italy: An Inquiry", unpublished manuscript.

Chan, S-H., J. Martin and I. Kensinger (1990), "Corporate Research and Development Expenditures and Share Value", *Journal of Financial Economics* 26, 255-266.

Daniels, R. and R. Morck (1995), *Corporate Decision Making in Canada* (Calgary: University of Calgary Press).

DeSoto, H. (1989), *The Other Path: The Invisible Revolution in the Third World* (New York: Harper & Row).

Eckbo, E. and S. Verma (1994), "Managerial Share Ownership, Voting Power, and Cash Dividend Policy", *Journal of Corporate Finance* 1, 33-62.

Hall, B. (1990), "Corporate Restructuring and Industrial R&D", *Brookings Papers on Economic Activity* (Washington, DC: The Brookings Institution), 85-135.

Hermalin, B.E. and M.S. Weisbach (1991), "The Effects of Board Composition and Direct Incentives on Firm Performance", *Financial Management* 20(4), 101.

Horner, M. (1988), "The Value of the Corporate Voting Right", *Journal of Banking and Finance* 12, 69-83.

Jensen, M. (1986), "The Agency Costs of Free Cash Flow", *American Economic Review* 76, 323-329.

Jensen, M. and W. Meckling (1976), "Theory of the Firm: Managerial Behaviour, Agency Costs and Ownership Structure", *Journal of Financial Economics* 3, 305-360.

Johnson, B., R. Magee, N. Nagarajan and H. Newman (1985), "An Analysis of the Stock Price Reaction to Sudden Executive Deaths: Implications for the Managerial Labor Market", *Journal of Accounting and Economics* 7, 151-174.

Kindelberger, C.P. (1978), *Manias Panics and Crashes* (New York: Basic Books).

King, R.G. and R. Levine (1993), "Finance and Growth: Schumpeter Might be Right", *Quarterly Journal of Economics* (August), 717-737.

Lakonishok, J. A. Shleifer, R. Thaler and R. Vishny (1991), "Window Dressing by Pension Fund Managers", *American Economic Review* 81, 227.

Lakonishok, J., A. Shleifer and R.W. Vishny (1992), "The Impact of Institutional Trading on Stock Prices", *Journal of Financial Economics* 32, 23.

Lease, R., J. McConnell and W. Mikkelson (1983), "The Market Value of Control in Publicly Traded Corporations", *Journal of Financial Economics* 11, 439-467.

Lenway, S., R. Morck and B. Yeung (1996), "Rent Seeking, Protectionism and Innovation in the American Steel Industry", *Economic Journal* 106(435), 410-421.

Levy, H. (1982), "Economic Evaluation of Voting Power of Common Stock", *Journal of Finance* 38, 79-93.

MacIntosh, J. (1995), "International Securities Regulation: Of Competition, Coopera-
    tion, Convergence, and Cartelization", unpublished manuscript, University of
    Toronto.
McConnell, J. and C. Muscarella (1985), "Corporate Capital Expenditure Decisions
    and the Market Value of the Firm", *Journal of Political Economy* 14, 399-412.
Megginson, W. (1990), "Restricted Voting Stock, Acquisition Premiums and the
    Market Value of Corporate Control", *Financial Review* 25, 175-198.
Morck, R. and B. Yeung (1995), "The Corporate Governance of Multinationals", in
    Daniels and Morck (eds.), *Corporate Decision Making in Canada*.
Murphy, K., A. Shleifer and R. Vishny (1991), "The Allocation of Talent:
    Implications for Growth", *Quarterly Journal of Economics* (May), 503-530.
Olsen, M. Jr. (1996), "Distinguished Lecture on Economics in Government: Big Bills
    Left on the Sidewalk: Why Some Nations are Rich, and Others Poor", *Journal of
    Economic Perspectives* 10(2), 3-24.
Rajan, R. (1992), "Insiders and Outsiders: The Choice Between Relationship and
    Arm's Length Debt", *Journal of Finance* 47, 1367-1400.
Robinson C. and A. White (1990), "The Value of a Vote in the Market for Corporate
    Control", unpublished manuscript.
Romano, R. (1995), "The Politics of Public Pension Funds", *Public Interest* 119
    (Spring), 42-53.
Rydquist, K. (1987), "Empirical Investigations of the Voting Premium", unpublished
    manuscript.
Sachs, J.D. and A. Warner (1995), "Economic Reform and the Process of Global
    Integration", *Brookings Papers on Economic Activity* (Washington, DC: The
    Brookings Institution), 1-118.
Shleifer, A. and R. Vishny (1996), "Property Rights", *Economic Journal* 106(435),
    309-319.
Smith, B., B. Amoaku-Adu and J. Schnabel (1989), "Characteristics and Trends of
    Restricted Shares Listed on the Toronto Stock Exchange", Working paper
    (Waterloo, ON: School of Business and Economics, Wilfrid Laurier University).
Weinstein D. and Y. Yafeh (1995), "On the Costs of a Bank Centred Financial
    System", unpublished manuscript.
Weisbach, M.S. (1988), "Outside Directors and CEO Turnover", *Journal of
    Financial Economics* 20, 431.
Zingales, L. (1994), "The Value of the Voting Right: A Study of the Milan Stock
    Exchange Experience", *Review of Financial Studies* 7(1), 125-148.
_____ (1995), "What Determines the Value of Corporate Votes", *Quarterly
    Journal of Economics* (November), 1047-1073.

Session Four
CANADIAN REGULATORY CHALLENGES

REGULATORY ISSUES:
A LOOK FORWARD

Nick Le Pan, Office of the Superintendent of Financial Institutions

I. INTRODUCTION

My assigned topic is regulatory issues, looking forward. I want to identify six and talk in more detail about one. The issues I cover are more regulatory and supervisory than issues of broad policy or industry structure (though a couple do have implications for some of the industry structure issues). The sixth, which is the major one I am going to spend some time on, is the technology issue related to SmartCards and the Internet.

II. FROM QUANTITATIVE TO QUALITIATIVE CONTROL

The first issue is the trend away from quantitative towards qualitative controls. That is a trend within institutions, a trend within regulatory structures, and a trend that the Basle Committee on Banking Supervision is going to spend some more time focusing on. It involves the adequacy of internal control systems, governance best practices, the role and reliance on internal and external audit and so on. We at the Office of the Superintendent of Financial Institutions (OSFI) spend a lot of time on that now. It is more important than previously as credit risks become relatively less important relative to trading risk, settlement risk, operational risk, etc. I want to note two specific issues from the White Paper.

One, we have indicated that OSFI is going to provide guidance on board of directors' responsibilities in the form of a best-practices paper. Second, we have raised the issue of whether there ought to be a legal responsibility of boards of directors of financial institutions to depositors and policyholders which arguably there is not today in statute law. In some jurisdictions there is such responsibility in common law, perhaps not so much in Canada. But when we think about governance issues, one of them relates accountabilities to whom and for what. There are some fascinating issues looking forward. Internationally, how much can one move towards more commonality of focus across jurisdictions on adequacy of internal controls? The Basle Committee will be examining this. Most of the high profile problems that everybody is aware of were really internal control problems. The Daiwa case and the Barings case are internal control and accountability problems, not derivative problems. The key issue here is: What is the right way to move forward in light of the fact that there are gaps in internal control structures around the world?

III. ENHANCED DISCLOSURE

The second major issue is enhanced disclosure. As people who follow the debates over Bill C-100 now C-15 (which is about to come into force) will know, one of the trends is towards more disclosure. I think the real issues here are the speed of the trend towards more disclosure and then how much more disclosure. This is particularly relevant in the case of supervisory judgements and supervisory ratings. They are not now disclosed — should they be? What I have not seen and what we really do not have experiments on or much understanding, is what happens as you move from one regime of no disclosure to another with more disclosure. The interesting analogy in my mind is the case of the move from left-hand to right-hand driving. The right analogy is what happened the *first* time the world thought that there would be a move from left-hand to right-hand driving, that is, before one had the trust that it was possible to make the switch. Because right now in any jurisdiction everybody has the trust that it is possible to move from left to right since others have done it. There is a trust that you can manage that transition. The idea that we would publish tomorrow on the front page of every newspaper in Canada that the Government of Canada or some of its regulatory authorities has downgraded a particular financial institution, is not something that I would argue the system at the moment has much experience in figuring out how to accept. No country currently does this, so there is no experience to fall back on. And the risk is that we will create or exacerbate a problem in the financial system.

IV. INTERNATIONAL REGULATORY COOPERATION

A key issue in international regulatory cooperation is related to the fascinating concept of a lead regulatory convenor for conglomerate groups in the financial services industry. This concept goes across jurisdictions — jurisdictions within countries, between banking and securities and insurance regulators, and jurisdictions between countries. This is about trying to identify more of an accountability structure in the regulatory community for who has the responsibility to share information? Who has the responsibility to coordinate crisis management? And so forth. Lots of people in the economics and legal professions have written about the issues of regulatory cooperation and what happens as you move increasingly into global financial markets. I think one of the very important and interesting developments over the next few years is how to make some of that real. What is the optimal level of that kind of co-operation in order to maintain an adequate level of trust in the system? But at the same time the reality of political and public expectations, of liquidation law and of deposit insurance schemes is that home-country depositors and policyholders are expected to get priority.

One of the interesting implications of a consideration of what functions are done by whom is the evolution of a different notion of what is functional regulation versus institutional regulation. Traditionally one thought about, say, the banking function versus the securities function. We know that separation does not correspond to the bank as an institution versus the securities dealer as an institution, but is our definition of function right? Consider the management of trading and market risk within credit institutions such as banks that are also in the securities business or insurance companies that are increasingly getting into the derivatives business. It is often the case that the management of those risks is centralized within one entity or another. And trading risk is different than credit risk. Then the issue is not functional regulation between bankers or securities or insurance regulators. The issue is who is looking at the trading risk within the whole institution and who has the comparative advantage to do that? And who is looking at credit risk within the whole institution? And who is looking at customer protection regulation — "know your client" disclosure rules and privacy role when the various parts of the institution are giving advice. Solvency regulators are not usually expert in those consumer protection fields. This type of re-categorization may advance what has become sterile jurisdictional debate in Canada.

V. INSTITUTIONAL CLOSURE

The fourth issue is that closure of financial institutions is becoming more and more possible. The Canadian experience has come a long way. In the early 1980s the notion of closing two small western banks was thought to be a potentially serious problem for the financial system. This has evolved to where we have closed some large deposit-taking institutions called trust companies. We also closed the third largest insurance company. A number of people thought there might be a problem for system stability, but it did not appear.

In Bill C-15, OSFI now has a legislative mandate for early intervention. That mandate indicates that closure is not something that necessarily means the regulatory system has failed. I personally believe that this is very important. The notion that closure of a problem financial institution is more and more possible is, I think, a very important and salutary one in the system. While we in Canada have some considerable experience when it comes to closures, we do not have, and nor do many other jurisdictions have, experience in closing an institution where most of the deposit liabilities are not deposit insured. Nor do we have much experience in closing an institution that has multiple businesses across jurisdictional boundaries. We did recently in the area of life insurance with Confederation Life, and it is not pretty. That does not mean we should not do it, but this is an evolutionary kind of thing and how one moves between here and there is a non-trivial exercise. Increasing the public's understanding that closure is possible is very important, as is the related issue of reasonable expectations of what the regulatory system can achieve.

VI. WHO DOES WHAT?

The fifth issue relates to who is in what business? I will not discuss who retails insurance or who leases cars. But I want to note that who is in what business has some important ramifications that should not be forgotten as one moves forward. Just a couple of plumbing kind of implications to illustrate this. There is a lot of talk about whether non-deposit-taking institutions should be in the payments system, for example. But tell me whether what then ends up being accepted by a non-deposit-taking institution is or is not a deposit. And where will it rank in an insolvency? In Canada, currently, life insurance liabilities rank by statute ahead of everybody else in an insolvency. Now, if we have institutions who are non-deposit-takers in the deposit-taking business, that needs to be sorted out. We must sort out what consumer protection regime, if any, is going to apply. The answer may be the same as currently but it is a non-trivial issue to think these things through. Some of this debate on who is in what business tends to be at the level of who gets to sell what product to whom through what distribution channel and who has what competitive position. There are a lot of other ramifications, depending on how the details are worked out. Also related to that are risk control systems. We watched the risk control attitudes develop over several years in deposit-taking institutions as evolution occurred in the clearing and settlement systems in Canada. People began to focus in middle and senior management on systemic risk. It is a non-trivial job to figure out what systemic risk is, what systemic risk isn't, and how you manage that within an institution, how you measure it and what MIS systems you need. There are a lot of institutions that might want into the payments system who do not have a sense of how to manage systemic risk at this time.

VII. TECHNOLOGY

The final issue is technology. Max Frisch said that "technology is the art of arranging the world so we don't have to experience it". Arthur C. Clarke said that, "any sufficiently advanced technology is indistinguishable from magic". Now, it is possible for me to take a plastic card, put it into some kind of "reader" and suddenly it has value. I can then take this card into a store and use it to purchase something. I can't see the value, but I know it is somewhere on the card, somewhere in that little kind of "thing amajig" in the smart card. Is this magic?

I will not be exhaustive here, but rather highlight some of the issues as I see them. Suppose I signed on the Internet and had it search for the best deposit rates around the world and made a deposit. Then I swiped my card, accessed my account, bought the product and paid for it. But then one day I sign on and the first national bank of "wherever" doesn't respond. Access is "temporarily not available". And they don't answer their phone. And then in a day or so the message on the screen says "business is suspended". A participant at a recent Internet seminar noted in a preamble to a question that "efforts by regulators to regulate content on the Internet constitute law by the clueless over places they have never been, using tools they don't have". You can imagine the question.

I want to cover some issues about SmartCards or E-cash and then some of the issues raised by Internet commerce. In the case of SmartCards, we will consider E-cash that is close to or indistinguishable from a medium of exchange. This is the version where you literally have a stored value card, a plastic card that you can walk into a machine, a banking machine of some form or other, you can add value to it, sort of like telephone cards and you can go around and effect transactions and the value gets subtracted. It is no longer linked to an account. To analyze the issues from a regulatory policy perspective one has to go back briefly to what is the whole purpose of regulation. Regulation in part is about trust and confidence in the financial system. Regulation is in part about consumer protection of people who, arguably, the political process thinks do not have adequate access to information to protect themselves and therefore ought to be protected by regulators and consumer protection plans. Regulation is also about controlling systemic risk. Chuck Freedman will address this in this volume. Regulation is about effective and efficient markets and the legal and institutional structures and disclosure that support those.

I defy somebody to tell me under the legal structure in place today just what is the status of the "value" that gets put on one of those cards, and what is going to happen if the issuing institution fails? Now, I think that if we are going to try and close one of those institutions one day, regulators, issuers, consumers and the like ought to know that. So part of the issue of E-cash and SmartCards is making sure that one gets the legislative, legal and institutional arrangements underpinning them sorted out. And there is a lot of work going on in many countries along these lines.

Another interesting and related question is who ought to be allowed to issue this value? And should it be deposit insured? Again, thinking on this is evolving in various countries including in Canada. There are no formal positions in either my organization or the ministry, but I think it is worth sharing some of my thoughts on the issues.

Who ought to issue this value? I think this kind of value can be a substitute for a piece of paper called a five-dollar bill. To the extent that this E-cash is a medium of exchange in the economy, there are some real issues about who ought to be able to issue it and those relate to public confidence. The idea that it ought to be allowed to be issued by private institutions is not new. We have had private banks issuing currency in Canada historically. They exist today in the world. But should an unregulated entity be allowed to issue this value? At what point is some degree of regulation necessary in order that there is sufficient confidence in the medium of exchange that the economic basis of transactions is not undermined? Currency issued by private banks historically traded at a discount, the farther away you got from the issuing institution. Why? Because the inefficiencies of information transmission allow contacts to evaluate the likelihood of the issuing institution honouring its promise to pay. At what point do you need to make sure that this kind of value is issued by a regulated institution precisely because you do not want too large a chance of losing public confidence in the medium of exchange? For the pilot projects that are being done in Canada (and Canada is actually ahead of the United States in terms of pilot projects), we are not prepared at this point to allow E-cash to be issued by an unregulated entity. Maybe we should at some point but we are not going to prejudice that decision now. But regulation may not have to be the full panoply that applies to a bank that is taking on credit risk, for example.

Now why are these cards different from phone cards? Why not regulate the phone card industry? I think the real issue is at what point does use of the phone card for economic transactions generally become so prevalent that it becomes a medium of exchange.

Even if it was accepted that issuance ought to be by regulated institutions the question then arises as to what one means by regulated institutions — an insurance company or a money market mutual fund? If non-deposit-taking institutions are to be allowed to issue this value I think certain principles are important:

- they should be subject to the same rules as deposit-takers for the activities they are engaged in,

- regulation has to apply to limit loss of public confidence in the medium of exchange. For example, we could require E-cash to be backed by high quality assets,

- control over creation of money should be a federal responsibility, and

- there should be consumer disclosure of the terms and conditions, and the liability of the issue in case of failure.

Legally, whether or not this value is a deposit affects whether it would be subject to deposit insurance. Even if it legally was a deposit the policy question is "Should it be subject to deposit insurance?" There are lots of arguments for and against deposit insurance. I am not aware of too many arguments that the medium of exchange ought to be deposit insured. We do not insure the bills and coins now, but they are issued by an entity that, presumably cannot fail — central banks. And I am not clear why deposit insurance ought to be a substitute for a general government backstop of the medium of exchange, if a backstop is necessary to preserve public confidence. The costs of deposit insurance are distributed quite differently from the cost of a general backstop.

As an issue, security is a bridge between E-cash and the Internet commerce since some of the issues are similar as one looks at virtual banks that only operate on the Internet or in some kind of electronic means.

I was recently with a senior risk manager of one of the major institutions who told me that, in his opinion, security and inscription were "the" issues of the 1990s. And I thought "the" issue for whom? Security is clearly the issue for people who want to provide these kinds of services. It is an issue for consumers. There is no question that institutions have an incentive to hold themselves out as providing secure systems. But everybody must recognize that there are no absolute guarantees in the security business.

I am less sure that, beyond some minimum, security issues are key for regulators. It seems to me that at a minimum we ought to make sure that somebody who clearly has a substandard system or does not have even rudimentary risk controls does not get in to business. But where do you stop? I do not want to face the moral hazard problem of effectively approving security systems given that I know that there is going to be a problem in a security system some day from one of these institutions. It is important that the incentives be still on the institutions to make sure that their systems are up to snuff. But one can hear the call for regulatory action given that the ability for an individual entity or an individual person dealing with one of these virtual banks to assess the adequacy of the security system is even less than it is for them to assess the financial health of a major deposit-taking institution. So the consumer protection arguments for security approvals by regulators are potentially going to be pretty high. And yet there are obvious moral hazard problems as one goes down that route.

There are other implications of electronic commerce and Internet banking. Obviously that trend has different implications for risk controls and appropriate risk control procedures. Disaster planning and business resumption planning is different for an institution that is technology driven than it is for one with people in it. And there is no question that there are many legal issues around these kinds of institutions, such as in what jurisdiction are the transactions actually occurring. This has implications for taxes and what consumer disclosure regimes apply.

The last issue related to the Internet I want to talk about is the implication for regulatory structures and access control. Traditionally, of course, access control to markets in one form or another has been a tool for regulators. The Bank Act says that if you want to engage in a banking business in Canada, you cannot do it unless you have a foreign bank subsidiary or other establishment in Canada. The Insurance Companies Act goes even further. It says that if a Canadian buys an insurance policy from somebody who is abroad, and the policy is delivered to that Canadian from an insurance company that has a Canadian operation, that Canadian operation must take account of that insurance policy and its capital treatment in Canada and in its books. Now, you tell me how that all works in a world in which my 11-year-old can sit in the second floor of my house and dial up an institution on the Internet. In that kind of world the ability to have control of access is different than it is today. So what is the right response? My sense is that we need to move more towards disclosure-based regulation. One can imagine calls for an international seal of approval for every institution that is operating in the Canadian jurisdiction. I am not sure if that is feasible. Maybe we should move towards negative disclosure. OSFI has its own Internet website and suppose it published a list of all the institutions who are regulated and who are deposit-insured in Canada. The decision to deal with any particular company is then a personal responsibility.

VIII. CONCLUSION

I do want to emphasize in closing that a value that is indistinguishable from magic does not necessarily scare me as a regulator. Magic can be fun and can be profitable. And as long as people are responsible and regulators and policy-makers continue to think through the implications and think what they have to do to fulfil their responsibilities, it can be useful for everybody.

LARGE-VALUE CLEARING AND SETTLEMENT SYSTEMS AND SYSTEMIC RISK

C. Freedman and C. Goodlet, Bank of Canada

I. INTRODUCTION

During the past few years, there have been significant efforts around the world to develop and improve electronic clearing and settlement systems for payments, and for securities and foreign exchange transactions. In part, these efforts have been driven by the need to process efficiently the sharp increases in the volume and value of transactions. The other principal factor behind the pressure for change has been the increased understanding of, and concern about, the various risks that can exist in clearing and settlement systems that handle large-value transactions, and the recognition of the need to contain such risks.

In this paper, we briefly describe the risks that can arise in clearing and settlement systems. We then discuss the public policy objective of controlling risks, particularly systemic risk, in clearing and settlement systems, and some of the approaches to risk containment in such systems. The rest of the paper focuses on recent developments in Canada in clearing and settlement systems for large-value payments, and for securities and foreign exchange transactions,

This paper originally appeared in *North American Journal of Economics and Finance* 7(2) (1996), pp. 153-162, and is reprinted by permission from JAI Press.

with particular emphasis on the mechanisms used to minimize systemic risk. The final section examines the role of the Bank of Canada as the regulator of large-value clearing and settlement systems under proposed legislation.

II. RISKS IN CLEARING AND SETTLEMENT SYSTEMS

The process of clearing and settling financial instruments is subject to various risks — legal, operational, credit, liquidity and systemic.

The importance of a legal framework that sets out the rights and responsibilities of all parties in all circumstances is evident. Uncertainty about the outcome in particular situations can cause institutions to incur risks that can be large and unmanageable. It is also important that the system be operationally sound and able to cope with various disaster scenarios. Credit risk refers to the possibility that a payor or its bank will be unable to settle the payment obligation for full value at the time the obligation is due, or at any later time. Liquidity risk refers to the possibility that a payor or its bank will not be able to settle its payment obligation for full value when it comes due, but will be able to do so at some later time. With both credit and liquidity risks there is a possibility that the receiving institution will have to find replacement funds. However, credit risk involves the potential loss of some or all of the principal owing, while liquidity risk results in the lesser cost and inconvenience of having to find funds at short notice to replace the payment that was not completed at the required time, but that will be completed later. Liquidity risk is, nonetheless, a serious matter for financial institutions since they may have to borrow funds or sell assets in unfavourable circumstances to avoid failing to meet their own payment obligations.

In recent years, systemic risk has been the focus of a great deal of attention by central banks and others. It refers to domino or spillover effects, whereby the inability of one financial institution to fulfil its payment obligations in a timely fashion results in the inability of other financial institutions to fulfil their obligations in that clearing and settlement system or in other systems, or in the failure of that clearing house or other clearing houses. Systemic risk has both a liquidity and a credit component, i.e., liquidity problems at one institution can lead to liquidity problems for other institutions or for clearing houses, or the failure of one institution can lead to the failure of other institutions or to the failure of clearing houses.

III. THE PUBLIC POLICY OBJECTIVE OF CONTROLLING RISKS IN CLEARING AND SETTLEMENT SYSTEMS

What is the public policy objective of controlling risks in clearing and settlement systems? Increasingly, the primary focus of public policy is the appropriate control of systemic risk in such systems.[1]

If a system handles only small-value retail payments, it is unlikely that it will generate such large interinstitution exposures that the inability of one participant to settle its obligations will lead to the inability of other participants to settle their obligations. Since systemic risk is unlikely in such a system, the need for extensive risk-proofing is reduced.

In contrast, systems that handle large values, and that therefore generate large credit and liquidity risks and hence systemic risk, will need strong risk-proofing measures to contain such risks. A well-designed clearing and settlement system that handles large-value payments will be able to provide the following benefits to participants in, and ultimate users of, the system:

- participating institutions will be certain that once a transaction has been accepted by the system, that transaction has settled or will settle no matter what else happens;

- given this certainty of settlement, the participating institutions will be able to provide customers with unconditional use of any funds received through such a system.

To achieve these benefits, the risks associated with a large-value clearing and settlement system must be properly controlled, with appropriate mechanisms allowing credit and liquidity risks to be monitored and managed in the system.

---

[1]There are, of course, other public policy issues with regard to clearing and settlement systems, such as efficiency, competition and access.

Since exposure is typically created by the extension of intra-day credit in the system, these mechanisms involve limits on the amount of exposure that any one participant can create for other participants. Collateral is frequently used to ensure containment or elimination of the risk of spillover effects associated with such intra-day credit arrangements.

IV. APPROACHES TO RISK CONTAINMENT

In some systems, if a participating financial institution fails, the surviving participants are protected, at least in part, by a reversal or unwinding of the transactions involving the failed institution. But while such an approach may be acceptable in systems that handle low-value, retail-type payments, it has become increasingly unacceptable in systems that handle large-value transactions. Unwinds are unacceptable because: (i) they would be highly disruptive in today's complex financial system; (ii) they do not eliminate systemic risk; (iii) users of a system with unwinds do not receive irrevocable funds; (iv) unwinds can leave institutions facing significant liquidity and credit risks; and (v) given the above, expectations can be created that the central bank or government will "bail out" a system facing an unwind in order to protect the financial sector and the economy from the resulting disruption.

Because it is so important that payment systems and other systems that handle large-value transactions provide certainty of settlement to the participating financial institutions and finality of payment to the ultimate receivers of funds, the central banks of the G-10 countries meeting at the Bank for International Settlements (BIS) have developed a set of minimum standards that should be met or surpassed by all such systems. While these so-called Lamfalussy standards were originally developed in the context of cross-border and multi-currency netting schemes, they have also gained widespread acceptance as the *minimum* standards for domestic clearing and settlement systems (Bank for International Settlements, 1990 and Board of Governors of the Federal Reserve System, 1994).

One of these minimum risk-proofing standards requires that the system be able to complete daily settlement even if the participant owing the single largest possible amount is unable to pay. This effectively rules out unwinding in almost all circumstances. Large-value payment systems developed recently have gone further, with risk-proofing procedures that permit settlement in all circumstances, including the failure of more than one large institution. In most countries, this has been done through the development of a real-time gross settlement (RTGS) system as the principal (or only) system for large-value payments. Typically, such a system has, at its centre, a mechanism for permitting payment orders to be approved if, and only if, the sending financial institution has sufficient funds in its account at the central bank to cover the payment. If access to intra-day credit is permitted (as a means of funding these payments), such credit will typically be supplied by the central bank, usually through repurchase transactions with participants or through the provision of overdraft facilities to participants. In most cases, this overdraft credit is largely or fully collateralized, so that the central bank is almost completely protected from loss in the event of the subsequent failure of the financial institution sending the payment order. With the payment order settled in central bank liabilities, which carry no default risk (since a central bank cannot fail), the financial institution on the receiving end of the payment order can treat any payment accepted by the RTGS as "good funds", which cannot be reversed, and hence can offer the same type of certainty or finality to its customer, the ultimate beneficiary of the payment order.

V.   THE DEVELOPMENT OF A LARGE-VALUE PAYMENT SYSTEM IN CANADA

Over the years, Canada has benefited from one of the most efficient paper-based cheque-clearing systems in the world. In spite of the vast size of the country, Canadian financial institutions have traditionally given same-day credit for cheques (even though they do not receive the funds to cover these cheques until the next day) and have cleared most cheques overnight. In addition, the near absence of failures among chartered banks has reduced the private sector's concerns about risk. All of this has undoubtedly lessened the incentive to develop an electronic large-value payment system in Canada, compared with countries that have less efficient payment systems or where there are stronger perceptions of risk associated with the operation of the payment system. In recent years, however, largely motivated by concerns about their exposures, the major Canadian financial institutions, under the aegis of the Canadian Payments Association (CPA) have been planning a large-value transfer system (LVTS), which is expected to be operational in the second half of 1997.

While the LVTS controls risk differently from the typical RTGS system, it has all the essential attributes of an RTGS system (Freedman, 1996). The key characteristic is that each payment message will be processed in "real time" and be subject to risk-control mechanisms. The LVTS will provide certainty of settlement even in the event of the failure of one or more participating financial institutions, intra-day finality to customers receiving payment, and the incentives and capabilities for participating financial institutions to monitor their positions in real time and to limit their maximum exposures to other financial institutions.[2]

The LVTS will use multilateral netting arrangements to reduce total exposures (for a given volume of payments) in the system and will ensure that each participant faces a cap on the total amount of exposure it can create in the system. Any exposure created by an individual participant through its use of intra-day credit will be fully collateralized. Thus, even if the largest participant fails to meet its payment obligations at the end of the day, the combination of caps and collateral ensures that the liquidity required to settle will be available and that any credit losses can be safely absorbed.

There are two streams of payments in the LVTS, Tranche 1 payments and Tranche 2 payments. Under Tranche 2, each participating institution grants a bilateral line of credit to every other institution (including zero, if it does not wish to have any credit exposure to a particular institution), and this establishes the maximum intra-day net amount that the latter can owe the former. The sum of all the bilateral lines of credit extended to an institution, multiplied by a specific fraction (currently set at 0.3 for the LVTS), establishes the maximum net debit cap of the sender (i.e., the maximum exposure that can be generated) for each financial institution during the day. A Tranche 2 payment message sent by a participant that wishes to use the intra-day credit provided by other participants has to pass both the bilateral cap and the sender net debit cap tests associated with Tranche 2 before it is accepted. Each participating financial institution puts up collateral equal to the

---

[2]The amount of their maximum exposures can be adjusted each day.

largest bilateral line of credit it has extended to any other institution multiplied by the fraction noted above (0.3). If a participating institution fails, the loss-allocation procedures provide for the division of any losses on the basis of the bilateral lines of credit established by survivors vis-à-vis the failed institution (and not on the actual intra-day credit used on the day of failure). The collateral pledged by the participants is sufficient to deal with the failure of the institution with the largest possible amount owing to the system (i.e., the institution with the largest sender net debit cap). This part of the system has been described as "survivors-pay" since surviving financial institutions largely absorb the losses associated with a failure.

There is also provision in the LVTS for a Tranche 1 payment, in which the sending institution fully collateralizes its own payment. This facilitates payments above the maximum level permitted by the risk-control procedures under Tranche 2 and ensures that institutions that are extended small or zero bilateral lines of credit by other participants can still have access to the system. This tranche can be described as "defaulter-pays", since, in the event of failure, it is the defaulter's collateral that ensures settlement.

At the end of the day, the overall net amounts to be paid and received are transferred among the participants on the books of the Bank of Canada.

The structure outlined above, while consistent with the Lamfalussy minimum standard for risk-proofing, has two drawbacks. First, while capable of dealing with the failure of the institution with the single largest possible net debit (or largest possible amount owing to the system), the system may be unable to cope with the failure, during the business day, of two or more large institutions with very large net debit positions at the time of failure. This leaves open the theoretical possibility that a participant will not receive a payment that it expected because of multiple failures. Hence, participating financial institutions may be unwilling to extend finality to their customers, since they cannot be absolutely certain that their own claims will result in the receipt of good funds at the end of the day. Second, the requirement for large amounts of collateral to back the LVTS (even if the amount is less than would be required in an RTGS) implies a significant cost of operation for the system, even though the cost of collateral is probably less than 25 basis points (calculated as the differential between the rate on treasury bills and that on wholesale term deposits at banks).

To deal with these problems, the Bank of Canada has taken two initiatives. First, the Bank has offered to guarantee settlement of the LVTS under all circumstances. This resolves the problem raised by the extremely unlikely possibility of the failure, during the operating hours of the LVTS, of more than one participating institution with the total amount owing to the system at the time of failure greater than the available collateral. This guarantee by the Bank to the LVTS is akin to the provision of an insurance policy against a catastrophic event that is highly unlikely to occur, and on which there is an extremely large amount deductible (in this case the collateral put up by the institutions to cope with the failure of the participant with the single largest possible net debit to the system). Furthermore, there is virtually no moral hazard in these arrangements, since the loss arrangements under Tranche 2 ensure that the participating institutions have the incentive to continue to behave prudently in monitoring each other's risk because so much of their own collateral is at stake before the Bank suffers any loss.[3]

The second initiative taken by the Bank has been to offer a new form of collateral for use in the LVTS (and in the other major clearing and settlement systems), which should be considerably less costly for the participating financial institutions than pledging treasury bills. This collateral takes the form of "Special Deposit Accounts" (SDAs) at the Bank of Canada, which will pay a rate of interest close to the cost of one-day funds to the largest banks. For a financial institution that raises one-day funds in the market and invests them in the SDAs, the overall cost will be, at most, a few basis points.

Thus, the architecture of the system, combined with the guarantee provided by the Bank of Canada, will result in the LVTS having all the essential attributes of an RTGS system. The objective of risk-proofing the large-value payment system will be met since certainty of settlement at the end of the day will be ensured under all circumstances, and participating financial institutions will be required to offer intra-day finality to their customers. Although the LVTS relies upon a Bank of Canada guarantee, in all but the most extreme situations the participating institutions themselves will bear the loss resulting from a participant failure.

---

[3]The guarantee does not come into play in the case of Tranche 1 payments, since they are fully collateralized by the sender.

VI. CLEARING AND SETTLEMENT OF SECURITIES IN CANADA

While the payment system (particularly the part that handles large-value payments) is the central clearing and settlement system in Canada, there are other important clearing and settlement systems associated with securities transactions and with foreign exchange trades that also handle large-value payments. Risk-proofing these systems has the same objectives — namely, certainty of settlement and receiver finality. These systems are typically designed to take advantage of the fact that the exchange of value between the seller and the buyer may occur completely within the system. For example, in the securities clearing system, the seller transfers ownership of a security to the buyer, who can pay the seller within the system. This allows these systems to be mostly self-collateralizing when dealing with liquidity and credit risks by using a technique known as delivery versus payment (DVP). In addition, these systems are able to take advantage of the receiver finality capability offered by LVTS or RTGS systems.

In Canada, the Canadian Depository for Securities Limited (CDS) has created the central mechanisms for clearing and settling trades in securities. Some years ago, it became clear that, for reasons of efficiency, it was essential to move from paper-based transactions in Government of Canada domestic marketable securities to an electronic clearing and settlement system ("immobilization" of securities). For cost and other reasons the decision was made to use the facilities of CDS rather than have the Bank of Canada build an entirely new system. This led to the introduction of Government of Canada bonds into the Debt Clearing Service (DCS) of CDS in mid-1994, and the introduction of Government of Canada treasury bills into the DCS at the end of 1995 (after the risk-containment measures on the DCS had been enhanced).

Since the decision was taken to use DCS as the clearing and settlement system for Government of Canada debt, the principal challenge has been to risk-proof the DCS to minimize systemic risk. The key mechanism in meeting such an objective in securities clearing and settlement has been to design the system on a DVP basis.

There are a number of ways of achieving DVP. The mechanism used in Canada is based on gross, or item-by-item, settlement for securities transfers throughout the day (with no reversal or unwinding possible), and on continuous netting of corresponding payment obligations, with end-of-day settlement of the net amounts owed and owing. (The use of netting significantly reduces the amounts at risk in this system.) To ensure that payment is made, the system relies upon "assured payment", in which a small number of the largest financial institutions participating in the system extend credit to the others and provide collateralized guarantees for end-of-day payment.

Thus, there are fundamentally two types of participants in DCS — receivers of credit and extenders of credit.[4] The receivers of credit, the majority of institutions participating in the system, receive lines of credit from extenders that enable them to purchase securities. If, at the end of the day, they are unable to pay for the net value of securities purchased and sold throughout the day, the extenders are required to make the end-of-day payments. Receivers of credit grant the extenders a security interest in the securities bought by the receivers on that day and, if an extender is required to make payment for a receiver that is unable to fulfil its end-of-day payment obligation, the extender is entitled to take possession of those securities (the so-called delivered or "unpaid-for" securities). The amount that each extender can owe to the system (either on behalf of those to which it has extended credit or on its own behalf) is capped, with the cap linked to the size of each extender's regulatory capital.

What happens if an extender is unable to meet its end-of-day obligation, either for its own net purchases during the day or on behalf of those receivers of credit that are unable to fulfil their obligations at the end of the day? In such a case, the system has a loss-allocation procedure whereby the remaining extenders are required to fulfil the obligation to the system of the failed extender. This loss-allocation procedure is backed up by a security interest in the unpaid-for securities of the failed extender and of any failed receivers for which it is supposed to make payment, as well as a pool of "paid-for" collateral (about $600 million at the time of writing). The sum of these two types of collateral (unpaid-for and paid-for) was expected to be sufficient to cover the failure of the extender with the single largest net debit to the system, i.e., to meet the crucial Lamfalussy standard. Thus, in case of a single extender failure, the system was expected to be able to settle without unwinding and without causing undue liquidity strains for participating financial institutions.

---

[4]This is something of an oversimplification, since there are two other groupings or rings — one composed of four institutions known as settlement agents, and the other composed of the Caisse centrale Desjardins.

In addition, as long as end-of-day payments take place through the exchange of cheques (i.e., until the LVTS is operational), an extender is required to pledge further collateral as a "top-up" when any cheque that is greater than the size of the pool of paid-for collateral is presented by an extender as payment to the CDS. This ensures that if an extender fails between the time of completion of payment exchange on the DCS (about 5:00 p.m.) and the final settlement of cheques on the books of the Bank of Canada at noon the following day, there will be sufficient paid-for collateral to cover the amount of the cheque.

While on the surface this system seemed satisfactorily risk-proofed, it turned out, after the introduction of Government of Canada bonds in mid-1994, that it had one significant problem that raised concerns about systemic risk. The DCS was an "open" system in that it permitted purchases and sales of Government of Canada bonds to be settled on the system in return for payment on the system or for payment outside the system (e.g., payment in a foreign currency or by transfer of a security not on the system). Such so-called "free deliveries" could result in a participant owing large amounts at the end of the day on the DCS, with virtually no backing of unpaid-for securities left in its account to function as collateral if it was unable to make payment.

To deal with this problem prior to the introduction of treasury bills into the DCS, the Bank of Canada and the participants in the DCS reached an agreement to make the DCS much more of a "closed" system, by severely limiting the amount of such free deliveries. This was done by introducing a "pre-edit" procedure for all transactions entering the system, which limits to a relatively small amount the difference between the value of the security being transferred at the time of settlement and the payment being made on the system. It is expected that these differences will not cumulate during the day to more than the amount of the pool of paid-for collateral in the system.

With these arrangements in place, the risk-proofing of the DCS can be considered to be satisfactory, although there is still room for improvement. Once the LVTS is operational, the DCS will use the LVTS for its end-of-day payments, thereby eliminating the need for overnight collateral.

Another risk that can be eliminated once the LVTS is available is "banker risk". When a private sector financial institution acts as the banker for the DCS, receiving payments from participants that owe money to the clearing house and making payments to participants entitled to receive money from the clearing house, the risk exists that the banker could fail between the time it receives payments from those owing money and the time it is supposed to make payments to those owed money. One way to eliminating this risk is for the Bank of Canada to become the settlement agent or banker for the DCS. The Bank is prepared to consider undertaking this function after the LVTS is operational, since it would not face any liquidity or credit risks once the LVTS was used to make end-of-day DCS payments.

VII. CLEARING AND SETTLEMENT OF FOREIGN EXCHANGE TRANSACTIONS IN CANADA

Another important type of clearing and settlement system deals with the netting and settlement of foreign exchange transactions. The distinguishing characteristic of this type of transaction is that payment is made in one currency against the receipt of a second currency. Settlement of these transactions thus involves two or more national payment systems. A major risk-control mechanism in multilateral clearing and settlement systems for foreign exchange transactions is payment versus payment (PVP).

One such system, called Multinet, is currently being developed in North America. Multinet is a clearing house that permits multilateral netting of forward and spot foreign exchange transactions. By netting these transactions, with itself as counterparty, Multinet ensures that if a participating financial institution fails, only the net amounts owed by, and owing to, the failed institution are relevant, not the gross amounts. In the case of forward foreign exchange transactions, it is the cost of replacement of the net amount of these transactions to which surviving financial institutions are potentially at risk, and this is covered by collateral.

The exposure at the time that these transactions are settled has received the most attention and is the cause of most concern (Bank for International Settlements, 1996). This so-called "Herstatt risk" (named for a German bank that failed in 1974) is an especially significant problem when currencies of countries in widely differing time zones are exchanged.[5] But even in the case of U.S. dollar-Canadian dollar transactions, settlement can pose difficulties because the two parts of the transaction do not take place simultaneously. The approach that Multinet proposes to take in the case of U.S. dollar-Canadian dollar transactions is to require payment of all amounts owing to Multinet in both U.S. dollars and Canadian dollars, before permitting the outpayment of funds in the two currencies to the institutions to which Multinet owes funds. In normal circumstances, all in-payments will arrive by 2:00 p.m. and all out-payments will be made at about 2:15 p.m. If an institution fails to deliver its payment to Multinet in one currency, it will not receive the payment owing from Multinet in the other currency. Multinet will then use the latter "blocked" funds to meet its requirements in the currency in which the defaulting institution failed to make payment.

One of the essential elements of a PVP scheme of the sort used by Multinet is the ability to use national payment systems with certainty of settlement and finality of payment for both halves of the transaction. Multinet plans to use Fedwire for its U.S. dollar transactions and the LVTS for its Canadian dollar transactions. However, in the period before the LVTS is operational, there is significant risk associated with the Canadian dollar transactions since there is no mechanism to ensure intra-day finality of payment in Canadian dollar transactions. An agreement has been reached on interim arrangements (including the use of collateral) to minimize this residual risk.

The international financial community has recently directed considerable attention to the problem of Herstatt risk. Because of time zone differences, the solution used to deal with Canadian dollar-U.S. dollar transactions cannot be automatically applied to U.S. dollar-yen transactions or U.S. dollar-mark transactions, which represent the bulk of foreign exchange transactions. A collateral pool has been used by another multilateral clearing and settlement system, called ECHO, which recently began operations, to deal with some of the risks in settling such transactions. Multinet also proposes to use such a pool in dealing with non-North American currencies.

---

[5]In practice, the situation is even worse because of market conventions regarding timing that result in a much longer period during which payment messages cannot be reversed. See Bank for International Settlements (1996).

Central banks are contributing to the solution of Herstatt risk by extending the hours of operation of their real-time payment facilities. Thus, by mid-1997, the Federal Reserve system will operate Fedwire from 12:30 a.m. to 6:30 p.m., instead of 8:30 a.m. to 6:30 p.m., as is currently the case. This change will permit Fedwire to overlap the operating hours in Europe and Japan, since the system at the Bank of Japan has also extended its hours.

While overlapping hours are a necessary element of a solution, they are not sufficient, since there will likely be little liquidity available in a country during the hours when most of its financial markets are closed, making it potentially difficult to obtain funds in a currency when there is a failure to deliver by a financial institution. There are also issues relating to the application of insolvency regimes and the ability to pledge collateral outside a participant's domestic financial and legal system that require consideration. Some of these issues are being examined by committees at the BIS.

VIII.   THE OVERSIGHT OF MAJOR CLEARING AND SETTLEMENT SYSTEMS IN CANADA

As is clear from the above discussion, the Bank of Canada has been involved in the development of automated clearing and settlement systems for some time, partly because the final settlement of transactions among financial institutions takes place through the transfer of funds between the accounts that these institutions hold at the Bank of Canada. The Bank also has strong links to the Canadian Payments Association, which operates the existing payment system and is building the LVTS.[6] In addition, since the Bank is the ultimate source of liquidity to the financial system and thus acts as lender of last resort, the Bank is concerned about the security and soundness of clearing and settlement arrangements. Poorly designed systems have the potential to disrupt the operation of financial markets, causing severe problems for financial institutions and making the implementation of monetary policy difficult. Historically, central banks, as lenders of last resort, have played a major role in dealing with these types of disruptions. For these reasons the Bank is very

---

[6]By law, the Chairman of the CPA must be an official of the Bank of Canada.

Session IV

supportive of international and domestic initiatives aimed at managing and controlling risk in major clearing and settlement systems.

Internationally, particularly through its membership in the G-10 group of central banks, which meet at the BIS, the Bank of Canada has actively participated in discussions on the identification and management of risks in clearing and settlement systems and on the establishment of agreed minimum standards for risk control.

Domestically, reflecting the Bank's central role in this area, the federal government has brought forward legislation (the Payment Clearing and Settlement Act) that would give the Bank a more formal and explicit responsibility for the oversight of clearing and settlement systems with the objective of controlling systemic risk. This formal oversight responsibility means that private sector operators of clearing and settlement systems that have been designated as having the potential to cause systemic risk would be required to obtain Bank of Canada approval of arrangements to monitor and control risks in their systems. The Act is carefully drafted so that the oversight function would apply only to those systems that involve payment obligations and that have systemic risk potential, and does not seek to have the Bank regulate any associated financial market, or the unrelated activities of participants in these systems.

Under the Act, the Bank will: (i) review all eligible clearing and settlement systems[7] for their potential to generate systemic risk; (ii) designate those systems with the potential to create systemic risk as being subject to the Act; and (iii) regulate the designated systems on an ongoing basis for the appropriate control of systemic risk. In carrying out this latter function, the Bank may enter into agreements with clearing and settlement systems concerning the control of systemic risk, issue directives to the clearing house in these arrangements if systemic risk is being inadequately controlled and enforce compliance of these directives, conduct audits of any designated clearing

---

[7]A clearing and settlement system is eligible for review if it clears or settles payment obligations or messages and: (i) it has three or more participants, at least one of which is a bank; (ii) clearing or settlement of payment obligations is at least partly in Canadian dollars; and (iii) payment obligations are ultimately settled through accounts at the Bank of Canada.

house, and charge back to the designated systems the direct costs associated with these activities.

The Act also contains provisions to increase the legal certainty regarding the enforceability of netting arrangements and to ensure that the settlement rules of designated clearing and settlement systems (including the rules related to the pledging and possible realization of collateral and the processing of entries to settle payment obligations) are immune to stays or other legal challenges. These provisions are intended to provide legal certainty that the rules of a designated clearing and settlement system will operate as designed in the event of a participant failure.

REFERENCES

Bank for International Settlements (1990), *Report of the Committee on Interbank Netting Schemes of the Central Banks of the Group of Ten Countries* (Basle: Bank for International Settlements).
_____ (1996), *Settlement Risk in Foreign Exchange Transactions* (Basle: Bank for International Settlements).
Board of Governors of the Federal Reserve System (1994), "Policy Statement on Privately Operated Large-Dollar Multilateral Netting Systems", *United States Federal Register* 59(249), 67, 534-67, 541 (Washington, D.C.).
Freedman, C. (1996), "The Large Value Transfer System in Canada" (Ottawa: Bank of Canada), mimeo.

Session Five
INDUSTRIAL ORGANIZATION AND THE CANADIAN FINANCIAL SECTOR

FINANCIAL SECTOR INDUSTRIAL ORGANIZATION — IS BANK CONCENTRATION ANTI-COMPETITIVE?

Harry Hassanwalia, Royal Bank of Canada

I. INTRODUCTION

Canada's financial system has been through some very far reaching reforms in 1987 and 1992. However, the forces of global competition and technological change are proceeding at an accelerating pace. Therefore, significant as our previous reforms have been, we cannot avoid the need to continually update them. This was recognized by the government when it reworked the financial sector legislation in 1992 by incorporating a sunset provision for review of that legislation in 1997. As a result we are now in the midst of another scheduled review. The recently released White Paper noted the need for a full review of the forces shaping our industry so that an appropriate legislative and regulatory framework can be designed.

In the discussions prior to the release of the White Paper a number of issues were raised. Among these was the issue about whether the degree of concentration in the financial system had reached alarming proportions. Then there were the questions of banks networking insurance or leasing cars. Other issues included the question of deposit-taking powers for insurance companies and their participation in the payments system, whether banks should be allowed to merge and whether there is need for further deposit-insurance reform. These are some of the high-profile issues.

The long-awaited White Paper (*1997 Review of Financial Sector Legislation: Proposals for Changes*) was released by the Government of Canada on June 19, 1996. While many of the above important issues would seem to have been in need of review, the government decided not to act upon most of them during the 1997 round. The White Paper's proposed legislative amendments address only some, but not all, of the important issues that had been raised prior to the paper. Most of the remaining issues would seem to fall under the broader review of specific study groups.

One is the Task Force on the Future of the Canadian Financial Services Sector, which will be established to provide advice to the government on public policy issues related to the development of the appropriate framework for the financial sector in the twenty-first century. The mandate and composition of this will be announced in fall 1996, and the expectation is that it would report back within 18 months.

The second is the Department of Finance Advisory Committee to Review the Payments System. This committee will have a range of experts on payments issues, including industry participants, academics, consumers and other key users. This committee will contribute to the work of the task force.

It seems, therefore, that these study groups will be examining most of the substantive issues facing the Canadian financial services industry.

Through much of Canada's postwar history, the issue of bank concentration and the implications for reduced competition have continued to surface time and again. The fact that the proposed changes for the 1997 round do not lift insurance networking restrictions upon banks nor permit banks to broaden their reach into auto leasing demonstrates to some extent a continuing concern that banks are already too big and too concentrated. This is also likely behind the implicit public policy restricting bank mergers.[1]

John Chant's paper (this volume) examines whether there are any public interest reasons for allowing bank mergers by looking at the issues of scale

---

[1]While the Bank Act (1992) does not prohibit bank mergers, such mergers may not receive the required ministerial approval. There is a government policy (colloquially termed "big shall not buy big") to generally not permit mergers between large financial institutions.

and scope economies, the cost of capital and a number of other issues. While such an investigation is important, it may not be the appropriate approach for setting direction of public policy. It implies a regulatory philosophy of restricting all activities unless permissiveness can be shown to be in the public interest, an approach not conducive to innovation and efficiency.[2] The more relevant question may be not why a particular market-based solution must be allowed, but rather why it should be disallowed. And this then may require identifying concerns with bank mergers. One such concern might be the short-run job losses as a result of streamlining of operations in merged banks, but this would have to be viewed against the benefit of security of long-term survival of the merged institution against competition from ever larger, more diversified and more efficient (due to better economies of scale) international competitors.[3] Another concern could be that the resulting larger banks become "too big to fail" and so obtain an implicit protection from failure from the government. The one that this paper particularly focuses on is whether mergers and the ensuing concentration will lower competition. In other words, is there a link between concentration and competition? And there are other ancillary questions associated with that.

II.   CONCENTRATION VERSUS LACK OF COMPETITION —
THE VIEW FROM ECONOMIC THEORY

Economic theory does not provide a clear linkage between concentration and lack of competition. High industry concentration can be consistent with highly

---

[2]Early public debate regarding the opening up of the Canadian securities industry was characterized by a philosophy of restrictiveness and led to very modest proposals for change. The eventual proposal to open up fully the industry emerged only after the adoption of a market-oriented philosophy with the onus being on those that would restrict market solutions to demonstrate the public interest in doing so. By analogy, instead of asking why banks should be allowed to merge, the more appropriate question might be to ask why they should be prevented from merging.

[3]The fact that evidence of scope and scale economies in banking is ambiguous might be a reflection of the fact that most of the studies are based on U.S. banks, which have neither the size, the geographic reach, nor the multiproduct nature of modern financial services enterprises.

competitive markets if the dominant firms cannot exercise market power. It is the conduct of institutions and the level of competition in markets that matters more than simple concentration measures. Recent research has confirmed that the number of firms or the relative concentration ratios of firms in an industry are not indicators of the degree of competition in the industry. For instance, Fama and Laffer (1972) showed that if individual firm behaviour to reduce output and increase price is accompanied by offsetting behaviour of other firms in the industry, an industry with a relatively small number of large institutions continues to be very competitive. Further support for this view is found in the concept of market "contestability" where competitive discipline is brought upon an industry through the threat of new entrants (Baumol *et al.,* 1982). Empirical studies on the Canadian financial system by Nathan and Neave (1989) and by Shaffer (1993) have also concluded against the presence of monopoly power.

It seems that two important ingredients for high concentration to reduce competition are barriers to entry and absence of close substitutes. In today's financial markets it may be extremely difficult to meet these two conditions given ease of entry, global competition and the presence of innovative substitutes as a result of financial engineering. Of course, this does not mean that there will not be any cases of market failure. There will be market failures from time to time in any sector or in any particular market. But that is the raison d'etre for competition policy.

III. FOUR KEY QUESTIONS

From a public policy point of view then, there are at least four key questions about bank concentration in Canada that one might wish to ask. These are:

•   Are Canadian banks increasing their concentration?

•   Is there a link between bank concentration and lack of competition?

•   Do Canadian banks earn excessive profits?

•   What about their spreads and fees?

We take up each of these in turn.

IV. ARE CANADIAN BANKS INCREASING
THEIR CONCENTRATION?

There needs to be objective analysis of this because it is very easy to point to partial statistics such as the shift from 0% to 75% control of the securities business that banks managed to corner since they were permitted to own securities firms in 1987. Or that in 1992 they were given the power to buy trust companies and they bought up all the big ones. More appropriate analysis would attempt to answer what this rise in share really means in terms of market control over the financial intermediation business in Canada.

Chart 1 shows the trends in the top two and top five bank shares of total bank assets in Canada going back 115 years. Neither the two largest banks nor the

Chart 1:   Concentration Among the Chartered Banks
          (% of total bank assets belonging to top two and five banks)

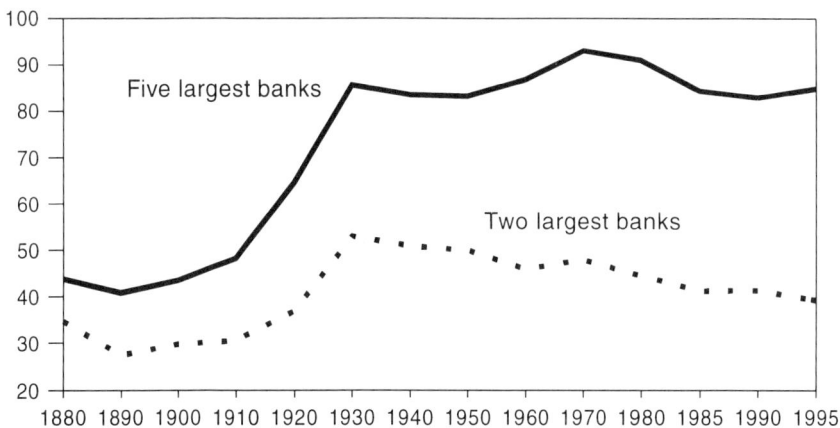

Source: E.P. Neufeld (1972), "The Financial System of Canada", Supplement to the *Canada Gazette*.

five largest banks show any trend towards a rising share of banking assets. In fact, the share of the two largest has been on a declining trend since 1930.

But there could be some questions about the usefulness of these ratios, since even if the top two and top five banks may be losing share relative to other banks, the banking industry itself might be gaining against the other intermediaries. Banks do not just compete with other banks; they also compete against all the other players, such as credit unions and trust companies on both the deposit and asset side of the business, against the insurance companies on the asset side of the business, against pension funds and mutual funds on the liabilities side and so on.

Moreover, this ratio is also biased by the fact that both the numerator and denominator include what banks do outside the country, which is not really relevant if one is interested in gauging the trend in the banks' domestic market power.

Chart 2 shows the shares of various intermediaries in the total domestic private sector financial intermediation pie. That is the banks' share of domestic, private intermediary assets. If anything, concentration has been falling. From a position of 75% of the domestic financial intermediation market at the time of Confederation, the share of banks has steadily come down to 37%. The share of banks has been on a steady though slightly volatile downward trend. While the banks' recent acquisitions of brokerage houses, trust companies, mutual funds and some insurance companies has led to some slight up-tick in their relative share of the market, there is no indication that they are headed towards the dominance that they once had.

This historical review is important so that we understand that the current dominance of banks is not a new phenomenon; it has been with us since Confederation. If anything it is lower today, even after all the mergers and acquisitions, than it has been in the past. Certainly it is lower today than it was even in 1950.

It might be argued that this aggregate asset base comparison is not meaningful, but that one should look at the dominance in individual markets. Such a market-based analysis would show that banks have increased their dominance in some markets and decreased it in others. In those that they have increased

**Chart 2:   Financial Intermediary Domestic Assets as a
Proportion of all Private FIS, 1870-1994**

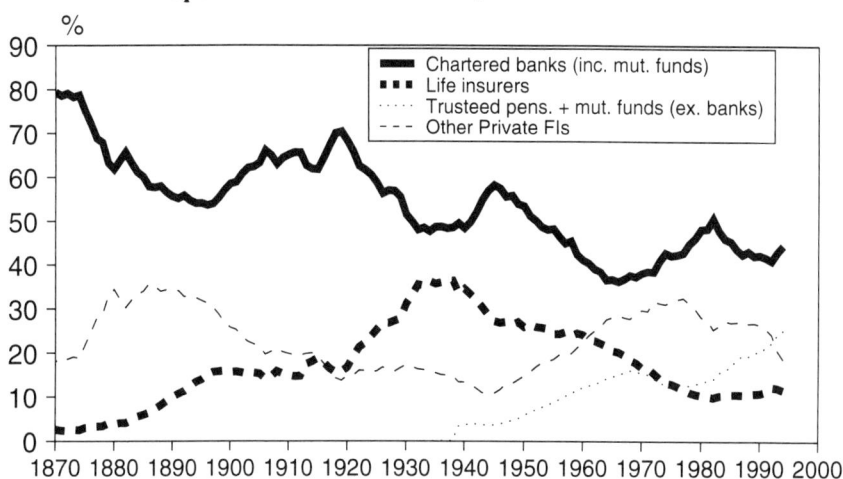

Sources: Dominion Bureau of Statistics, Statistics Canada, Bank of Canada
Review and Investment Funds Institute.

their dominance, the next logical question is to ask what happened to the state
of competition, an issue that is examined below.

Chart 2 also shows trends for other industry groups. One group that has had
a large drop in share recently is the near banks. Their drop coincides with the
rise in share of the banks and reflects recent bank acquisitions of trust
companies. The life insurance sector experienced a long-term decline in its
market share from the 1930s until the early 1980s, but since then its market
share seems to have stabilized. This long-term decline occurred because of
competition from pension plans and mutual funds in capital market assets and
competition from banks and near-banks in mortgage credit.

An interesting sector is the suppliers of long-term capital in Canada, the
mutual funds and the trusteed pension plans. Mutual funds are of a relatively
more recent vintage in terms of their importance but the trusteed pension plans
have been there for a long time. And they have been rising and they will likely
continue to rise, because of disintermediation and the trend towards increasing
importance of capital markets in the supply of credit.

Industrial Organization and the Canadian Financial Sector   *157*

In summary, as far as the domestic market is concerned, analysis over the past century shows that banks have had higher concentration in the past and there is no evidence that they will increase their concentration to levels they had in the past. If anything, the recent spate of merger and acquisitions by them seem to have slowed their gradual decline.

This is as far as the domestic market is concerned. However, even in the global arena, the situation as far as Canadian banks are concerned is not very different. The pace of consolidation, mergers and acquisition among international banks has been accelerating for some time as they strive to achieve economies of scale and scope. Canadian banks relative to global banking are not getting larger, but rather smaller. The size rank of Canadian banks has been slipping (see Chart 3). So neither when compared to the domestic market, nor when compared to the global market can it be said that Canadian banks are increasing their concentration. On this subject of relative global size, it is sometimes suggested that exchange rate distortions are part of the reason behind Canadian banks relative decline in size. While that may well be the case, it does not lessen the competitive consequences that banks have to face, since the prices of new technology investments required to remain competitive, with the rapid pace in technological change, are determined in international markets, not in Canada in Canadian dollars. So while size rankings may have been affected by exchange rate distortions, that is small comfort as far as international competitiveness of banks is concerned.

Chart 3: World Ranking of Canada's Largest Banks
(Assets, U.S. $ Millions)

1970			1984			1994		
Rank	Bank	Assets	Rank	Bank	Assets	Rank	Bank	Assets
12	RBC	9,599	20	RBC	65,654	59	RBC	123,382
19	CIBC	8,629	34	CIBC	52,811	65	CIBC	106,302

Source: *The Banker* (Top 500 and Top 1000 issues).

V. IS THERE A LINK BETWEEN CONCENTRATION AND COMPETITION?

As the long-term trends for Canadian banks reveal there is no sign of an increase in their aggregate concentration whether in the domestic or international market. But that is not the case as far as some individual markets are concerned. When banks entered the securities business they increased their share from virtually nothing to 75%. They got into the residential mortgage business and the consumer credit business in the 1960s and have increased their share in those markets substantially. So in aggregate they have not increased their concentration but there are markets in which they have gained share and equally there are other markets where they have lost share. In order to gauge the linkage between concentration and competition, it is therefore instructive to examine those markets in which banks have increased their dominance. For instance, the theoretical linkage between concentration and lack of competition would suggest that in these markets where banks increased their dominance, it should have been accompanied by the exercise of increased market power and decreased levels of competition. On the other hand, if in fact, as we expect, those markets were contestable, increased dominance would not have provided any opportunity for exercise of market power.

For this reason it is useful to examine the long-term trends in prices in those markets where banks have increased their dominance. The three markets examined below are the securities market, the residential mortgage market and the consumer credit markets, because we have enough historical data on them over a sufficiently long time.

Securities Business

Banks were given the power to acquire securities dealers in 1987. Most of the acquisitions were consummated in 1988, after the stock market crash of October 1987.

As Chart 4 shows, the share of the banking industry in the securities business has climbed to the 75 to 80% range from virtually zero in 1987. But despite this rise in bank concentration in this market, prices as measured by commissions as a percentage of TSE and MSE volumes have come down.

Chart 4: Expansion by Banks and Price Securities Industry

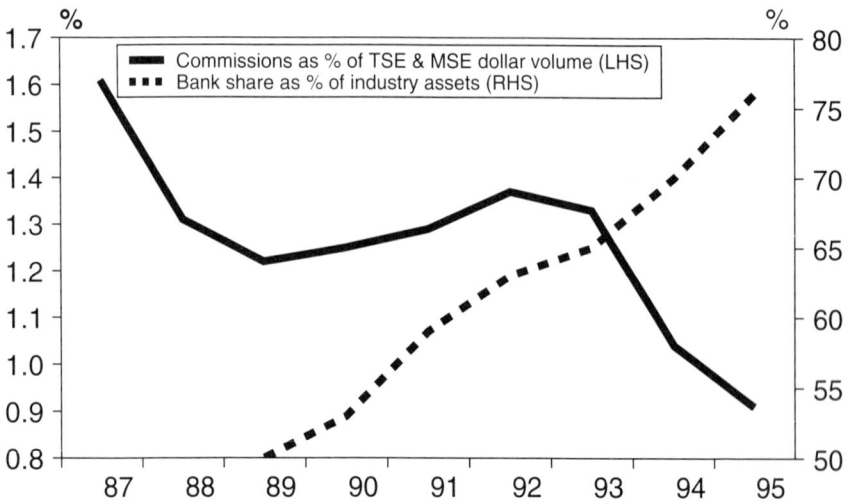

Sources: Statistics Canada, Bank of Canada, IDA.

Commissions are just an indication of aggregate price. So even as bank dominance of this market increased prices if anything went down. This is not to imply that banks went in and lowered prices. It just indicates that competition was enhanced by opening the market to new players. It may very well have been the existing players that initiated the lower prices. It does not have to have been the new entrants that did it. What is important is that the opening of the market, while leading to a rising concentration with banks, resulted in enhanced competition and lower prices.

Another important measure relates to volumes. For instance, curtailment of quantity is an indication of lack of competition. In fact, however, the opposite happened. Chart 5 shows that trading volumes, as a ratio of GDP, increased by orders of magnitude. Volumes on the Toronto and Montreal stock exchanges measured in millions of dollars ranged between 5% and 10% of nominal GDP in the 1950s through to the early 1980s, and then rose to the present level of over 25%.

One of the difficulties with inferring too much from the securities market is that this covers a relatively short time span, only eight years. There is this view

Chart 5: TSE + MSE Volumes – Millions of Dollars
(as % of nominal GDP)

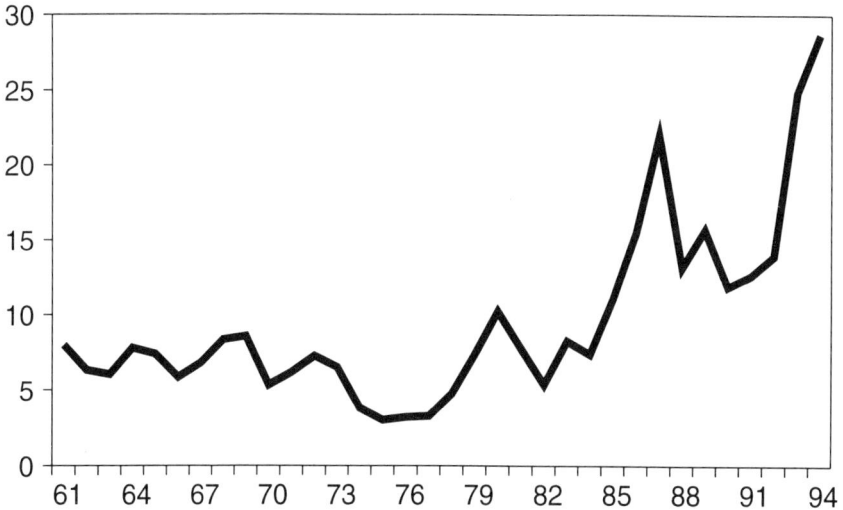

Sources: Bank of Canada, Statistics Canada.

that banks are big and after they get into a new market, they will lower prices to drive out competition and when the competition is levelled, they will go out and jack up the prices. So the relatively short span of time covering the experience in the securities market does not provide enough evidence to counter the charge of potential predatory pricing.

Fortunately, there are two other cases of bank entry and domination of markets that cover a much longer time span. These are the entry of banks into the residential mortgage and the consumer credit markets.

Residential Mortgages

Banks began to enter the residential mortgage market in a major way in the mid-1960s. During the past 30 years they have increased their share of this business more than five fold, from about 10% to over 50% today. Despite this trend towards dramatic market share gains by banks, which has extended over 30 years, there is no upward trend in prices (see Chart 6). In fact, the spread

**Chart 6: Bank Market Share and Spread in Residential
Mortgage Market**

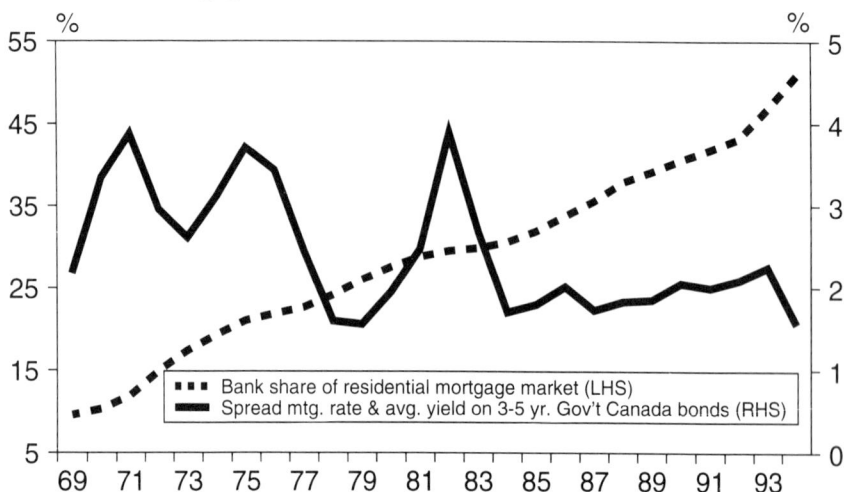

Bank share of residential mortgage market (LHS)
Spread mtg. rate & avg. yield on 3-5 yr. Gov't Canada bonds (RHS)

Sources: Statistics Canada, Bank of Canada.

between mortgage rates and interest rates on Government of Canada bonds of
comparable maturity has maintained a flat to somewhat downward trend, even
as banks increased their market share.[4] This would tend to confirm that bank
dominance has not been accompanied by any predatory pricing. Moreover, as
banks were gaining market share, the total amount of residential mortgage
credit was expanding faster than the economy; the dollar volume of residential
mortgage credit as a percentage of nominal GDP has increased from about
17% over 25 years ago to about 43% today (see Chart 7). Volumes rose much
faster than they had before.

---

[4]The spread against Government of Canada bond rates is not and should not
be interpreted as a measure of "profit", since the marginal cost of funds for banks is
not equal to the rate at which government can raise funds. The use of Government of
Canada bond rates is simply to provide a benchmark for the overall level of market
interest rates.

Chart 7:   Expansion by Banks and Volume of Credit
(Residential mortgage market)

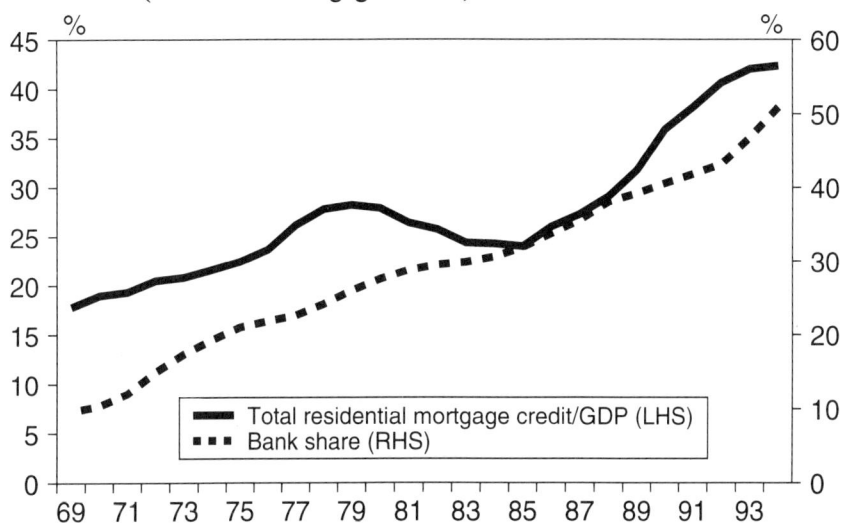

Sources: Statistics Canada, Bank of Canada.

Consumer Credit

The third market is the market of consumer credit. The consumer credit market, into which the banks began to make major inroads again in the mid-1960s, has also been characterized by a substantial rise in volumes as banks expanded their presence (Chart 8). The dollar volume of consumer credit as a percentage of nominal GDP has gone from about 8% in the 1950s to the present level of around 14% of GDP. Over this same period, banks increased their market share from about 30% to almost 70%.

Prices, as measured by the spread between total interest payments on consumer credit as a percentage of total consumer credit and the bank rate, have been quite flat over the last four decades, with a slight downward trend (see Chart 9).

This review of the three markets which banks entered and came to dominate shows that while bank entry did lead to rising concentration in those markets

Chart 8: Expansion by Banks and Volume of Credit
(Consumer credit market)

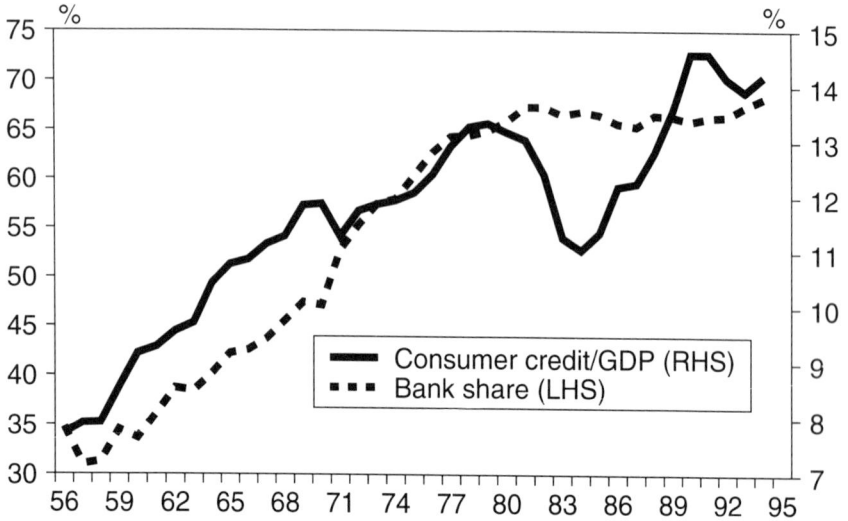

- Consumer credit/GDP (RHS)
- Bank share (LHS)

Sources: Statistics Canada, Bank of Canada.

Chart 9: Bank Market Shares and Spreads on Consumer Credit

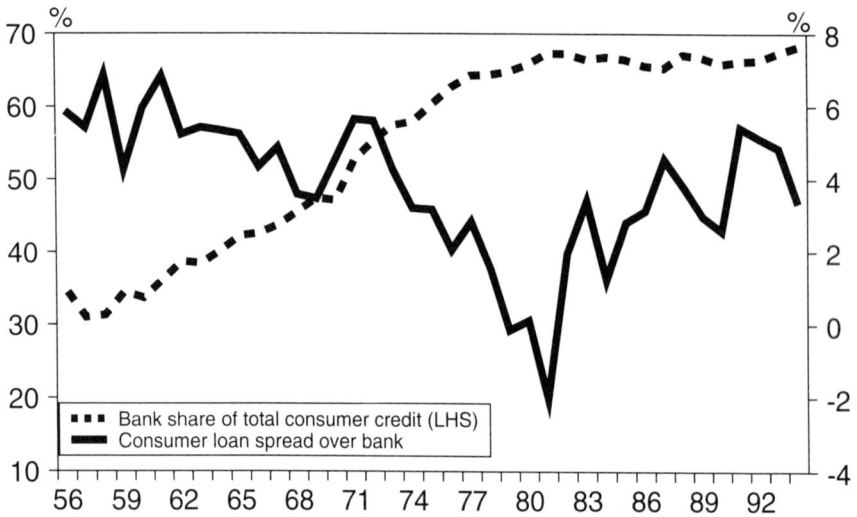

- Bank share of total consumer credit (LHS)
- Consumer loan spread over bank

Sources: Statistics Canada, Bank of Canada.

by banks, prices if anything went down, volumes certainly rose much more than they had before and product variety and innovation also increased.

International Evidence on Concentration and Competition

The question of concentration and potential implications for competition can also be examined in the context of international trends in banking. If high concentration reduces competition, one might expect bank-loan spreads to be higher in countries with higher levels of bank concentration. However, Chart 10 shows that there is no correlation at all between the degree of bank concentration in various countries and bank loan spreads charged in those countries. Not only is the apparent linkage between concentration and lack of competition refuted in Canada, it is also refuted in major countries around the world.

There is a trend, however, that does stand out and that is a clear negative correlation between the degree of bank concentration in a country and the size

Chart 10: Concentration Versus Spreads
(11 countries)

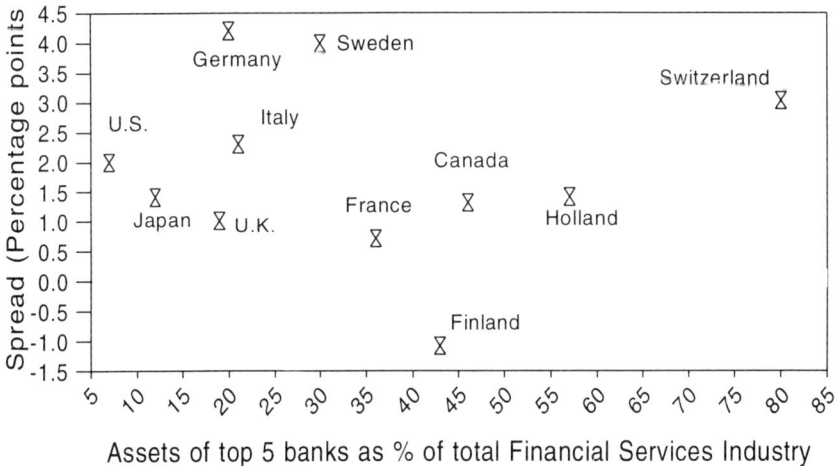

Assets of top 5 banks as % of total Financial Services Industry

Sources: OECD and IMF.

of that country (see Chart 11). That is, the smaller the country, the higher the degree of concentration in its banking sector. This seems to imply that there is a gravitation towards some universal size of bank. While this observation cannot be treated as a rigorous test, it nonetheless is consistent with the presence of economies of scale. The smaller the country, the smaller its banking sector and, therefore, if economies of scale require banks to be large, the fewer the banks it will have and the higher its level of concentration. It would seem that if Holland, for example, had the same kind of concentration as Germany, it would have very small banks which may not be able to be globally competitive.

VI. DO CANADIAN BANKS EARN EXCESSIVE PROFITS?

Any discussion about concentration and competition relating to Canadian banks is incomplete without a discussion of profits. There is no question that

Chart 11: Concentration Versus Population
    (11 countries)

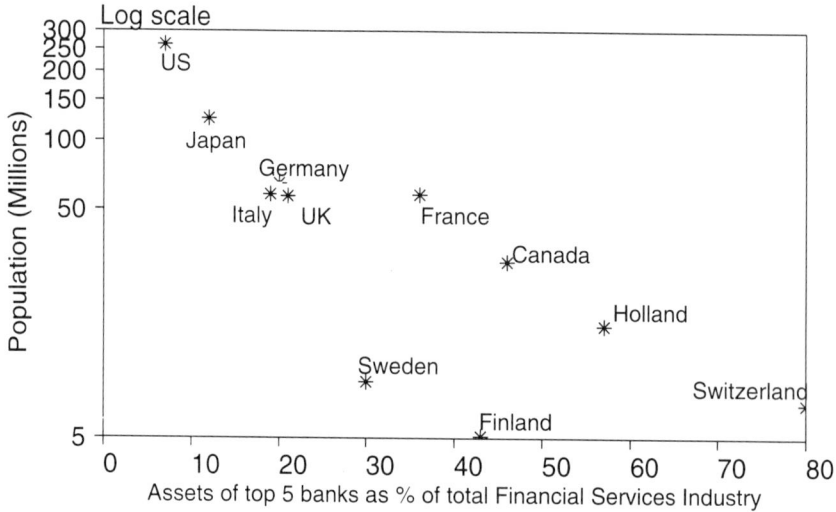

Sources: OECD and IMF.

banks are large institutions in Canada and they earn huge profits when measured relative to the other players in Canada. But that by itself simply is a reflection of their size. What is more relevant is their level of profitability relative to their size, as measured, for example, by return on equity.

There are a number of ways of carrying out profit comparisons. One way is to compare Canadian banks relative to banks in other countries. Second, one could compare Canadian banks relative to other industrial sectors in Canada. Finally, one could compare individual banks to other large profitable individual Canadian companies.

Canada - U.S. Comparisons

Chart 12 shows the average return on equity from 1990 to 1994 for the big six Canadian banks relative to the largest ten U.S. banks and the largest 28 U.S. banks. Based on this comparison, it does not appear that the big six Canadian banks are earning excess profits. Given that the United States has very low bank concentration with thousands of banks, the fact that Canadian banks' profitability is lower is yet another challenge to the notion of linking concentration and competition. Of course, there is some question about whether aggregate concentration ratios are meaningful in the United States with the fragmented regional structure of the banking sector.

In any event, on the basis of return on equity measurements it does not seem that Canadian bank profitability is out of line with U.S. banks. One may ask whether it is appropriate to conduct a comparison with U.S. banks. An important reason for this comparison is that Canadian banks are competing with U.S. banks for capital as Canadian and U.S. capital markets are quite integrated, and under NAFTA this integration is going to increase rather than decrease.

Chart 12: Average Return on Equity 1990-1994

%

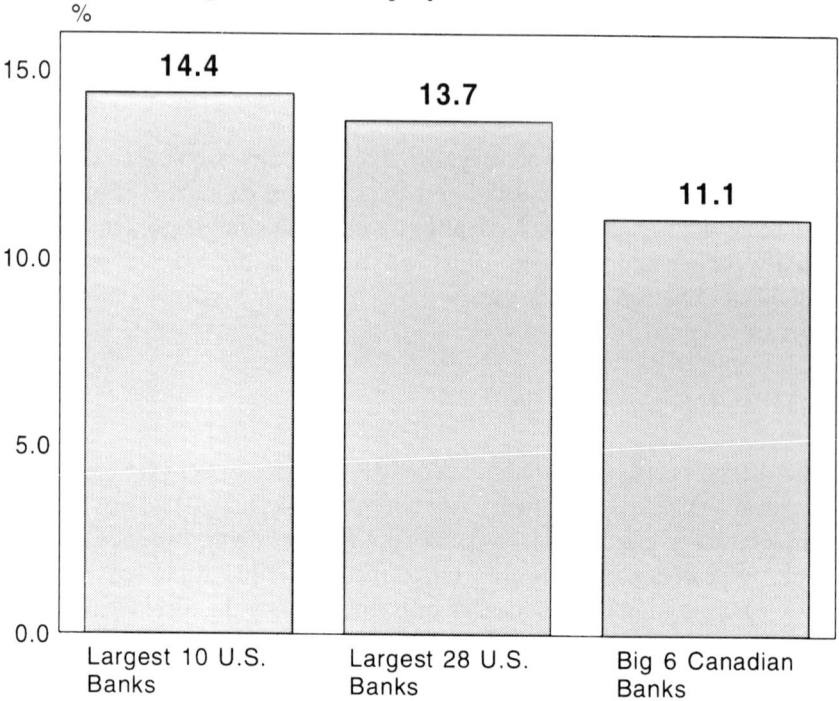

	14.4	13.7	11.1
	Largest 10 U.S. Banks	Largest 28 U.S. Banks	Big 6 Canadian Banks

Note: More recent averages (1990-1995) would put the percentages at 14.6, 14.2 and 11.5 respectively.

Sources: *Banking in the 1990s*, CS First Boston, annual surveys (1991 through to 1996); *Bank Annuals*, Salomon Brothers, annual surveys (1991 through to 1996); annual reports of individual Canadian banks.

Domestic Interindustry Comparisons

Chart 13 shows the profitability on domestic operations for various industry sectors in Canada.[5] The banking industry is about in the middle. However, a

---

[5]In order to perform consistent comparisons between industry sectors, only profitability on domestic operations is used. Moreover, the banking sector covers all banks, not just the big six.

Chart 13: Average Returns on Equity on Domestic Operations
    (1990-1995Q1)

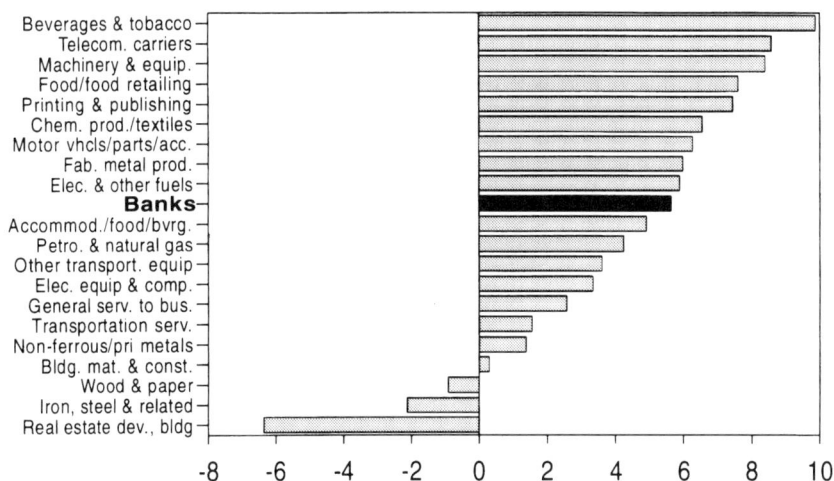

Source: Statistics Canada.

weakness of these broad industry comparisons is that they cover a very wide size range of firms, and this may understate the results for banks by the inclusion of small less diversified and perhaps less profitable banks. The next comparison, therefore, looks at individual companies.

Intercompany Comparisons

Chart 14 compares the performance of the Royal Bank to that of other large Canadian companies. Again this shows that among the largest 500 companies in Canada, the rate of return for the largest bank in Canada is about in the middle of the pack.

Costs and Efficiency

Lack of excessive profitability does not necessarily imply lack of market power. For instance, a firm could have market power and earn rents on the price side which do not get passed into excessive profits because of cost

Chart 14: Comparing Return on Total Shareholders' Equity with Canada's 500 Largest Companies

Year	Royal Bank ROE*	# companies higher than Royal Bank (including crown corps.)	# companies higher than Royal Bank (excluding crown corps.)
1995	14.32	134	127
1994	14.15	135	127
1993	3.89	241	231
1992	1.4	255	238
1991	13.84	68	60

* Based on total shareholders' equity.

Source: *Financial Post* 500 surveys from 1992 to 1996 for 1991 to 1995 data.

inefficiencies. Therefore, it may be useful to look beyond profitability to the productivity of the firm. A commonly used measure by bank analysts to gauge bank productivity is the efficiency ratio, the ratio of non-interest expenses (NIE), a proxy for input, to gross revenues, a proxy for output. The greater the efficiency, the lower this ratio should be. It is not a perfect measure, as it is sensitive to the product mix of a bank. Chart 15 shows that Canadian banks are more efficient according to this measure than U.S. banks.

VII. WHAT ABOUT THEIR SPREADS AND FEES?

There is a more direct way of gauging the presence of rents on the price side. The price trends in the three markets of residential mortgages, consumer credit and securities markets that were discussed earlier have already shown that bank dominance did not lead to price increases. Another way of examining

Chart 15: Efficiency Ratio - NIE/Gross Revenues
(average for 1990-1994)

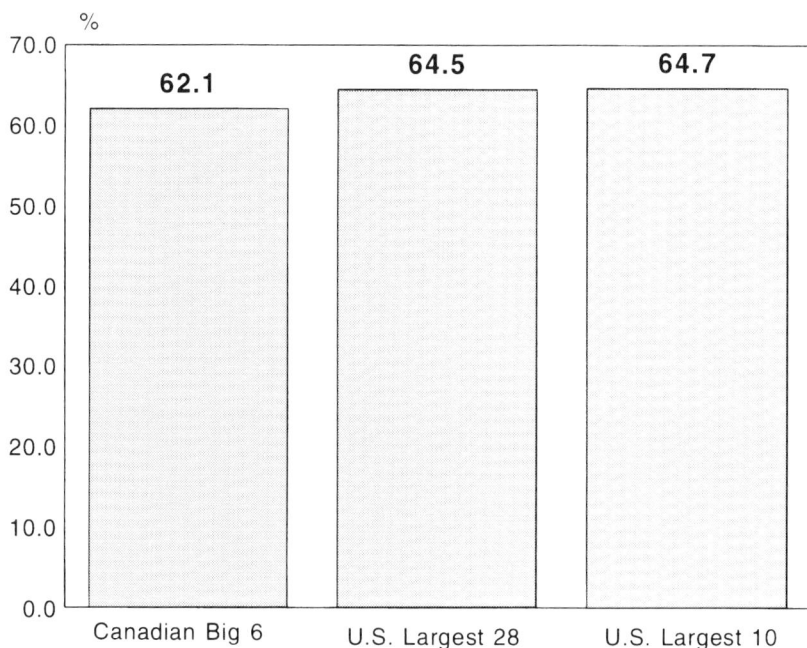

Note: More recent averages (1990-1995) would put these ratios at 61.9, 64.3 and 64.3 respectively.

Sources: *Banking in the 1990s*, CS First Boston, annual surveys (1991 through to 1996); *Bank Annuals*, Salomon Brothers, annual surveys (1991 through to 1996); Annual reports of individual Canadian banks.

prices is pricing comparisons by borrower size. Chart 16 shows the loan spread over cost of funds in the United States and Canada for various sizes of borrowers. As expected, the line slopes downward implying that as the size of the borrower rises the risk is lower and so the spread gets narrower. But the interesting thing is Canada's spreads are consistently lower than those in the United States. Moreover, the relatively more favourable pricing in Canada is the greatest at the smallest borrower level.

Chart 16: Pricing Comparison by Borrower Sales
(Spread over costs of funds, July 1995)

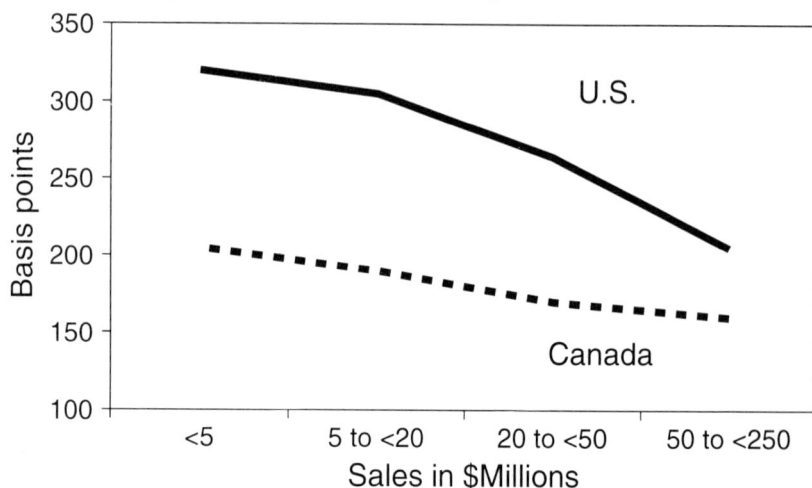

Source: Loan Pricing Corporation.

Finally, Chart 17 shows a comparison of service charges for a basket of 13 commonly used services between Canada and the United States. Again, what is clear is that Canadian prices are lower than those in the United States.

VIII. CONCLUSIONS

While there may be many reasons to be concerned about bank consolidation and the ensuing concentration, this paper suggests that the possible negative implications for competition do not seem to be among them, likely reflecting low barriers to entry and large numbers of substitutes for banking products. Moreover, at an aggregate level the control over domestic financial inter-mediation by banks today is lower than it has been in the past and there is no indication that it will rise to previous heights. Certainly, bank concentration today is even lower than in 1950.

Chart 17: Bank Fees: Canada Versus United States

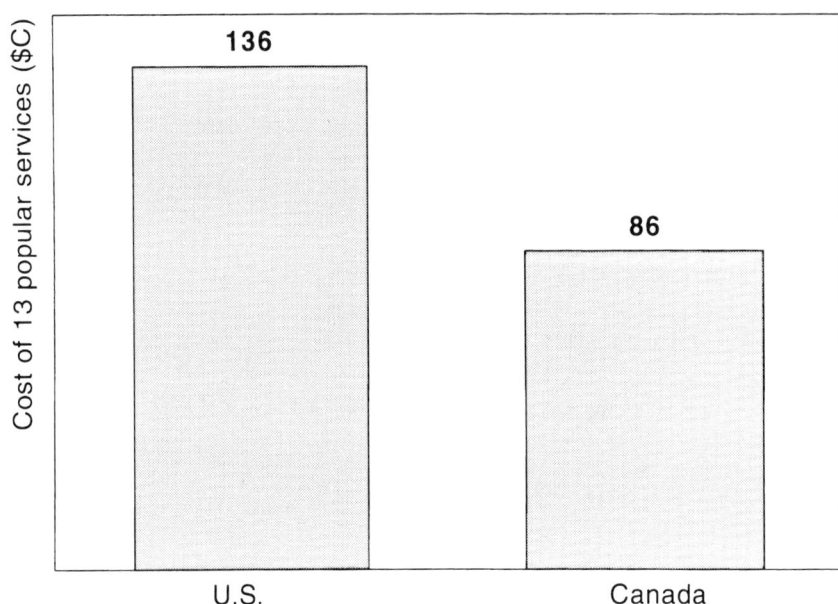

Sources: Individual Canadian banks; Siefer Consultants (1995).

Despite this apparent reduction in aggregate bank concentration in the Canadian financial sector, banks have increased their dominance in certain pockets of the financial industry. The three clear areas where bank dominance has increased are residential mortgages, consumer credit and securities. Yet market developments in these three areas show that bank entry was followed by increased volumes, improved access for consumers and new product innovation, while at the same time prices generally either stayed flat or declined.

Other comparisons that look at bank profitability and pricing trends in Canada also do not provide any support for the apparent linkage between concentration and lack of competition.

REFERENCES

Annual reports (1995), of the 'big six' chartered banks (Royal Bank, Bank of Montreal, Canadian Imperial Bank of Commerce, Bank of Nova Scotia, Toronto-Dominion Bank, and National Bank).

Banking in the 1990s: Who Will be the Winners by 1997? Bank Annual, CS First Boston (Equity Research-Americas), 1995 issue.

Bank Act 1996, Statutes of Canada 1991 c.46 plus amendments, Annotated, Guy David and Louise Pelly (Toronto: Carswell, Thomson Canada Ltd).

Bank Annuals, Salomon Brothers, various issues.

Baumol, W.J. (1982), "Contestable Markets: An Uprising in the Theory of Industry Structure", *American Economic Review* 72(1), 1-15.

Baumol, W.J., J. Panzar and R. Willig (1982), *Contestable Markets and the Theory of Industry Structure* (New York: Harcourt Brace Jovanovich).

Edey, M. and K. Hviding (1995), *An Assessment of Financial Reform in OECD Countries*, OECD Working Paper No. 154 (Paris: Organization for Economic Cooperation and Development).

Fama, E. and A. Laffer (1972), "The Number of Firms and Competition", *American Economic Review* 62 (September), 670-674.

Nathan, A. and E. Neave (1989), "Competition and Contestability in Canada's Financial System: Empirical Results", *Canadian Journal of Economics* 22(3), 576-594.

Neufeld, E.P. (1972), *The Financial System of Canada: Its Growth and Development* (Toronto: Macmillan).

Shaffer, S. (1993), "A Test of Competition in Canadian Banking", *Journal of Money Credit and Banking* 25(1), 49-61.

Siefer Consultants (1995), *Service Charge Survey & Pricing Guide 1995* (Storm Lake, IA: Siefer Consultants).

The Banker, Top 1000 and previously Top 500 issues (London: Financial Times Magazines), annual issue (currently July, previously June), distributed by Seymour International Press.

MERGERS, OWNERSHIP AND THE
TEN PERCENT RULE: COMMENTS

John L. Evans, Evans Strategic Policy

I think that Harry Hassanwalia has done an excellent job of describing the results of the study that was done by he and John McCallum earlier this year (1996). And I should say at the outset that my comments should not be taken to be directed at either Hassanwalia or the Royal Bank in particular.

Indeed, when it comes to ownership, the Royal Bank has taken a somewhat different view from the other Canadian banks. Back in the 1970s, the CEO of the Royal pointed out that the 10% ownership regime was really not necessary, that foreign banks should be allowed to come into Canada and that Canadian banks could compete quite effectively with foreign banks in this country. I am convinced that the Royal Bank has always been a pro-competitive element within the banking industry, but that is not to say that the Canadian banking industry has itself been pro-competitive.

I think that those of us who went through the 1980 Bank Act revision and subsequent updates and experienced the battles between the trust industry and the banking industry as to the 10% ownership rule will know the banks have taken some very strenuous positions with regard to the ownership of Canadian financial institutions.

In this regard, I would like to say a few things about the recent conversion of some banks to a more open ownership position. I likened it, in a recent article, to the conversion of Saul on the road to Damascus. I am referring here to the apparent (and I mention apparent because it was put forward first of all by the new CEO of the Royal Bank which is not inconsistent with previous comments that have been made by Royal Bank CEOs over the years) 180 degree change of heart with regard to the issue of ownership. This view that the 10% ownership rule should be abandoned was subsequently reiterated by the outgoing head of the Canadian Bankers Association. The reason for this, of course, is that the 10% ownership rule causes some problems for potential Canadian bank mergers.

Now, you will recall that ever since bank management was handed total immunity from shareholder discipline in 1967 with the introduction to the Bank Act of the 10% ownership rule, the Canadian banks have continuously promoted the view that this rule is the only thing keeping Canadian banking from falling into the hands of the devil himself. Certainly in the early 1980s this devil took the form of industrial and commercial organizations that were acquiring Canadian trust companies. Indeed the rule was felt to be so essential to the health of the financial system that the banks advocated its extension to all forms of financial institutions. The White Paper in 1982 called for the imposition of a 10% rule on the trust and loan industry. The rationale for the application of the 10% ownership rule to Canadian trust and loan companies was, I think, primarily to stop the takeover of Royal Trust. No action was taken. In any event, the Canadian trust industry has now been all but absorbed into the banking system, and by 1992 any changes that allowed the trust industry to move beyond its domain in business operations were simply too late.

In my view, the sanctity of the 10% rule has come to be one of the great myths of our time, and I do mean myths. But what is this we hear now from the Canadian bankers and the CEO of the Royal Bank of Canada? Both are now calling for the abandonment of this "golden rule of Canadian banking". This new view of the world is apparently being forced on the banks by their need to pursue a new Holy Grail. And this Grail is world-class size. Specifically, the big five Canadian banks feel they are too small to be real players on the world banking scene. To overcome this obstacle they must be allowed to merge, one with another. In order to merge, of course, the 10% ownership rule must be sacrificed and this is all being done in the name of the public good.

Not yet discussed are the details of how the 10% rule should be removed. For example, will it apply to all forms of ownership of Canadian banks? In other words, will bank ownership be open to anyone with sufficient capital and integrity to meet the regulatory requirements? Does this mean that Canada

Trust will finally be allowed to call itself what it has long been, a bank? Does it mean that Imasco will be allowed to acquire the Toronto Dominion Bank and merge it with Canada Trust? Does it mean that Power Corporation, for example, will be allowed to do what it was denied the right to do in the 1980s, acquire a bank? Will any group of highly respectable entrepreneurs be allowed to form a new bank? Will the life and health insurance industry, for example, be allowed to collectively buy or form a bank? Will, perish the thought, a huge foreign bank be allowed to acquire one of the Canadian banks? Is this what the removal of the 10% ownership rule will in fact mean?

If merger is made feasible, why wouldn't the banks merge with foreign institutions since, in fact, NAFTA and WTO would allow foreign banks to take over Canadian banks in the absence of the 10% rule. If this is so then why would Canadian banks not merge with foreign institutions to attain greater size, not to mention the greater access to foreign markets that would come along with such a merger? Some very interesting options come into play when the 10% rule is withdrawn. And I am not sure that any of the current advocates of the new Holy Grail have thought this through to any great extent. None of these options are what the big five banks or the Canadian Bankers Association have in mind. Rather, I think they have a more limited view of the world. More than likely they would prefer to have the 10% rule suspended so as to allow mergers among themselves, but nothing more than that.

Now, this brings us to some really interesting issues. The Canadian public already believes, whether or not it is true, and Hassanwalia has provided some very interesting evidence to the contrary, that the banks have far too much power over Canadians' daily financial lives. And in politics, let me tell you, perception is definitely reality. The public also believes that there is far too much concentration in the industry, whether or not this is true. As such, I highly doubt that mergers among the big five banks would go down well either with the public or with the politicians. And I distinguish between government and politicians. They are separable and distinct.

Now what benefits would such mergers bring to the average Canadian? I think that is the question that has to be addressed if in fact the Canadian public is to be convinced that such mergers should be allowed. Would they ensure that employment in the Canadian banking industry expands? Not likely, since it is clear that the application of new technologies will result in fewer not more jobs in the banking industry. Would they mean that Canadians would receive their financial services at lower prices than before? Not in my view. Canadian banks are already beyond the size necessary to realize all the economies of scale that are likely available. This evidence was provided by John Chant in this volume. The issue of scale economies has also been examined and reported on by Coopers Lybrant, Ernst & Young, and by other academics. All have come to the conclusion that beyond a certain level, and I think John said it was around $25 billion, or somewhere in that $25 to $50 billion asset range, the economies of scale have been fully realized. In fact, the evidence indicates that the cost curves of the institutions actually start to rise beyond the $50 billion U.S. point. Beyond that point a firm incurs diseconomies, usually associated with the fact that as it gets larger, the management problems that accompany size, the complexity of the organization and all, cause the cost structure to start to increase. Furthermore, the institution becomes incapable of responding to the changing environment in a dynamic fashion and of keeping up with changing times.

So, would mergers mean that Canadians would receive their financial services at lower prices? Not necessarily. Any price reductions to consumers that do result in the future will undoubtedly come about as a result of increased distribution efficiencies, and the realization of such efficiencies is not, I would contend, a function of size. Now will internationally competitive banks, what-ever this means, make Canada a powerhouse in the world? Will they lead to increased consumer benefits? Again, not in my opinion. Competitiveness in financial services, both domestic and international, results from innovation and flexibility, from intensified consumer orientation, from ruthless cost contain-ment, but not, I would contend, from sheer size. What greater size will deliver is the opportunity in the short run for Canadian bankers to sit among the world's banking elite. It will serve to feed the egos of certain CEOs, those who are left after the mergers that is, but it will do precious little for the folks back home. I would suggest that we should remember how much we all benefited from the bank forays into LDC loans in the early 1980s.

Beyond these concerns there is a much larger one which I feel must be avoided. Canadian banks are the central elements in the financial system in this country. There is no doubt about that. They are already, I would suggest, too big to be allowed to fail. That is not too big to fail, they certainly could do that, but they are too big in this country to be allowed to fail. The different treatment between how Royal Trust was treated and how Central Guaranty Trust was treated shows where too big to be allowed to fail applies. Royal Trust was not allowed to fail: it was merged as an ongoing entity. Central Guaranty was kind of merged, but the smaller trust companies that have experienced problems have just been decimated, for example, Standard Trust. So you can see that somewhere along the size line a financial institution becomes too big to be allowed to fail. You find other ways of resolving those institutions. I do not necessarily agree that that is the way it should be done. I think the interesting comment on failure in the earlier paper by Randall Morck was, "let's go ahead and just scrap them and give the debt holders ownership of what is left". If the shares are worth 5% of pre-failure value, then that is what creditors get. I think that is a really innovative suggestion that should be looked at more closely.

If the banks become even larger, it is likely that the already too comfortable relationship between the banks and the government would become truly unbearable. I am referring here to the translation of shear economic power into political power in this country. What this country needs is more competition, not more market management. But bank mergers would result in the latter, not the former, all with greater assistance from the government.

If an institution is too big to be allowed to fail, it becomes in the interests of the government to ensure that this institution prospers, not excessively, but prospers nonetheless. I think you can look at a merged series of banking institutions in this country down to say three institutions and draw analogies that run roughly parallel to the health and safety afforded to Hydro-Québec or Ontario Hydro. They do not make a lot of money but they make comfortable returns. This leads to public policies which protect institutional interests rather than consumer interests, and that run counter to the policies that the government should be pursuing in the future. If the interest of the institutions and the government get too closely entwined, and the institutions become indistinguishable from public utilities and recent evidence clearly shows how efficient public utilities are, then the consumer interest is sure to take a back seat.

Now you may say that the Canadian banks do not lead such a privileged life. After all, did the government not just deny them new insurance powers? Did they not deny them auto leasing powers as well? But consider that the current government will need to face the electorate just when the legislative changes are scheduled to be made. No government in its right mind would take on the insurance and auto dealer lobbies at such a time. End of debate. But if a second factor is needed, add the fact that in the case of insurance the banks really do not need any further powers to move aggressively into this market.

They won the war in 1992. They lost a postwar skirmish in the White Paper. Banks can now set up insurance distribution networks outside their branches which, after all, is where insurance is sold in any event, and where most financial services will be sold in the not-too-distant future. They are going to be sold electronically, not in branches of financial institutions. I will guarantee you that five years from now there will be a dramatically smaller number of brick and mortar branches of banks than there are today. The fact is, banks have the power they need in the insurance area now. They can own an insurance company. They can retail insurance. They just cannot retail it through their branch network.

Now, return to the public utility issue. Utility status is like a two-edged sword. It makes for a comfortable existence for management but it may preclude changes necessary to increase operational efficiency. Consider the case of the banks. In the not-too-distant future they are going to have to begin shutting down a large number of branches as they move to more efficient electronic distribution. And make no mistake, they are moving very aggressively in the area of electronic distribution. Closing branches can lead to unrest among certain classes of customers who prefer to receive their financial services face to face. You saw reference to this in the White Paper — access to financial services by underprivileged groups. That is just the tip of the iceberg. Think of the political fallout then from merging banks and consolidating branches at the same time as you are shutting down branches and converting to electronic distribution. Low-income Canadians and others in society will feel they are being shut out of the system, and these groups generate a great deal of political sympathy. They will be saying they do not have access. Now, I would not want to be a bank that is put in this situation and have to try to justify my actions in an environment that is becoming ever more concentrated. As concentration increases it becomes harder to do the things that need to be done from a business perspective. Citibank has faced some rather interesting times in New York City in closing down branches. They have closed down a large number very quietly but now the political reaction is being felt. So you can imagine what will happen when the number of bank branches we have today begins to decline, and we are consolidating dramatically at the same time. You can imagine the kind of political outcry that is going to be heard.

So if you couple the need to close branches for efficiency reasons with the need to close branches due to mergers, what we have is the making of what I would call a first class political bun fight. It seems to me that the banks might want to think twice before stepping into this one given the kind of reception that they received in respect of insurance and auto leasing powers. Overall, I think it might be wise for the banks to rethink the merger idea. If they open up the 10% ownership rule they may be opening up their protected market, and I believe it is a protected market, to competition that they are not prepared for in exchange for very little benefit. And if they merge one with the other, then certainly in my view they will be opening up the door to greater public and political oversight and much greater levels of interference.

Now, there is a public policy alternative to this and it is something that I have been thinking about, and of which I was reminded as Maurice Levi was giving his paper. This is the applicability in Canada of the type of regulatory regime introduced in New Zealand. New Zealand has, quite simply, decided to get out of the business of regulating financial institutions. Now, New Zealand is a special case. Ninety percent of bank assets are held by foreign financial institutions. Only 10% are held by domestic institutions. But it is still a very interesting example. New Zealand says "we're out of the business". No deposit insurance, only full disclosure. The home country of an institution operating in New Zealand will be responsible for regulating that institution. Now if you look at the European Union, you will see a similar model. Institutions can locate in any country in the union, and do business in any other country. But the institution's home country is responsible for regulation and deposit insurance coverage.

Now you could think of a scenario in which Canada would say "we're going to get out of the business of regulating financial institutions. We're going to follow the New Zealand or EU examples. We're going to request that all Canadian banks choose a country of jurisdiction in which they will re-incorporate. They will be allowed to do business freely in Canada so long as their new home country agrees to provide adequate regulation acceptable to the Bank of Canada, and they agree to provide Canadian depositors with deposit insurance as though the deposits were held in that country".

For example, the Royal Bank could reincorporate in the United States and provide Canadians with U.S. $100,000 deposit insurance, rather than $60,000 Canadian. I think the Royal Bank might have a marketing advantage. Considering this kind of an environment, I have to ask myself would Canadians care? Is there some reason why Canadians would be worse off in this environment than they are in the current one? New Zealand does not seem to think so.

What is the big deal? Banks lend money, it is a Canadian that owes a foreign institution the money, and the Canadian law determines how foreign institutions can exercise their right of relief in case a Canadian fails to pay. And from the point of view of depositors, if the United States government stands behind deposit insurance in the United States and it stands behind deposit insurance in Canada, are we any worse off than the situation where the Canadian government stands behind deposit insurance in this country? I do not think that would be seen as a big problem. Now there are surely problems with this model. But it is clearly conceivable and one that might be contemplated when the White Paper task force decides to look at the question of ownership in anticipation of the next revision of the Bank Act.

Session Six
A NATIONAL SECURITIES COMMISSION

A NATIONAL SECURITIES COMMISSION FOR CANADA?

Jeffrey G. MacIntosh, University of Toronto

I. INTRODUCTION

Following the recent First Ministers' meeting in Ottawa in June, it was announced that eight provinces (excluding Quebec and British Columbia) and the prime minister had endorsed the concept of a national securities regulator, to be called the "Canadian Securities Commission" (McKenna and Freeman, 1996, p. B1). Assuming that the first ministers' plans come to fruition, Table 1 (in the appendix) indicates that the road to the creation of a national securities commission has not been a short one. As early as 1935, the Royal Commission on Price Spreads recommended the creation of a federal body to oversee the primary distribution of securities. As Table 1 shows, the Royal Commission's call for a national regulator has been oft-repeated both at the federal and provincial[1] levels, although not until the first ministers' recent agreement has there been such widespread support for a national securities regulator.

The author would like to thank Katherine Swinton for her helpful comments. Note that this paper is current only as of Fall 1996.

[1]Throughout, the word "provincial" should be understood as including both the provinces and the territories.

This paper canvasses the substantive issues implicated in the debate concerning the wisdom of creating a national securities regulator. Inevitably, the paper covers ground already canvassed by Professor Daniels, particularly in the enumeration of pros and cons for a national regulator (Daniels, 1992). My debt to Professor Daniels' earlier exploration of these issues is gratefully acknowledged.

The focus of the paper is the question of economic efficiency; that is, would the aggregate benefits of moving to a national securities commission exceed the aggregate costs. Clearly, however, other issues are important, both on a normative plain and in shaping the discussion that has taken place on the idea of a national securities commission. I begin, however, with a brief discussion of some of the political factors that have made it difficult for the provinces and the federal government to agree on a national regulator.

II. POLITICAL ISSUES

The substantive discussion below indicates that there are many good reasons for creating a national securities regulator, as opposed to ten provincial (and two territorial) regulators. Why, then, has it taken so long for most of the provinces and the federal government to agree to a national regulator?

A large part of the explanation lies in the political concerns that have tended to push aside the substantive pros and cons. These concerns include the following:

Loss of Power to the Eastern Establishment

The specter of domination from the east (both real and imagined) has long been a potent force in western politics. The western provinces have historically been leery of moving to a national regulator because of the perception that this would cede further political power to the eastern commercial/political establishment and sacrifice local control. This concern has made itself felt with particular force in British Columbia, which (with Manitoba, Ontario and Quebec) declined to lend their support to the federal government's 1994 proposal for a federal securities regulator. Reluctance to cede further power to the eastern establishment undoubtedly underlies (at least in part) British Columbia's aversion to participating in the federal government's current proposal for a federal regulator.

Loss of Power to Ontario

It is likely that a national commission will be dominated by Ontario-appointed commissioners, given that the vast bulk of securities-related transactions currently occur in Ontario. The 1994 proposal for a federal securities Act, for example, would have resulted in half of the commissioners being appointed from Ontario. While Ontario already plays the role of lead jurisdiction in matters of securities law policy, a formalization of Ontario's role may not sit well not only with the western provinces and Quebec,[2] but the other provinces as well.

The Systemic Difficulty of Altering an Existing Distribution of Power in a Federal System

Any adequate description of the distribution of powers in a federal system probably ought to begin with the observation that the existing distribution of power, whatever it happens to be, will be difficult to change. Politicians are people who thrive on the exercise of power and all its attendant perquisites. It simply goes against the grain for politicians to cede power willingly to another level of government. Despite all of the plaudits that have been bestowed on the practice of "cooperative federalism" in Canada, this political reluctance to part with power creates a systemic inertia that operates to slow down, and in some cases completely derail a transfer of power between levels of government.

---

[2]See McKenna and Freeman (1996, p. B1) quoting Lucien Bouchard, Premier of Quebec, opposing a national regulator on the basis that this would centralize power in Ontario.

Quebec and the Sovereignty Debate

The sovereignty issue is one that infects virtually every important political debate in Canada. Particularly when nationalist feelings are running high, the federal government is disinclined to do anything that will fan the flames of separatist sentiment. Moves that aim at centralizing power in the hands of the federal government run a risk of doing just that.

Indeed, the sovereignty debate is in essence a debate about the appropriate degree of centralization of political power in Canada. Extreme sovereigntists favour the corner solution of absolute decentralization (at least for Quebec). Sovereigntists who are less extreme in their views are willing to tolerate some degree of national control. All separatists, however, favour a significant transfer of power from the federal government to Quebec. It is a matter of indifference to them whether other provinces share in this bounty, although for strategic reasons, Quebec often finds it convenient to ally itself with other provincial decentralists.

Sovereigntist sentiment is, without question, the controlling factor in Quebec's approach to the prospect of a national regulator. More to the point, the substantive merits of a national regulator are substantially irrelevant in the current political environment in Quebec. Ceding political power, in any arena, to the federal government is radically inconsistent with the PQ's political agenda. While Quebec will be forced to bring its regime into reasonable harmony with national legislation (or see business flow elsewhere), it seems clear that so long as separatist sentiment is a significant force in Quebec politics (and whether or not the PQ retains power[3]), Quebec will decline to opt into any national system.

Bureaucratic Turf Wars and Job Loss

Politicians are not the only constituency with an interest in maintaining or expanding spheres of influence. A transfer of power may also result in loss of influence and prestige for civil servants.

---

[3]Even the former Liberal government, cognizant as it was of the force of separatist sentiment, favoured a decentralist approach.

Bureaucrats have a more direct and pressing interest than politicians, however. A transfer of power may cost bureaucrat jobs. Whenever a significant number of jobs are on the line, resistance to change will be substantial. This greatly adds to the systemic inertia that militates against a transfer of power from one level of government to another.

There are two circumstances in which jobs may be lost, both related to economies of scale (Cf. Daniels, 1992, pp. 90-91). First, it may be that the existing provincial commissions are operating at an insufficiently large scale to exploit economies of scale in their local operations. Second, combining the various provincial commissions will eliminate duplication of functions, resulting in administrative savings.

It may well be, as Daniels suggests, that provincial operations are already sufficiently large to exploit local economies of scale (*ibid.*, p. 90). However, the move to a national commission is certain to eliminate duplicative effort. Instead of each provincial commission having a policy arm, for example, there need be only one policy-making body within a national commission. Thus, creating a national commission is virtually certain to eliminate civil service jobs.

The strength of bureaucratic anxiety about job loss will vary considerably from one province to another. A national regulator is almost certain to be located in Toronto. Thus, civil servants in Ontario will likely feel less threatened by the nationalization of securities regulation than regulators in Nova Scotia, Manitoba, or other provinces.

Turf Battles Within Provinces

It would be a mistake to perceive any province as having unambiguous political and bureaucratic sensibilities. For one thing, the priorities and perceptions of the relevant minister may differ from those of the provincial securities regulatory body (as has sometimes been the case, for example, in Alberta). While the various provincial commissions ostensibly operate under the control of the minister, they have often operated in a substantially independent manner. This has created a situation in which there is likely to be a good deal of discussion, negotiation and compromise between the relevant ministry and provincial commission about what position the province should take.

The situation is further complicated in that there may be more than one ministry that has political and/or bureaucratic capital at stake. In Ontario, for example, the OSC is formally under the control of the Ministry of Finance. However, the Ministry of Economic Development, Trade, and Tourism will very likely wish to have a say in whether a national commission should be created. On top of this mixture must be added the often inconsistent agendas of various interest groups, such as lawyers, accountants, corporations and other service providers and consumers.

In short, any negotiation between the provinces will be proceeded by negotiations within provinces. As the number of negotiations swells, the inertial mass that must be displaced to achieve a multiprovince agreement increases.

An Ontario Veto?

Over 80% of Canada's securities-related business is situated in Ontario.[4] The practical result is that if Ontario declines to participate in a national commission, it is very unlikely that the federal government will proceed. Ontario's decision not to support the 1994 federal proposal was much more pivotal in the federal government's abandonment of that proposal than was opposition from British Columbia, Manitoba and Quebec.

Horse Trading: Securities Regulation as a Pawn in Broader Federal-Provincial Negotiations

At any given time, there are likely to be a variety of ongoing negotiations between various provincial governments and the federal government concerning a wide variety of matters. Individual negotiations often become bargaining chips suitable for trading for items that the province values more highly. Thus, a province whose politicians and administrators are in private sympathetic to the idea of a national commission (or whose resistance is weak) may steadfastly refuse to accede to a federal proposal in order to wrest a concession from the federal government in respect of some completely unrelated matter. There are indications, for example, that British Columbia Premier Glen Clark

---

[4]Freeman and Feschuk (1996, p. B1) quoting Ed Waitzer, Chair of the Ontario Securities Commission.

will endorse a national commission if the federal government will make concessions regarding salmon fishing.[5]

III. CONSTITUTIONAL BASES FOR PROVINCIAL AND FEDERAL AUTHORITY

The constitutional bases for provincial and federal authority are dealt with at length by Anisman and Hogg (1979, p. 192). These are briefly summarized below.

The Provincial Governments

It is absolutely clear that the provincial governments have authority to legislate securities law. This certainty derives from a 1932 decision of the Privy Council,[6] which held that the provinces may constitutionally regulate securities markets by virtue of their authority to make law in relation to "property and

---

[5]*The Globe and Mail* recently reported that:

> British Columbia is increasingly referred to as the Quebec of the West Coast - a distinctive province more attentive to its own agenda than that of the rest of the country. In Mr. Clark, it now appears to have a Premier willing to express those differences to the fullest. "It makes it difficult for British Columbia to co-operate on the federal government's agenda when they're not co-operating at all on an issue of concern to British Columbia," he said. Mr. Clark seemed to be suggesting that the province could reconsider its refusal to participate in a national securities commission if it felt that its agenda on salmon was taken seriously. (McKenna and Freeman, 1996, p. B1)

See also Dalglish (1994, pp. 13-14) quoting Ontario Premier Bob Rae as saying that "Ontario would be willing to consider federal regulation of securities under a couple of conditions: that other provinces are also interested in talking about it, and depending on what other items are on the table with the federal government".

[6]*Lymburn* v. *Mayland* [1932] A.C. 318. See also *Multiple Access Ltd.* v. *McCutcheon* [1982] 2 S.C.R. 161 (S.C.C.).

civil rights in the province".[7] Additional authority to regulate securities markets derives from the province's ability to incorporate companies with "provincial objects",[8] but only insofar as the regulation is ancillary to company law objectives.[9]

The Federal Government

It is less clear that the federal government has the constitutional power to comprehensively regulate securities markets. The possible bases for federal authority are:

a. "The Peace, Order and Good Government of Canada" (the so-called "residual clause").[10]
b. "The Regulation of Trade and Commerce".[11]
c. "Banking, Incorporation of Banks, and the Issue of Paper Money".[12]
d. "Savings Banks".[13]
e. "The Criminal Law".[14]
f. Federal works and undertakings.[15]

---

[7]*Constitution Act, 1867* (formerly the *British North America Act*, and referred to below as the "BNA Act"), s.92(13).

[8]BNA Act, s.92(11).

[9]See, generally, Anisman and Hogg (1979).

[10]BNA Act, s.91(1).

[11]BNA Act, s.91(2).

[12]BNA Act, s.91(15).

[13]BNA Act, s.91(16).

[14]BNA Act, s.91(27).

[15]BNA Act, ss.91(10)(a), (c).

The first enumerated power has already been found by the Supreme Court of Canada in *Multiple Access Ltd.* v. *McCutcheon*[16] to support insider trading provisions found in the federal corporations legislation. However, it seems doubtful that *Multiple Access* would support comprehensive securities legislation. In his judgement, Laskin C.J. held that:[17]

> In one of its aspects, insider trading legislation, dealing as it does with fundamental corporate relationships, may certainly be characterized as company law.

The federal insider trading provisions were thus supported under the federal government's power to pass laws in relation to companies with federal objects.[18] It seems extremely unlikely that the court would be willing to characterize all aspects of securities regulation as an adjunct of company law.

The broadest of the powers enumerated above, and the head of power most likely to support a comprehensive scheme of securities regulation, is "the regulation of trade and commerce". The trade and commerce power may be contrasted with the provincial power to regulate in relation to property and civil rights in the province. The latter was intended to enable the provinces to regulate in relation to intraprovincial matters, while the former was designed to allow the federal government to regulate in relation to interprovincial matters.

The courts have held that there are *two* branches of the trade and commerce power. The first is the "interprovincial" branch. Under this branch, the federal government can regulate where the activity in question is predominately interprovincial in character. The second is the "general" branch. In *General Motors of Canada Ltd.* v. *City National Leasing*,[19] Dickson C.J outlined five

---

[16][1982] 2 S.C.R. 161 (S.C.C.).

[17]*Ibid.*

[18]*Ibid.* The origins of the federal government's power may be found in *Citizens Insurance Co. of Canada* v. *Parsons* (1881), 7 App. Cas. 96, at 117. See also *John Deere Plow Co.* v. *Wharton* [1915] A.C. 330 (P.C.).

[19][1989] 1 S.C.R. 641 (S.C.C.).

"indicators" of the constitutionality of federal legislation under the general trade and commerce power:

> *First,* the impugned legislation must be part of a general regulatory scheme. *Second,* the scheme must be monitored by the continuing oversight of a regulatory agency. *Third,* the legislation must be concerned with trade as a whole rather than with a particular industry... [Fourth,] the legislation should be of a nature that the provinces jointly or severally would be constitutionally incapable of enacting; and [fifth,] the failure to include one or more provinces or localities in a legislative scheme would jeopardize the successful operation of the scheme in other parts of the country.

Dickson C.J. also held that the more the federal scheme intrudes upon provincial powers, the less likely it is that the scheme will be held to be constitutional. This element of the test recognizes the inherent conflict between the provinces' power to regulate in relation to property and civil rights, and the federal government's power to regulate in relation to trade and commerce. Indeed, according to Dickson C.J., the five indicators are themselves barometers of how much the federal scheme intrudes upon provincial powers.

How likely is it that the federal government could support a scheme of securities regulation under the general trade and commerce power? The first three of Dickson's indicators could easily be met by a federal scheme of securities regulation. The legislation need merely be a comprehensive general scheme for the regulation of securities markets, administered by a securities regulatory body. The fourth indicator is more problematic. As noted above, the provinces have clear constitutional authority to regulate securities markets. Under this authority, many of the provinces have adopted comprehensive schemes for the regulation of securities markets. Thus, on the face of it, it seems difficult to argue that securities legislation is of a nature that the provinces are constitutionally incapable of enacting.

As is often the case, however, first appearances may be deceiving. The provinces are fully capable of enacting securities regulatory schemes that have the predominantly local character envisioned in the phrase "property and civil rights *in the province*" (emphasis added). However, provincial regulatory schemes may be constitutionally incapable of dealing with transactions with a cross-border element.

Consider, for example, the case of a company headquartered in B.C. and trading on the Montreal Stock Exchange, with 20% of its shareholders in Ontario. Suppose that a resident of Great Britain agrees to purchase a controlling block of shares currently held by a resident of Manitoba. This change in control may materially affect the welfare of shareholders wherever situated. Do any of the provincial commissions have jurisdiction to regulate the transaction?

As a practical matter, B.C., Quebec, Manitoba and Ontario will probably all assert jurisdiction.[20] There are serious doubts, however, about whether any of these provinces actually have jurisdiction. Aside from the fact that the trans-action will technically fall within the domain of the securities legislation of Manitoba alone (since the offer to purchase control will constitute a "takeover bid" only within Manitoba), the transaction clearly has a transprovincial character; indeed, it has a transnational character. The courts have struggled mightily with the question of whether transactions or events involving out-of-province elements can properly be brought within the purview of the provincial property and civil rights power. While I am unable here to review these cases in any detail, suffice it to say that the courts (including the Supreme Court of Canada) have often given inconsistent answers to this important jurisdictional question.[21] Admittedly, a recent Ontario Court of Appeal holding[22] suggests that all that is required for a province to assert jurisdiction is that there be some affect on the capital markets of that province. However, in my view this test is overly broad and inappropriate. A test based simply on an affect within a province would allow the provinces to take jurisdiction over transactions occurring anywhere in the world simply because there are repercussions for provincial shareholders. This does not, in my view, capture the essentially local character which the framers of the constitution intended that "property and civil rights in the province" should have. It also goes significantly beyond existing constitutional jurisprudence and potentially

---

[20]See, e.g., Ontario Interpretation Note replacing Policy Statement 1.5; Dey (1983).

[21]Contrast, for example, *Interprovincial Cooperatives* v. *The Queen*, [1976] 1 S.C.R. 477; *R.* v. *Thomas Equipment*, [1979] 2 S.C.R. 529.

[22]*Re The Securities Act*, R.S.O. 1980, c.466, as amended (1992), 58 O.A.C. 277 (O.C.A.), leave to appeal to S.C.C. refused (27 May 1993).

involves an enormous expansion of provincial powers. If the affects test is accepted, this would require a comprehensive rethinking of how the provincial and federal powers interact, and the reopening of many of the countless jurisdictional questions which the courts have dealt with since Confederation.

The same Ontario Court of Appeal holding also upheld the application of provincial securities regulation to a transaction with interprovincial and international elements on the ground that the pith and substance of the regulated activity was intraprovincial securities transactions. The court (following prior jurisprudence) held that so long as the pith and substance of the regulatory scheme falls within a permissible head of provincial power, provincial regulation may also touch transactions with interprovincial elements.

While the court's explication of the law is correct, the decision is nonetheless premised on the factual assumption that the balance of securities-related activity is intra-, rather than interprovincial. While once true, this assumption is no longer valid. Certainly in dollar terms, the vast amount of securities-related business now possesses extrajurisdictional elements. In my opinion, securities markets have evolved to the point where it has become impossible to hold that the regulation of extrajurisdictional transactions is merely an incidental feature of provincial securities schemes. The very core of securities market activity in modern capital markets is interprovincial, and often international in nature.

The jurisprudence thus leaves ample doubt about whether any of the provincial securities commissions have jurisdiction over the hypothetical transaction posed above. Nor should it be thought that this hypothetical transaction is merely fanciful. Regulators deal every day with transactions involving insider trading, takeover bids, registration of securities market professionals, and primary and secondary market disclosure in which there are significant interjurisdictional elements. In short, all that is the bread and butter of modern securities regulatory schemes is plagued by deep and as yet largely unaddressed jurisdictional problems.

Arguably, only the federal government can constitutionally regulate transactions involving a significant out-of-province element, or in which there is at least a preponderance of multijurisdictional elements. Thus, it may well be that

Dickson C.J.'s fourth test for the assertion of jurisdiction under the federal trade and commerce power is met.[23]

The fifth element, however, may also present difficulties. As indicated earlier, the federal government has manifest its willingness to participate in a cooperative federal-provincial securities scheme despite the fact that all provinces will not willingly participate in the scheme. The government's willingness to proceed on this basis arguably constitutes an admission that the failure to include one or more provinces in the scheme would not jeopardize its successful operation in other parts of the country.

It should be noted, however, that in his judgement in *General Motors*, Dickson C.J. held that none of the five indicators that are indicia of constitutionality are indispensable. Rather, they are intended to constitute a "preliminary checklist of characteristics, the presence of which in legislation is an indication of validity under the trade and commerce power".[24] Thus, the failure of a federal scheme to be national in scope is not inevitably fatal.

Moreover, a national scheme would undoubtedly work more effectively if all provinces were to participate. For example, as discussed below, a key impetus to achieving a national regulatory structure is to economize on the transaction costs of regulatory compliance. In this respect, a national scheme would undoubtedly smooth the waters more than a scheme omitting some of the provinces.[25]

---

[23]The response of the provincial regulatory authorities thus far has largely been to ignore jurisdictional problems, and simply assume jurisdiction (often under the rubric of the "public interest powers"). Securities market actors rarely challenge the assertion of such jurisdiction because of the need to maintain an amicable long-term relationship with regulators. See Janisch (1989).

[24]Nor do these indicators constitute an "exhaustive list of traits that will tend to characterize general trade and commerce legislation." *General Motors of Canada Ltd.* v. *City National Leasing* [1989] 1 S.C.R. 641 (S.C.C.).

[25]It should also be noted that under the general trade and commerce power, the incidental or ancillary doctrine would allow federal securities legislation to touch wholly intraprovincial securities transactions, if the efficacy of the legislative scheme requires that intra-, as well as interprovincial transactions be included. See *General Motors of Canada Ltd.* v. *City National Leasing* [1989] 1 S.C.R. 641 (S.C.C.).

The "interprovincial" branch of the trade and commerce power may also present a constitutional opening for federal securities legislation. Here, the tension between the provincial power in relation to property and civil rights and the federal trade and commerce power is again evident. If the preponderance of regulated activity is intraprovincial in character, then the provinces may regulate (and the regulation may incidentally affect interprovincial transactions). If the preponderance of regulated activity is interprovincal, the feds may regulate (and the regulation may incidentally affect intraprovincial transactions). Thus, the question is whether securities regulation is predominantly intra- or interprovincial in nature. As noted above, it seems clear that at this point in time, the predominance of securities-related activity is interprovincial. On this view, the federal government may regulate securities markets under the "interprovincial" branch of the trade and commerce power. Indeed, as noted above, if the preponderance of transactions contains extraterritorial elements, the very constitutionality of provincial securities regulatory schemes, as applied to out-of-province transactions, is called into question.

In my view, therefore, the federal government possesses the power to regulate securities markets at least under the interprovincial branch of the trade and commerce power, if not under the general branch as well.

IV. OTHER CONSTITUTIONAL BASES FOR A NATIONAL COMMISSION

A national commission may also be created by delegation of provincial authority in either of the following three ways:

Provincial Adoption by Reference of Federal Legislation

The provinces may adopt by reference federal securities legislation,[26] as it stands from time to time, with each province delegating its authority to

---

[26]"Legislation" in this context is meant to include not only primary legislation but secondary legislation as well.

administer the legislation to a common (and federally controlled) regulatory body.[27] This method appears to form the basis for the 1994 federal proposal.

Delegation by both Provincial and Federal Governments to a Common Regulatory Body

Another constitutionally permissible means of setting up a national commission would be for the provinces and the federal government to pass and maintain identical legislation, and jointly delegate administration of the provincial and federal enactments to a single regulatory body.[28] Although in theory this regulatory entity might be under either provincial, federal, or joint provincial-federal control, for practical reasons (e.g., ease of amending the law) it would make greatest sense to leave control in the hands of the federal government.

Both above-noted mechanisms for establishing a federal commission (adoption by reference, and maintaining identical legislation with administrative interdelegation) accomplish the same substantive result as a direct delegation of provincial authority in the securities arena to the federal Parliament. Curiously, however, the Supreme Court has held that a province cannot delegate its constitutional powers *directly* to the federal Parliament (nor can the Parliament delegate its powers directly to a province).[29]

---

[27]Formally, this would likely be done by the federal government passing a securities statute and ceding administration of the statute to a federal regulatory body, coupled with legislation in each participating province ceding power to the federal body to act in relation to securities matters wholly within a province as it would act in relation to matters spanning more than one province. See *A.G. Ont.* v. *Scott*, [1956] S.C.R. 137 (S.C.C.); *Coughlin* v. *Ontario Highway Board*, [1968] S.C.R. 569, 53 D.L.R. (2d) 30; *Re Agricultural Products Marketing Act*, [1978] 2 S.C.R. 1198 (S.C.C.). See generally Hogg (1992, pp. 14-21 to 14-24).

[28]See *Prince Edward Island Potato Marketing Board* v. *H.B. Willis Inc.*, [1952] 2 S.C.R. 392, 4 D.L.R. 146. See generally Hogg (1992, pp. 14-18 to 14-20).

[29]*Attorney General of Nova Scotia* v. *Attorney General of Canada*, [1951] S.C.R. 31, [1950] 4 D.L.R. 369.

Delegation of Provincial Authority to a National (but not Federal) Commission

The provinces need not delegate their powers to the federal government in order to constitute a national commission. They may also choose to collectively delegate their authority to a national commission with no connection at all with the federal government. The national commission might in such a case administer a single uniform act agreed to by all the provinces (and duly enacted in each participating province), or it might administer the different laws of the different provinces. A national regulatory body created in this fashion would be under the joint control of the provinces, with the distribution of control to be determined by bargaining between the provinces.

V. THE PLUSES AND MINUSES OF VARIOUS MEANS OF CONSTITUTING A NATIONAL COMMISSION

Unilateral Federal Action under the Trade and Commerce Power

Use of federal constitutional authority to constitute a national commission would solve one problem; it would cure jurisdictional infirmities in the application and enforcement of securities law where the dealings in question cross provincial (or national) boundaries.

It would also cure another problem: that of instability. By instability I refer to a situation in which any province can unilaterally withdraw from a national commission and revert to its own legislative scheme. By overcoming the instability problem and replacing the existing provincial regulatory edifice with a single federal scheme, unilateral federal action under the trade and commerce power would greatly simplify the securities regulatory system for its users.

The efficacy of a move to a federal commission, however, depends entirely on whether the federal legislation displaced provincial securities law, or merely added another tier of securities regulation on top of existing provincial enactments. Should the latter be the case, then creating a federal securities enactment would only add to the inefficiencies of the current system. While one or more of the provinces might voluntarily withdraw their securities legislation to remove the second tier, they might reintroduce it at any time, leaving the problem of instability untouched.

Whether federal legislation will displace provincial legislation turns on the application of the constitutional doctrine of paramountcy. If paramountcy is found to operate, then the federal legislation is said to "suspend" the operation of provincial legislation that is otherwise constitutionally valid. So long as the federal law continues in force, the provincial law simply ceases to have any application.

Should paramountcy apply, the federal government need not negotiate with any province about the creation of federal securities legislation. It can simply legislate, and the federal legislation would then displace the provincial securities enactments. This is clearly the least cumbersome legal route to a federal securities statute. It is also the only one that resolves the danger of instability, and that which yields the cleanest and simplest regulatory structure.

Would paramountcy operate in the securities law context? The answer is uncertain. On one view, paramountcy should operate only where there is an express inconsistency between a provincial and federal enactment, such that compliance with one is defiance of the other. On another view, paramountcy should operate even where there is no inconsistency, if the federal law can be said to "occupy the field". The former view yields a much smaller scope for the operation of the doctrine.

After reviewing Supreme Court of Canada decisions on the doctrine of paramountcy, Hogg concludes that:

> The inexorable conclusion is that there is no room for an imputed inconsistency based on covering the field or negative implication. The sole test of inconsistency in Canadian constitutional law is express contradiction. (1992, p. 16-13)

Multiple Access Ltd. v. *McCutcheon*,[30] a case involving a challenge to federal insider trading laws found in the Canada Business Corporations Act,[31] is illustrative of the express contradiction test. A civil action for insider trading was commenced in Ontario under identically worded Ontario legislation, and the defendants in the action applied for a ruling that the doctrine of paramountcy rendered the Ontario legislation inoperative. In denying the defendants' petition, the court held that:

> In principle, there would seem to be no good reasons to speak of paramountcy and preclusion except where there is actual conflict in operation as where one enactment says "yes" and the other says "no"; "the same citizens are being told to do inconsistent things"; compliance with one is defiance of the other.[32]

Thus, the doctrine was held not to operate where the federal and provincial provisions merely duplicate one another, without actual conflict.

What if a provincial securities enactment does not merely duplicate the federal legislation, but adds to its requirements? Does this constitute an express conflict? There are a good many Supreme Court holdings addressing this issue. They uniformly hold (save for the *Hall* case referred to below) that provincial legislation that merely adds to federal requirements is not suspended by the doctrine of paramountcy (see Hogg, 1992, pp. 16-07 to 16-13). As Hogg suggests (*ibid.*), these cases implicitly hold that there is no "covering the field" test of paramountcy. Provincial and federal enactments may cover the same or similar subject matters without the provincial legislation being suspended by the doctrine of paramountcy. Thus, for example, should a provincial law require more exhaustive prospectus disclosure than the federal law, the provincial law would continue in full force.

Without a "covering the field" test (save as noted below), federal legislation is inadvisable. Paramountcy would only come into play to the extent that the federal and provincial enactments command citizens to do inconsistent things.

---

[30][1982] 2 S.C.R. 161 (S.C.C.).

[31]R.S.C. 1985, c. C-44.

[32]*Multiple Access*, at 191.

Moreover, the doctrine would operate only to suspend those parts of provincial legislation that are in conflict with the federal legislation; it would not touch the balance of the provincial enactment, which would continue in force (Hogg, 1992, p. 16-18).

A recent holding of the Supreme Court, however, appears to lean away from the express contradiction test. In *Bank of Montreal* v. *Hall*,[33] a provincial enactment purported to qualify a bank's right under federal bankruptcy legislation to seize security, by requiring the bank to meet certain procedural and substantive tests prior to realization on its security. The Supreme Court held that the provincial legislation, standing alone, was constitutionally valid. However, its operation was suspended by the doctrine of paramountcy. The federal provisions dealing with seizure were held to be central to the purpose of the federal statute, which was to meet a "pressing need" for uniform national legislation. The court further held that there is actual conflict in operation, and hence paramountcy will come into play, "when application of the provincial statute can fairly be said to frustrate Parliament's legislative purpose" (*ibid.*). This exposition of the doctrine greatly broadens the circumstances in which paramountcy will be found to operate, and arguably creates a "covering the field" test for paramountcy. Unfortunately, the waters are further muddied by two Supreme Court decisions that follow *Hall*.[34] These decisions appear to embrace the express conflict test.

The *Hall* case provides some footing for the view that federal securities legislation might be found to *completely* displace provincial securities laws, whether or not there is any express inconsistency between the two laws. Suppose, for example, that the federal law as well as the various provincial laws require that a prospectus be assembled in connection with a public offering of securities, but that the provincial disclosure requirements are materially more demanding than the federal requirements. Suppose further that the prospectus disclosure requirements are sufficiently different that issuers making national offerings in Canada suffer a significant competitive disadvantage compared to issuers making offerings in foreign venues. The existence of a competitive disadvantage would open the door to an argument

---

[33][1990] 1 S.C.R. 121 (S.C.C.).

[34]*Clarke* v. *Clarke*, [1990] 2 S.C.R. 795; *Husky Oil Operations Ltd.* v. *Canada (Minister of National Revenue - M.N.R.)*, [1995] 3 S.C.R. 453 (S.C.C.).

that there is a pressing need for uniform national legislation — a pivotal element in the application of the doctrine of paramountcy in *Hall*.

The need for national legislation has indeed clearly grown over time as securities markets have become more interprovincial and international in character. As capital has become more and more transnationally mobile, the existence of multiple regulatory regimes in Canada has begun to drive both issuers and investors to seek more user-friendly capital markets. Given the importance of Canada's capital markets to the national economy, this has created a tenable argument that there is a pressing need for a single national regulator.

The question of a "pressing need" for uniformity can also be linked back to the issue of the constitutionality of provincial securities legislation. As argued above, the increasing proportion of securities transactions that have a cross-border element continues to put more and more strain on provincial assertions of constitutional jurisdiction. This, too, arguably enhances the argument that there is a pressing need for uniform national legislation.

Whether the "pressing need" argument would succeed is not at all clear, however. As proponents of a decentralized system like to point out, the existing regulatory system is far from a complete failure. Moreover, the federal government has arguably shot itself in the foot by indicating that it is prepared to go ahead with a national regulator while excluding application of the legislation to those provinces that decline to participate. Thus, while in many ways (discussed below) moving to a national statute would be desirable, the situation may be insufficiently urgent to support the "pressing need" argument.

Hall also suggests that paramountcy will operate to the extent that the provincial legislation interferes with the achievement of Parliament's legislative purpose. Legislation that is either identical to or similar in all material respects to federal legislation would not likely be found to interfere with Parliament's legislative purpose. However, under the *Hall* test, legislation that is quite different from the federal legislation would run a greater risk of being found inoperative, particularly if the differences add materially to the burden imposed by the federal legislation or result in a materially different trade-off in regulatory costs and benefits.

Once again, take the case of mandated disclosure. Suppose that the federal legislation allows companies 140 days after the end of their fiscal year to file financial statements, management discussion and analysis, and the annual information form for that year. Suppose also that one or more provinces require filing within 30 days. While there is no express conflict between the federal and provincial enactments (both may be simultaneously complied with by filing within 30 days), the provincial enactments may nonetheless frustrate the federal government's regulatory purpose. In formulating its own law, Parliament may well have traded off the benefits of quick disclosure against the costs of reporting inaccuracies caused by overly-hasty reporting, and decided that a reporting period of 140 days results in the best balance between speed and accuracy. A reporting period of 30 days could well result in substantially less accurate reporting and hence frustrate Parliament's legislative intention.

Even without *Hall*, however, there appears to be a mechanism by which a determined federal government could effectively expand the doctrine of paramountcy and ensure that all the provincial securities enactments would be suspended in their entirety by the federal law. The Supreme Court holdings referred to above that reject covering the field test hold only that a federal enactment may not *implicitly* cover the field and displace a provincial enactment. These holdings do not extend to a situation in which the federal enactment *expressly* displaces similar provincial enactments. Both on principle and the basis of extant jurisprudence, Hogg (1992, pp. 16-13 to 16-14) concludes that express displacement is permissible. If this is indeed the case, the federal government need only write into its securities enactment that the federal law displaces all of the provincial securities laws. This simple solution would allow the federal government to bypass the often inconsistent jurisprudence on paramountcy and achieve the goal of a single, national regulator.

There is yet another potential problem in the use of the federal trade and commerce power however. An integral part of any remedial scheme of securities legislation is the provision of civil remedies for those harmed by wrongdoers. According to Dickson C.J. in *General Motors*, however, "[t]he creation of civil actions is generally a matter within provincial jurisdiction under s. 92(13) [property and civil rights in the province] of the *Constitution Act, 1867*".[35]

---

[35]*General Motors of Canada Ltd.* v. *City National Leasing* [1989] 1 S.C.R. 641 (S.C.C.).

This would suggest that a federal securities enactment could not contain civil remedies. However, Dickson C.J. also held that a civil right of action may constitutionally be incorporated into federal legislation, if the provision is "functionally related to the general objective of the legislation". In *General Motors* itself, a federal civil right of action was found to be constitutionally valid. Dickson C.J. held that the provision was "an integral, well-conceived component of the economic regulation strategy found in the *Combines Investigation Act*" (*ibid.*). The civil cause of action was found to complement and reinforce the criminal and administrative rights of action found in the statute.

A federal securities act would likely contain a variety of civil causes of action; historically, these have been an integral part of securities law enforcement. In my view, federal civil causes of action similar in scope to those found in current provincial legislation would almost certainly be validated under the *General Motors* test.

The constitutional questions raised in this section are unlikely ever to be reached. Practical and substantive considerations often yield to politics, and the issue of securities regulation is no exception. Without Quebec (and possibly British Columbia), unilateral action might be conceivable. However, the federal government's desire to pacify Quebec separatists is a major force in this, as in many other Canadian political debates. Unilateral passage of federal securities legislation would pour gasoline on the flame of separatist sentiment. By itself, this factor is almost certainly enough to keep the federal government from acting unilaterally, however desirable unilateral action may be.

Even without the separatist wildcard, the *modus operandi* of resolving jurisdictional disputes of this nature has increasingly become "cooperative federalism", under which a cooperative, rather than a unilateral solution is negotiated between the two levels of government. Moreover, in recent times there has been a substantial and continuing devolution of federal powers to the provinces (see Courchene, 1996). Against this backdrop, the provinces would undoubtedly take considerable umbrage at the prospect of unilateral federal action. This is unfortunate, as the best way to resolve the difficulties created by provincial securities legislation is a single federal enactment that displaces all the provincial enactments.

Provincial Incorporation by Reference of Federal Legislation

The provinces may validly adopt federal legislation by reference and delegate their authority to administer the legislation to a regulatory body under federal control. This solution addresses jurisdictional problems that currently plague securities regulation in that the commission charged with oversight of the federal statute would assume the totality of the federal and provincial powers in relation to securities regulation.

This mechanism for constituting a federal commission, however, is not without its flaws. It obviously fails to resolve the instability problem. Moreover, when provinces can credibly make threats to withdraw from a national scheme, the process of amending the law may be retarded. Instead of one level of government having complete control of the amendment process, the various participating provincial governments can insist (formally, or more likely informally) on the right to be consulted — or at least heard on an ad hoc basis — before amendments are made. If so, amending the securities laws will lead to cumbersome and time-consuming negotiations, yielding a legislative scheme that is difficult to change. With respect to matters in which developments are few and far between, this might pose little problem. However, securities markets are extremely dynamic, and the rapid evolution of such markets frequently requires a nimble response from regulators. The ability to respond to new developments by means of secondary legislative instruments greatly assists regulators in responding to new developments with alacrity. Nonetheless, a legislative superstructure cast in reinforced concrete is not likely to serve well the cause of enlightened capital market regulation.

Further, if the unanimous consent of all provincial governments is required to amend the rules (or the ad hoc consent of those that protest) the government will find that the only changes it can make are those that are uncontroversial. Failure to resolve the instability problem, in other words, will ultimately affect the substance of the legislation and the dynamism and imagination with which changes can be made.

Delegation by both Provincial and Federal Governments to a Common Regulatory Body

As noted, another way of overcoming jurisdictional difficulties associated with provincial securities regulation is for the provincial and federal governments to adopt identical legislation, and for each to delegate its power to administer its statute to a common regulatory body under federal control. As with adoption by reference, this solution resolves jurisdictional difficulties that now plague provincial regulation, and will result in uniform regulation across the country. The instability problem, however, remains.

Moreover, there is substantial doubt about whether the various provinces and the federal government would be able to keep their rules completely in harmony. There is ample historical precedent to enlarge this doubt. The so-called "Uniform Act" provinces (British Columbia, Alberta, Saskatchewan, Manitoba and Ontario) agreed on substantially identical rules early in the 1970s. However, since that time, the rules of these provinces have substantially diverged (see Anisman, 1986). If the various provincial and federal enactments did indeed drift apart, then many of the savings that would otherwise be realized through the creation of a national commission would be lost.

Delegation of Provincial Authority to a National Commission

Provincial delegation to a non-federal national regulatory body has one noteworthy advantage. By cutting the federal government out of the picture altogether, this solution might be more palatable to recalcitrant provincial governments than delegation to the federal government.

Otherwise, this solution suffers from the same problems as adoption of federal legislation by reference, including instability, and the danger that protracted negotiations will be required to amend the legislation. It also suffers from a problem of jurisdictional infirmity. The provinces can only delegate to a national commission that authority which they constitutionally possess. As noted, the provinces' ability to regulate in relation to transactions with an interprovincial or international character is increasingly problematic. A national commission operating under the authority of joint provincial delegation will have no more power to deal with cross-border transactions than the authority currently possessed by the provinces. Finally, this solution would require the maintenance of identical legislation in each province, a prospect which appears unlikely to bear fruit.

VI. A NATIONAL COMMISSION: SUBSTANTIVE PROS AND CONS

Transaction Costs

Primary Market Offerings

Every time a company seeks public capital, it must prepare and secure regulatory approval of a comprehensive disclosure document known as a prospectus. There are a number of types of public offerings. The first is the initial public offering ("IPO"), which occurs when the company seeks public capital for the first time. Once the company has gone public, it may raise further capital in the public markets. If it is sufficiently large,[36] it may take advantage of the prompt offering prospectus ("POP") system, under which a company is entitled to make abbreviated disclosure in its prospectus. A so-called "POP issuer" will reap the benefit of quicker prospectus review by regulatory authorities than would normally be the case, and will qualify for "expedited review", under which the issuer can sell across the country by clearing its prospectus through a single provincial regulatory authority.

A company seeking capital may also raise funds by means of a "private placement". Generally, a private placement is a sale of securities to investors who are sufficiently sophisticated to be able to protect their own interests without the benefit of a prospectus (and hence, no prospectus is required).

For primary market offerings, the problems created by having multiple regulatory authorities can be stated quite easily. The most obvious is the added

---

[36]For equity offerings, the firm must have a market float (i.e., value of publicly traded securities, excluding those exercising some measure of control) of seventy-five million dollars. See National Policy Statement No. 47.

direct costs (mostly fees for lawyers, accountants and other professionals) resulting from compliance with the different regulatory systems. Somewhat less obvious, but probably more important, are the opportunity costs created by the delays associated with multiple review of the issuer's prospectus. The opportunity cost can be divided into two components: internal opportunity costs (principally the extra managerial and employee time required to see that the prospectus is approved), and market opportunity costs. Market opportunity costs in turn include both the danger of losing a window of opportunity during which primary offerings can be sold at attractive prices, and harm to the company resulting from a delay in receipt of funds under the offering. For private placements, no advance review of offering documents is required: nonetheless, compliance with multiple regulatory systems can still create both direct and opportunity costs (given that professionals in various jurisdictions will have to be hired to ensure that the offering meets all applicable standards).

A preliminary examination of the magnitude of these costs is made in a report by Sawiak *et al.* (1996) to the Standing Senate Committee on Banking, Trade and Commerce (the "Kirby Committee"). Sawiak *et al.* conducted a survey of recent IPO issuers, companies listed on both a Canadian and U.S. exchange, securities market professionals ("registrants"), and securities lawyers. A large majority of seasoned (i.e., non-IPO) issuers and their professional advisors indicated that they would expect added direct costs in excess of $20,000 as a result of issuing securities in a province in which the issuer had not previously been active (*ibid.*, p. 21). Opportunity costs were not quantified (although the added direct costs include executive salaries). Many respondents, however, identified differing escrow requirements[37] in the various provinces as a factor tending to discourage the issuance of securities in Canada, as compared to the United States (Sawiak *et al.*, 1996, p. 22). Differing provincial requirements also tend to discourage rights offerings in Canada (*ibid.*). For seasoned issuers, anecdotal evidence suggests that the delay to market resulting from multiple compliance is on the order of 10 to 15 days.

---

[37]An escrow requirement requires directors, officers, significant block-holders, and others in some position of power or influence to put a certain percentage of their shares in the company into "escrow" for certain periods of time. While the shares are escrowed, they generally cannot be sold.

Companies that had recently done IPOs in Canada reported that differing requirements in differing provinces resulted in delays getting issues to market. The report states that:

> The most common negative effect reported was increased professional fees, albeit such increase was generally considered by the Securities Lawyers to be minor. The second most common response was a negative financial impact on the client which was attributable to the client receiving the proceeds of the initial public offering later than expected as a result of having to clear all jurisdictions' comments. The least cited effect was a lower selling price or smaller offering which was attributable to such factors as missing a market window of opportunity.

Thirty percent of securities lawyers estimated that the increase in professional expenses resulting from compliance with multiple requirements was less than $5,000 (*ibid.*, pp. 8-9). Sixty percent indicated that the added costs were between $5,000 and $10,000, and 10% indicated that they were more than $10,000. As a percentage of total IPO transaction costs, 40% indicated that the added costs were less than 1% of total transaction costs, 50% indicated that they were between 1% and 5%, and 10% indicated that they were in excess of 10% (*ibid.*). A number of respondents added that junior issuers are most affected by differences in the rules, and in particular that junior issuers in British Columbia and Alberta were deterred from accessing the more senior capital markets in Ontario and Quebec (*ibid.*, p. 11).

The report did not deal with international offerings in Canada. However, anecdotal evidence suggests that even a small additional cost can cause a foreign issuer to by-pass Canada in favour of larger capital markets. Canada is a relatively small market, and a large foreign corporation that is well known internationally can pick and choose which capital markets it chooses to raise money in.

The Sawiak Report also suggests that a national commission would result in more savings than continued attempts to coordinate provincial rules, such as through the National Policy Statements. Coordination has been only a partial success. National Policy No. 1 ("NP1"), for example, is supposed to operate, in effect, as a "mutual recognition" system. Under the policy, an issuer raising money pursuant to a prospectus in more than one province is supposed to be able to deal primarily with the regulator in a single ("principal") jurisdiction. While NP1 is often said to ease the administrative burden of conducting a multiprovince offering, non-principal jurisdictions often present the issuer with "comment letters" that frequently raise objections to the offering not raised in the principal jurisdiction (*ibid.*, p. 9). The adoption of "expedited review" (by all provinces save Quebec) for POP issuers is designed to cure this defect by formalizing the mutual recognition of prospectus approvals. However, any province may opt out and conduct its own review. Moreover, in some cases, provinces such as Ontario will provide the issuer with a "supplementary comment letter" without formally opting out.

This is not to deny that moves to harmonize and coordinate the current system have resulted in reduced costs for capital markets users. However, full harmonization is a chimera, oft-pursued but never achieved (Anisman, 1986). A national regulator is the only way to create a system with completely unified rules.

In one respect, however, a federal regulator may increase transaction costs. Currently, a company needs to translate a prospectus into French only if it is issuing securities in Quebec. It is conceivable that a federal regulator would routinely require prospectus translation, regardless of where the securities are to be issued.[38] This would add non-trivially both to the cost of assembling a prospectus, and to the time required before sales may begin.

Continuous Disclosure

Once an issuer has made a public offering, it acquires the obligation to make public disclosure of material events in the life of the company. This burden is known as the obligation to make "continuous disclosure".

The Sawiak Report deals with continuous disclosure, and again presents evidence that a national system would reduce costs for users of capital markets. Indeed, 86% of inter-listed companies, 76% of companies that had done an IPO, 88% of mutual fund managers, and 75% of securities lawyers were of the view that a national commission would reduce compliance costs (Sawiak *et al.*, 1996, pp. 16-17). A large majority thought that annual compliance costs would be reduced by more than $10,000 (*ibid.*, pp. 18-19).

---

[38]See, e.g., cl.36 of the 1994 Proposal.

This is in spite of the fact that, in theory, National Policy No. 40 ("NP40") institutes a (partial) mutual recognition scheme not unlike NP1 for primary offerings. Once again, the system works better in theory than in practice.

Registration (Licensing) of Market Professionals

Securities market professionals are required to register with the securities regulators in each province in which they carry on business. This obligation extends to brokers, dealers, underwriters, financial institutions and those advising others in their purchases of securities.

The registration requirement is not unlike a licensing regime, although the requirements for registration vary markedly for different types of professionals. The current system of registration is imbued with a protectionist flavour. In order to secure a registration, a registrant will generally be required to have an office in each province in which he or she carries on business. Thus, it is not possible for a broker registered in Alberta to communicate with a resident of Nova Scotia with a view to soliciting business, unless the broker is also registered in Nova Scotia. Some provinces will register non-residents, but will only permit them to conduct business outside usual business hours. Amongst other harms which these rules occasion, they have prevented mutual funds from setting up toll-free numbers connected to out-of-province locations.

The only exception to the policy of non-recognition of an out-of-province registration arises in British Columbia and Alberta, which have jointly delegated authority to approve registrations to the Investment Dealers Association. Thus, one registration covers both provinces.

By contrast, under a national system, one registration would allow a registrant to carry on business across the country. This would reduce transactions costs for those doing business in more than one province. That in turn would likely increase competition in many local markets, to the benefit of consumers.

While no mutual recognition system is currently in place, one has been proposed. Draft National Policy No. 54 would institute a principal jurisdiction system not unlike that in place for primary offerings and continuous disclosure. However, for reasons already given, this solution is likely to be inferior to the harmonization achieved when there is a single regulator.

The Sawiak Report also touches on registration. In this respect, survey questions were put to a number of different types of registrants, including regional and national investment dealers, investment fund managers, banks, trust companies and life insurance companies. The survey results indicate that some firms are deterred from registering in more than one province because of differing registration requirements. These are described in the report as "generally single office operations" (*ibid.*, p. 30). However, while many larger firms were undeterred from registering in more than one province, the added expense of multiple compliance was considerable. For example, 20% of registrants indicated that applying for registration in a province outside their principal jurisdiction resulted in added internal costs (e.g., employee salaries) of more than $100,000 (*ibid.*, p. 30). Thirty-seven percent indicated that ongoing internal compliance costs were in excess of $25,000 annually (*ibid.*).

These figures leave out fees paid to professional advisors and registration fees paid to the provinces. These too can be substantial. For example, to maintain registrations in all provinces other than the principal jurisdiction can cost an issuer in excess of $10,000 in professional fees and $25,000 in registration fees (*ibid.*, pp. 30-31).

In summary, the report states that the registration requirements are "costly, inefficient inconveniences which added substantially to the cost of compliance".

Takeover Bids

Companies making takeover bids for other companies must comply with provincial takeover rules. Compliance will involve either making mandated disclosures in a takeover circular, or finding an exemption from the disclosure requirements. The differential takeover rules are typically not a great source of additional cost or delay. Takeover circulars need not be approved in advance by regulators, occasioning less delay than the rules relating to primary offerings. However, while takeover rules are similar in the different provinces, variations may compel the acquiring company to seek exemptive relief from features of one of more province's takeover codes. This can be productive of additional direct expense (and in particular, legal expense) to make the takeover bid. More importantly, it can hold up the bid for a period of time, and time is often a crucial factor in making a takeover bid. A national commission would eliminate these additional costs.

Transaction Fees and Provincial Surpluses

Currently, provincial securities regulators collect fees from market users for a wide variety of securities-related transactions. In all of the provinces except Alberta and British Columbia, these fees flow into the province's general revenue account and generate a total surplus of approximately $50 million.[39] The provinces have demanded that the federalization of securities laws be accompanied by lump sum payments from the federal government to compensate for the loss of these revenue streams. The 1994 proposal would have divided $150 million between the provinces, and the figure on the table in the current round of negotiations is somewhere in the region of $200 million (Westell, 1996).

There is a very compelling argument that charging fees that significantly exceed administrative costs are a forbidden form of indirect taxation.[40] Whatever the merits of this contention, the question I address here is whether these fees would be higher or lower under a federal regulator. Under the current (1996) federal proposal, the federal commission would be self-funding (*ibid.*). However, the lump sum payment to the provinces would be a debt owed by the commission to the federal government. It may therefore be that, at least until the debt is paid off, securities market users could anticipate little reduction in aggregate fee burden, unless the commission decided to pay off the debt over a long period of time. Once the debt is paid, however, the

---

[39]Westell (1996). The *Report of the Task Force on Operational Efficiencies in the Administration of Securities Regulation* (1995) 18 O.S.C.B. 2971 (19 June 1995) at 2974 indicates that, as of the end of fiscal 1994, more than 50% of total regulatory revenues ended up in provincial general revenues.

[40]See Westell (1996) quoting both Ed Waitzer, Chair of the OSC, and Bill Hess, Chair of the ASC, as concurring in the view that provincial fees are open to judicial challenge. If so, then the federal government proposes to compensate the provinces for loss of illegal revenues.

commission will operate on a cost recovery basis (Freeman and Feschuk, 1996, p. B1). Thus, at least in the longer term, it is likely that the fee burden will be reduced.

Enforcement

Resolving Jurisdictional Problems

Creating a federal commission, at least under the federal trade and commerce power, would resolve lingering doubts about provincial authority to regulate cross-border trading. This would render enforcement of the laws less problematic.[41]

Efficacy of Enforcement

Where a transaction involves multijurisdictional elements, obtaining legal jurisdiction over out-of-province actors can present difficulties. The Bennett case is a good illustration. Ontario regulators sought to hold a hearing to investigate whether Bill Bennett, the former premier of British Columbia, and others had engaged in illegal insider trading. While Bennett's orders to trade were initiated in British Columbia, they were put through brokers in Ontario. The respondents declined, however, to appear at a hearing before the OSC, on the grounds that Ontario lacked jurisdiction. This led the OSC to apply to an Ontario court for an order appointing a commissioner to take evidence from

---

[41]Ontario has recently established a body known as the Securities Enforcement Review Committee, which will consist of representatives of eight entities; the Ministry of the Attorney-General, the Ontario Securities Commission, the RCMP, Ontario Provincial Police, Metropolitan Toronto Police, the Toronto Stock Exchange, the Canadian Investor Protection Fund and the Investment Dealers Association of Canada. See Den Tandt (1996, p. B1). The report quotes Larry Waite, the OSC's Director of Enforcement, as stating that: "If there's a case that involves someone outside the province, or in other countries, then the RCMP would run with it". B.C. has set up a similar committee. See McNish (1996, p. B1). These measures cannot, however, substitute for the ability of skilled securities regulators to mount Canada-wide investigations.

the respondents in British Columbia, and for the Ontario court to issue a request to a British Columbia court to compel the respondents to give evidence to the Ontario commissioner. The Ontario court declined the OSC's invitation, holding that neither the Ontario Securities Act nor any other Ontario legislation authorized it to make the orders requested.[42] While the Ontario statute now contains the required authority, there are grave doubts about whether an out-of-province court could constitutionally accede to an Ontario court's request (see Anisman and Hogg, 1979).

Mutual enforcement of orders made under the discretionary "public interest" powers also presents practical and constitutional difficulties. The public interest powers allow the regulators to make a variety of orders "in the public interest", including the revocation of a registration, the enjoining of a transaction, and the capacity to deprive a company or individual of the ability to carry on trading activity in the jurisdiction. These powers are amongst the most important that the regulators possess. Through the National Policy Statements, the regulators have agreed to mutually enforce some of these orders, but again the constitutionality of mutual enforcement is questionable. Moreover, it is difficult for regulators in one jurisdiction to police activities in all jurisdictions in order to determine if an order has been violated.

Administrative Economies in Enforcement

In some cases, more than one provincial commission will commence enforcement proceedings. In the *Bennett* case, for example, both British Columbia and Ontario scheduled hearings. While in some of these cases (as in *Bennett*) the various provincial commissions will agree to hold joint hearings, it would nonetheless economize on enforcement resources if there was a single enforcement branch, rather than a multiplicity (Daniels, 1992, p. 91).

---

[42]See *Re Ontario Securities Commission and Bennett et al.* (1990), 72 O.R. (2d) 77, 66 D.L.R. (4th) 756 (H.C.J.), aff'd (1991) 1 O.R. (3d) 576, 77 D.L.R. (4th) 576 (C.A.). See generally, Jordan (1993).

Inadvertent Breaches of Securities Laws

When capital market users must comply with the rules of a variety of jurisdictions, the probability of inadvertent breaches of securities laws is enhanced. It simply becomes much more difficult to ensure that every pertinent law has been complied with. By eliminating different provincial requirements, a national commission would greatly reduce the risk of inadvertent breaches of law, with commensurate savings in compliance costs.

Enforcement Activity in Smaller Provinces

At present, the quantum of resources that the different provinces devote to enforcement varies substantially, and in general commensurately with the size and wealth of the province. While under a national commission it is virtually certain that existing securities commissions would continue to perform at least routine enforcement actions, a national commission would likely spread enforcement resources more evenly across the country. This would tend to lead to a higher level of enforcement in those provinces and territories (such as P.E.I., the Northwest Territories and Newfoundland) that have not devoted significant resources to securities regulation.

Administrative Economies of Scale (Generally)

Exploitation of economies of scale is discussed above. As Daniels argues, local economies of scale may largely have been exploited already. However, there are likely to be administrative savings resulting from collapsing the various provincial commissions into one and eliminating duplication.

Regulatory Innovation

As securities markets have become more international in character, and as capital has become increasingly mobile, the importance of regulatory innovation and imagination has greatly increased. In years to come, it will no longer be sufficient to "stay the course" and follow the lead of other jurisdictions. An increasingly competitive capital market will result in "first mover" advantages to regulators who anticipate, rather than merely follow, regulatory trends (see MacIntosh, 1995).

Is a single federal commission more or less likely to be innovative and responsive? Certainly the current method of bringing provincial systems into harmony by means of National Policy Statements is only a partial success. The requirement for consensus renders the process slow and cumbersome. As noted above, however, whether a single national commission would improve upon the current situation depends on how it is constituted. If it is constituted under the federal trade and commerce power, then it will likely be easier to implement regulatory changes than if it is constituted by delegation or incorporation by reference.

The degree of innovation, however, is a function not merely of the speed with which new laws may be implemented. A number of other factors come into play. One of these arises from the maxim that "two heads are better than one". *Ceteris paribus*, it is more likely that an innovation will be produced when a number of different regulatory teams seek solutions to common problems, simply because more minds have been directed to the issue.

Another important factor is the incentive to innovate. As the "charter shopping" debate in U.S. corporate law has made abundantly clear, the rate at which regulatory innovations is produced is a direct function of the benefit that the regulating jurisdiction is able to realize in producing such innovations (Romano, 1993). Delaware's continued commitment to its corporate clientele, and its willingness to innovate in corporate law, is a function of the fact that a large proportion of its state budget depends on revenues derived from firms choosing to incorporate in Delaware.

The provinces derive economic benefit from securities transactions to the extent that they collect transaction fees for processing transactions.[43] These fees often exceed the actual cost of the service provided, leaving many of the provinces with fat operating surpluses that flow into the general revenue account. In Ontario, for example, the surplus generated by the OSC in 1995 was approximately $25 million (McKenna and Freeman, 1996, p. B1). These direct benefits are very small, however, compared to any province's annual

---

[43]These include, for example, capital fees levied on prospectus financings and registration fees.

budget. Thus, one would not expect that they would create the type of incentive that Delaware has to introduce innovative laws in order to attract corporate clientele.

Moreover, as Daniels and I both point out (Daniels, 1991; MacIntosh and Cumming, 1995), securities laws are applied not on the basis of the jurisdiction where the firm is incorporated, but on the basis of where its shareholders are resident (or perhaps even on the basis of whether there are connecting factors to the province[44]). This makes it very difficult for a province to attract business by introducing regulatory innovations, because other provinces can simply apply their own laws to cross-border transactions and trump the innovation, even if the transaction is carefully engineered to take place within the innovating jurisdiction.

So far as large firm transactions are concerned, the provinces have not in fact been very innovative in their securities laws. Most provinces (Quebec, of course, excepted) simply follow the lead of Ontario. Indeed, through the National Policy Statements and by other means, the provinces have sought to achieve some measure of harmonization and cooperation, rather than promote competition.

Nonetheless, the provinces have had an incentive to innovate in relation to small transactions that take place mostly, or entirely within a single province. While the direct benefits that result are small relative to provincial budgets, the indirect benefits may be substantial. These include bringing securities-related employment and economic activity into the province.

Vancouver's Howe Street (the locus of securities-related activity in British Columbia) is a case in point. Howe Street generates a huge amount of economic activity for the province of British Columbia, in addition to serving as the chief supplier of capital for local natural resource (and other) enterprises. Approximately 90% of the capital raised in Vancouver is raised privately through exemptions from the prospectus requirement, rather than through public offerings. The private placement rules are precisely the area of securities law in which British Columbia has been extremely innovative. Securities laws in British Columbia relating to private placements are very

---

[44]Re Asbestos Corporation (1992), 10 O.R. (3d) 577; 97 D.L.R. (4th) 144; 58 O.A.C. 277 (C.A.).

different from those in Ontario or Quebec (markets which tend to service large public companies) and much more accommodating to small companies (see MacIntosh, 1994). These more forgiving requirements have contributed not only to the vitality of local enterprise, but have attracted small firm financings from across the country. Alberta has innovated in a similar way in relation to intraprovincial sales of securities, with similar results for its local capital market and economy (see, e.g., Robinson, 1993).

The economies of both British Columbia and Alberta have also benefited from the distinctive characteristics of the Vancouver and Alberta Stock Exchanges. The less demanding listing standards found on these exchanges have attracted a large number of firms that are unable to list on the Toronto or Montreal stock exchanges. While substantial public companies with a large following in the investor community may locate virtually anywhere without affecting their ability to raise capital, small companies will often find it advantageous to locate in the community that is the source of their funding. Situating locally allows investors to become more familiar with the company and its principals, helping to resolve information asymmetries and lowering the firm's cost of capital.

Thus, the distinctive character of the public markets of British Columbia and Alberta has resulted in significant indirect benefit to the local economies. This is a point stressed by Daniels (1992, p. 94) in arguing in favour of maintaining the existing regime of provincial rules.

It is therefore no accident that British Columbia and Alberta (and particularly the former) have historically been vocal in their opposition to the creation of a national securities commission. The perceived danger is that a national regulator will impose uniform rules on all provinces both in relation to the exempt and the public markets. Another perceived danger is that national regulation will result in uniformity both in listing standards and other stock exchange rules. In net, British Columbia and Alberta fear that national regulation would bring to an end the distinctive character of the British Columbia and Alberta capital markets.

While these fears are not without foundation, the 1994 federal proposal, which apparently forms the basis for the 1996 proposal, was not insensitive to these concerns. The proposal would have allowed the provinces to craft their own prospectus exemption regimes. The proposal also indicates that the existing rules and by-laws of the various stock exchanges would be adopted holus bolus into the new federal law. Moreover, under the proposal the stock exchanges would continue to pass their own rules and by-laws. Finally, the proposal would have left the provinces with the ability to pass legislation constituting the stock exchanges. These concessions were likely made with a view to pacifying British Columbia and Alberta. While British Columbia declined to go along with either the 1994 or 1996 proposals, it is not known if the basis for the province's dissatisfaction is that these concessions are insufficient to guarantee the continued distinctiveness of the B.C. market.[45]

In my view, the 1994 proposal forms a solid foundation for a regime that will tend to encourage regulatory innovation, insofar as innovation is possible within the existing choice of law rules. I also note that I fully endorse Daniel's call for full mutual recognition by each province of the other provinces' securities laws, so that a corporation could select a jurisdiction whose securities laws would govern its securities-related transactions (with minimum standards to be set for provincial laws governing smaller firms) (Daniels, 1992, pp. 95-96). However, this does not seem to be a realistic possibility in the current regulatory or political climate. The 1994 proposal seems to be a happy medium between the ideal and the possible.

Forum Shopping: Shareholders' Welfare

The last section left out of account one important constituency: shareholders. It was more or less assumed that if the provinces benefit from regulatory innovation, then the enhanced incentive to generate innovations was a good thing. What, however, about the danger of a "race to the bottom", in which regulating jurisdictions produce laws that are good for themselves, corporate managers, and perhaps the local economy, but bad for the shareholders?

Happily, the evidence suggests that forum shopping by corporations in search of congenial corporate laws has not in the main harmed shareholders; rather, in most cases, shareholders' fortunes appear to have improved (Romano,

---

[45]Under the 1994 proposal, while the stock exchanges would continue to be able to formulate their own rules, these rules would be subject to veto or change by national regulators. Thus, under the 1994 proposal, the stock exchanges would not be completely under local control.

1993). The widely touted "race to the bottom" that is said to result from interjurisdictional competition for corporate charters appears to be more a chimera than a reality. It is very likely that the same is the case in relation to competition for securities business.

Similar comments apply to competition between stock exchanges for listings. Indeed, in my view, there is at present too little competition between Canadian stock exchanges. Moves to enhance the competitiveness of the stock exchanges are likely to result in savings for corporate users and investors alike (see Fischel, 1987).

Forum Shopping: Rogues

The balkanized system of securities regulation in Canada has created opportunities for boiler room operators and other rogues who have been excluded from the securities markets of one province to set up shop in another. While such operators may have their registrations revoked in one market, regulators in that market cannot deny them access to the securities business save in the province in which the order is made. Other provincial regulators may use the revocation of registration as a reason for denying a registration application (or revoking a registration) in their own jurisdictions. However, they will only do so if they are aware of the revocation of registration in another jurisdiction. By contrast, under a national system, a revocation of registration would apply across the country, denying rogues the ability to engage in roving scams.

The Opening Up of Markets and Enhanced Competition

As noted above, registration requirements have played a marginal role in confining at least some of the smaller registrants to a single province. Because a national commission would grant a single registration valid across the country, this would tend to result in greater competition between securities firms, benefiting consumers of professional securities market services.

Externalities

As noted by Daniels (1992, pp. 91-92), the existence of regulatory externalities may be a factor in the choice of the size of the regulatory entity. If regulation in one jurisdiction is creating negative externalities in an adjacent jurisdiction, then fusing the two jurisdictions under a common regulatory umbrella (staffed by representatives from each) may cure the problem.

Provincial regulation can be productive of externalities. A case involving the Asbestos Corporation is a good example. Going back some decades, the asbestos industry in Quebec has been a declining industry. This decline was of great concern to the Parti Québécois government elected in the 1970s, as it threatened tens of thousands of jobs in Quebec. Under then Finance Minister Jacques Parizeau, the Parti Québécois decided to indirectly (through purchase of an intermediate entity) acquire a controlling interest in Asbestos Corporation Ltd., one of the largest employers in the asbestos industry in Quebec. It seems clear from the subsequent history that the motivating reason for the purchase was to maintain employment in Quebec, rather than to earn profits for shareholders. Five years after the government's purchase of a controlling interest, the stock in Asbestos traded for a fraction of its initial value.

Quebec's action clearly resulted in an external diseconomy. The purchase resulted in a benefit for Quebec asbestos workers at the expense of shareholders. The Quebec Securities Commission is implicated in this externality insofar as it failed to take action to protect the shareholders of Asbestos Corporation, when such action appeared to be both possible and warranted.

The Asbestos transaction involved a number of extraprovincial elements. For example, Asbestos Corporation Ltd. was then headquartered in Toronto, traded over the Toronto Stock Exchange, and 30% of its shareholders were situated in Ontario. The purchase contract was effected with a company incorporated in Delaware and headquartered in St. Louis. On the basis of these and other factors connecting the transaction to Ontario, the Ontario Securities Commission asserted jurisdiction and commenced a hearing to determine whether the province of Quebec should be barred from access to Ontario's capital markets. Quebec challenged the jurisdiction of the commission.

In the end result, the Ontario Court of Appeal ruled that the question of jurisdiction was (as the commission had posited) to be resolved on the basis of the strength of the factors connecting the transaction to the province seeking to assert jurisdiction.[46] Curiously, however, and almost certainly because of political factors, the Ontario Securities Commission ultimately declined to take jurisdiction.[47]

While the Ontario Court of Appeal's ruling suggests that Ontario might have taken jurisdiction and corrected the externality, the legal position leaves abundant doubt as to whether a province suffering an externality will always be in a position to supply a remedy. Thus, under the current system, at least some externalities will go unredressed.

Externalities may occur in a wide variety of contexts. For example, should Ontario enjoin a takeover bid made in a number of different provinces, that may have the effect of killing the bid in all provinces, depriving investors everywhere of the benefit of the bid.

Nonetheless, externalities are probably the exception rather than the rule. In most cases, the different provincial commissions will share a common goal: the protection of investors. While a particular regulator's legal and/or constitutional mandates may prevent that regulator from protecting local investors from extraterritorial activities, in most cases the extraterritorial securities regulator will act in a manner that results in protection for the local investors. Thus, the externalities problem is probably less serious in practice than might initially appear to be the case.

In theory, moving to a national commission will eliminate externalities (at least, those occurring within Canada) by drawing all of those with an interest in a particular regulatory outcome under one umbrella (Daniels, 1992, p. 92). For example, if the Asbestos case had arisen under a national commission, it is possible that having a single government responsible to all affected constituencies would have pointed the way to a different, and more efficient outcome.

---

[46]*Re Asbestos Corporation* (1992), 10 O.R. (3d) 577; 97 D.L.R. (4th) 144; 58 O.A.C. 277 (C.A.).

[47]*Re Asbestos Corporation* (1994), 17 O.S.C.B. 3537.

As Daniels points out, however, in practice things may turn out somewhat differently (*ibid.*, pp. 91-92). Because of political factors, the federal government may be more responsive to some interests than others. In the Asbestos case, the federal government's desire to appease Quebec might have led to the same outcome that occurred under the provincial system of securities regulation.

Further, a national regulator body is likely to be dominated by Ontario appointees. The commission may thus tend to regulate in ways that are more congenial to Ontario than the other provinces, such as ratcheting up the level of regulation sufficiently to wipe out the junior markets in British Columbia and Alberta (and hence destroy any possibility of competition from those venues). On balance, therefore, moving to a federal regulator will not clearly result in substantial savings in mitigating regulatory externalities.

Securities Legislation, Industrial Policy and Prospectus Exemptions

Provincial legislators have sometimes used securities legislation as a means for implementing industrial policy. For example, Ontario's legislation presently has a prospectus exemption that makes it easier for firms to issue tax-favoured securities.[48] Many provinces have special regulatory regimes that apply only to labour-sponsored venture capital funds. While the use of securities legislation to further industrial policy is a questionable practice, nationalizing securities regulation threatens to deny the provinces of the ability to use securities laws in this way (Ontario Securities Commission, 1996).

The 1994 federal proposal, however, would have left prospectus exemptions in the hands of the provinces. Given the loose way in which exemptive procedures have been used in the past (e.g., to create the short form prospectus, shelf prospectus, bought deal, and multijurisdictional prospectus system) there seems to be little doubt that allowing the provinces the freedom to craft prospectus exemptions would be interpreted by provincial regulators as ceding them a wide freedom to create special prospectus regimes. Indeed, there is danger in this as well as opportunity. Allowing the provinces the freedom to create special prospectus regimes under the guise of designing prospectus

---

[48]*Regulation Made Under the Securities Act*, R.R.O., 1990, Regulation 1015, s.14(f).

exemptions would tend to defeat one of the chief aims of a national regulator: uniform laws administered by a single, national regulator. Thus, the powers left to the provinces must be crafted with sufficient care to foreclose the possibility of the provinces usurping the federal legislation by designing prospectus exemptions that are in fact alternative prospectus regimes.

Is Optimal Securities Legislation Different in Different Parts of the Country?

Daniels and I argue that securities markets can be notionally divided into two parts: that sector which is composed of large firms well followed by institutional investors, the press and analysts, and the sector composed of small firms, not well followed by any of the above (Daniels and MacIntosh, 1992). We suggest that there are good reasons for applying different corporate and securities laws to these two sectors. This same logic might be extended to argue that securities laws ought to be different in different parts of the country. The British Columbia market, for example, has a far higher proportion of comparatively unsophisticated retail investors than does Ontario. Moreover, most British Columbia firms fall into the second sector of companies, and tend to be concentrated in the natural resource sector, which historically has presented particular regulatory challenges.[49] For all of these reasons, it could be argued that securities rules in British Columbia should not in all respects mimic those in Ontario. In short, there may be a different balance between the costs and the benefits of regulation in different parts of the country.

Fortunately, however, differences between provinces will tend to lie in the small firm domain, which the 1994 federal proposal, and presumably the more recent proposal, leave to the provinces (by virtue of ceding the provinces control over prospectus exemptions and, to some extent, the stock exchanges).

---

[49]Indeed, in response to a perception that issuances by junior mining issuers are more likely to present problems than issuances by other firms, Ontario has for many years regulated prospectus offerings by such issuers with particular stringency. See Ontario Policy Statement 5.1.

Transition Costs

As Daniels (1992, pp. 94-95) points out, moving to a national regulator would create substantial transition costs. Both the direct costs of negotiating and constructing the new regime, and the costs of educating lawyers and users about the final product could be considerable.

Responsiveness to Regulated Communities

Regulatory responsiveness to members of regulated communities can wear a number of guises — some good and some bad. On the downside, over-responsiveness may be a symptom of "regulatory capture", in which the regulators design the rules in the interests of the regulated communities, rather than in the interests of the public at large. However, responsiveness to concerns of regulated communities can also enormously improve the policy-making process. Designing the policy process so as to routinely include feedback on proposed initiatives serves as an important information pipeline. This pipeline serves to inform regulators whose ox is likely to be gored by regulatory initiatives. Having a map of winners and losers will assist regulators in determining whether the rule change is a good or a bad one. Moreover, the information pipeline will also help the regulators decide how best to implement a particular regulatory strategy at minimum cost and without unanticipated side effects.

It is also important for members of regulated communities to build a relationship of trust with regulators. Where a trusting relationship exists, transactions can often be speeded on their way by obtaining informal regulatory approvals, rather than by setting the formal regulatory machinery in motion. Thus, members of regulated communities will want to have ready and low-cost access to regulators, in order to build a long-term relationship, and to communicate information or objections concerning proposed transactions or rule changes.

Finally, local regulators acquire expertise in understanding local capital markets. An understanding of local conditions, practices, and players allows regulators to respond more effectively and quickly to concerns raised by market participants, whether at the operational or policy levels. Such expertise facilitates responsiveness.

The U.S. literature on charter shopping suggests that regulatory responsiveness is indeed an important link both in designing and implementing effective laws. Delaware, which is the most responsiveness of all states to its regulatees, is the hands down winner of the charter shopping competition. And, as noted above, when firms move to Delaware, share prices tend to go up, rather than down (Romano, 1993). In short, responsiveness is an important part of the regulatory process.

Moving to a national commission would likely diminish regulatory responsiveness. A dealer in Halifax, for example, will no longer be able to walk or drive to the local securities commission offices to consult with senior policymakers on securities law matters. While local offices will be left in place, local officials will likely lack the authority to deal with many of the policy issues raised by market participants. While a long distance call is always an option, the comparative lack of personal contact will tend to break down the ties between regulators and regulatees. Moreover, given that there will almost certainly be fewer regulators on the job should a national commission be created (because of the consolidation of provincial operations in the move to a national commission), there will be fewer access points for capital market professionals and users. National regulators will often have less expertise in understanding local markets.

Should the power to grant prospectus exemptions be left with the provinces, and some degree of autonomy granted to the stock exchanges, this will ameliorate the problem of diminished responsiveness. Nonetheless, the importance of responsiveness in the regulatory process suggests that national regulators should make liberal use of regional offices with the authority to grant approvals on a wide range of commonplace transactions, such as prospectuses, interested party transactions, and the like.[50] It also suggests that regional offices should gather intelligence on the manner in which national rules impact on local communities, in order to facilitate the policy-making process.

---

[50]The 1994 proposal would have put regional offices in British Columbia, Alberta, and one of the Atlantic provinces. The absence of a regional office in Manitoba was a key reason in Manitoba's decision not to back the proposal. See McIntosh (1994d).

Transparency

Just as a move to a national commission would reduce responsiveness, so it would reduce the transparency of the regulatory process. Transparency is an important process value: as the maxim goes, it is important not only that justice be done, but that justice be seen to be done. At the policy level, for instance, transparency requires that the means whereby policy changes are formulated be open and well understood by those affected. Policy changes must also be supported by credible evidence and routinely justified by regulators to their regulated communities. The model proposed by the Daniels Committee and largely implemented in Ontario forms a sound basis for the procedures that should be implemented in a national commission (Ontario Task Force on Securities Regulation, 1994).

Political Accountability

Like responsiveness and transparency, the political accountability of the regulatory process is likely to decline with a national commission. At present, actions of a local group of regulators who are under the direction (and thus the responsibility of) local politicians can be challenged relatively easily, whether through the local press, personal contact with legislators, or by other means. Nationalization of the process will make it much more difficult to engage the political process in order to protest regulatory outcomes. The national press (of greater concern to national politicians than local press) will be far less sympathetic to local concerns than the local press. Senior politicians who might be in a position to influence the regulatory process will be both literally and figuratively more distant. Further, when national politicians must deal with concerns from across the country, many purely local concerns are likely to get pushed to the back burner.

Responsiveness and accountability are complementary. Politicians (as well as regulators) are likely to be responsive when they can be held accountable. Thus, designing a national commission with an eye to ensuring political accountability will aid in designing a commission that is responsive to those who are regulated.

Clarifying Which Law Will Apply

Under the current system it is difficult for market participants to know which law (e.g., that of Ontario? Alberta? both?) will apply to a given transaction (Daniels, 1992, p. 91). This interferes with the process of planning transactions, and introduces a legal wildcard into the evaluation of prospective investments, both by corporations and investors. A national regulatory system will make it clear which law will apply, obviating these difficulties.

International Negotiations

Another difficulty with the current system of provincial regulation is that there is no single voice that speaks for Canada's interests in international negotiations with other countries or securities regulators (Daniels, 1992, pp. 92-93). Indeed, not all provinces are represented in international forums. For example, only Ontario, Quebec and British Columbia are represented at meetings of the International Organization of Securities Organizations, the international body that attempts to coordinate securities regulatory activity around the world. This leaves Canada open to "divide and conquer" strategies on the part of other countries, diminishes the efficacy with which Canadian interests are represented, and leaves the interests of some provinces entirely unaccounted for. Daniels deals with these themes at greater length (*ibid.*).

VII. SUMMARY

There are both pluses and minuses in moving to a national commission. Overall, however, the pluses would appear to outweigh the minuses. So far as the large firm sector is concerned, the pluses include savings in administrative and transactions costs, ease of enforcement, clarification of which law will apply to a firm/transaction, and gains in advancing Canada's position in international negotiations. Negatives include the costs of transition to a national regime, and probable losses in transparency, responsiveness and political accountability.

It is important, however, how a national commission is to be constituted. While in many ways the preferred outcome would be for the federal government to use the federal trade and commerce power, political considerations make this unlikely to happen. While constituting a national commission by means of delegation is inferior in many respects, it appears to be the only choice on the table. Delegation by the provinces to a federal commission, the basis for the 1996 proposal, will simply have to do.

In the domain of intraprovincial transactions involving small firms, it is important to preserve an ability for the provinces to innovate and compete for securities-related business. The 1994 federal proposal, which would leave to the provinces a large measure of control in this area, appears to be a very good starting point.

Recent reportage in the press suggests that the on-again, off-again national commission is now off-again. Given earlier momentum in the direction of forming a national commission, however, it is to be hoped that this is but a temporary setback, rather than another nail in the coffin.

DATE	ORIGINATOR OF PROPOSAL	ACTION TAKEN (OR CONSEQUENCE OF PROPOSAL)
935	Royal Commission on Price Spreads[1]	None.
964	Royal Commission on Banking and Finance (the "Porter Commission")[2]	None, although the call for a national regulator inspired Ontario's subsequent "CANSEC" proposal.
967	Ontario Securities Commission "CANSEC" (or Canadian Securities Commission) proposal[3]	Proposal circulated to other provincial governments and to federal government.
968	Federal government[4]	None.
969	Report of the Canadian Committee on Mutual Funds and Investment Contracts[5]	None.
971	Remarks by Honourable Ron Basford, federal Minister of Consumer and Corporate Affairs[6]	None.
975	Federal government	Study commissioned under the direction of Philip Anisman. Volume of working papers published with draft federal securities legislation.[7] Perfunctory announcement by Andre Ouellet in Parliament in 1982 that the government would not proceed with the proposals.

1987	OSC Chairman Henry Knowles is quoted as supporting a federal securities regulator.[8]	None.
1989	OSC Chairman Stanley Beck predicts the coming of a federal securities regulator.[9]	None.
1989	Gilles Loiselle, federal Minister of State for Finance, and Don Blenkarn, Chairman of the Commons Finance Committee, call for the establishment of a federal securities regulator.[10]	None: Finance Minister Michael Wilson publicly repudiates idea of a federal securities regulator shortly after the Loiselle/ Blenkarn remarks.
1989	The Economic Council of Canada calls for the establishment of a federal-provincial agency to set minimum national standards for the bank, trust, insurance and securities industries (to be administered by the provinces).[11]	None.
1993	The four Maritime premiers jointly call for the establishment of a federal securities regulator[12]; proposal supported by Ontario Premier Bob Rae.[13]	None, although this call serves as an inspiration for the federal government's own proposal in 1994.[14]
1994	Federal Throne Speech calls for establishment of federal securities regulator.	Draft proposal circulated among the provinces[15]; plan ultimately abandoned due to opposition from Quebec, British Columbia, Manitoba and Ontario.[16] However, failure of the proposal prompts the creation of a joint provincial Task Force on Operational Efficiencies to improve the functioning of the current system.

1995	In her report on the mutual funds industry in Canada,[17] Glorianne Stromberg calls for the establishment of a national regulator to oversee the Canadian mutual funds industry.	None, although the Stromberg Report may have fortified the federal government's determination to proceed with its 1996 proposal.
1996	At urging of Ontario Finance Minister Ernie Eves, the Federal Throne Speech (Feb. 27, 1996) calls for the establishment of a federal securities regulator.[18]	Draft proposal circulated among the provinces; issue put on the agenda for the First Ministers' Conference in June 1996.
1996	Ontario Throne Speech endorses federal securities regulator.[19]	Provides further impetus to federal proposal.
1996	Sawiak Report[20] (commissioned by the Senate Banking, Trade and Commerce Committee, or the "Kirby Committee"), endorses federal securities regulator.	Provides further impetus to federal proposal.
1996	Paul Martin, federal Finance Minister, publicly endorses federal securities regulator.[21]	Further momentum given to federal proposal.
1996	First Ministers' Conference	The premiers of eight provinces (Quebec and British Columbia excluded) and the prime minister agree in principle to the establishment of a federal securities regulator to be called the Canadian Securities Commission.[22]

Notes: 1. Canada, Royal Commission on Price Spreads (1935).

2. The agency proposed by the Porter Commission would have regulated interprovincial and international securities trading. The commission expressed the view that:

> establishment of a federal regulatory body working in co-operation with provincial administrations could lead to higher standards, both in the industry and in the securities commissions, to better enforcement of the laws, to improved investor information, and to a reduction in duplication.

Canada, Royal Commission on Price Spreads (1935), p. 346.

3. "Cansec", November 1967 O.S.C.B. 61. The proposal and reaction to it is described in Banwell (1968), pp. 22-29.

4. Banwell (1968), pp. 29-32.

5. Baillie (1973), pp. 385-386.

6. See *ibid.*, p. 390.

7. See Anisman (1979).

8. See McIntosh (1987).

9. See Waitzer (1994).

10. See, e.g., Dalglish (1989b); Dalglish (1989a); Welsh (1989b); Welsh (1989a).

11. Economic Council of Canada (1989). See also Graham (1989).

12. The premiers made the proposal both publicly and by means of a letter to the prime minister. See Dalglish (1994).

13. "Federal Role in Canada Securities Likely -- Analysts", Reuters, August 26, 1993; McIntosh (1994d).

14. McIntosh (1994a).

15. See (1994) 17 O.S.C.B. 4401. See also September 20, 1994, "Ottawa pushing securities plan", *Canadian Press Newstex* (QL); McFarland (1994).

16. McIntosh (1994d); McIntosh (1994b); McIntosh (1994c); McFarland (1994).

17. Stromberg (1995).

18. Westell (1996); Graham (1996).

19. McKenna (1996, p. B7).

20. Sawiak *et al.* (1996).

21. Freeman and Howlett (1996, p. B1).

22. "Eight Provinces Agree on Securities Commission", Reuters, June 21, 1996; McKenna and Freeman (1996, p. B1).

REFERENCES

Anisman, P. (1979), *Proposals for a Securities Market Law for Canada* (Ottawa: Supply and Services Canada).
_____ (1986), "The Regulation of the Securities Markets and the Harmonization of Provincial Laws", in R. Cumming (ed.), *Harmonization of Business Laws in Canada*, Research Studies of the Royal Commission on the Economic Union and Development Prospects for Canada, Vol. 56 (Toronto: University of Toronto Press).
Anisman, P. and P. Hogg (1979), "Constitutional Aspects of Federal Securities Regulation", in *Proposals for a Securities Market Law for Canada*, Vol. 3 (Ottawa: Supply and Services Canada).
Baillie, J.C. (1973), "Securities Regulation in the Seventies", in J.S. Ziegel (ed.), *Studies in Canadian Company Law*, Vol. 2 (Toronto: Butterworths).
Banwell, P.T. (1968), "Proposals for a National Securities Commission", *Queen's Intramural Law Journal* 1(3), 22-29.
Canada, Royal Commission on Price Spreads (1935), *Report* (Ottawa: King's Printer).
Courchene, T.J. (1996), "ACCESS: A Convention on the Canadian Economic and Social Systems", a working paper prepared for the Ministry of Intergovernmental Affairs, Government of Ontario, August.
Dalglish, B. (1989a), "Business", *Canadian Press Newstex*, June 25 (QL).
_____ (1989b), "Securities-Loiselle", *Canadian Press Newstex*, June 27 (QL).
_____ (1994), "Trading Places", *Maclean's*, April 4.
Daniels, R.J. (1991), "Should Provinces Compete? The Case for a Competitive Corporate Law Market", *McGill Law Review* 36, 130-190.
_____ (1992), "How 'Broke' is the System of Provincial Securities Regulation?" *Canadian Investment Review* (Spring), 89.

Daniels, R.J. and J.G. MacIntosh (1992), "Toward a Distinctive Canadian Corporate Law Regime", *Osgoode Hall Law Journal* 29, 863-933.

Den Tandt, M. (1996), "Ontario Unveils Securities Crime Buster: Regulators, Police to Co-ordinate Moves", *The Globe and Mail*, June 19.

Dey, P. (1983), "The Extraterritorial Application of Securities Laws", *Ontario Securities Commission Bulletin* 6, 3481-3488.

Economic Council of Canada (1989), *A New Frontier: Globalization and Canada's Financial Markets* (Ottawa: Supply and Services Canada).

Fischel, D.R. (1987), "Organized Exchanges and the Regulation of Dual Class Common Stock", *University of Chicago Law Review* 54, 119-152.

Freeman, A. and S. Feschuk (1996), "Quebec, Alberta, British Columbia Wary of Ontario-Based Idea of Single Canadian Stock Regulator", *The Globe and Mail*, June 13.

Freeman, A. and K. Howlett (1996), "Keep IPOs at Home: Martin: Finance Minister Urges Setting up Federal Securities Regulator to Help Stanch Flow to U.S.", *The Globe and Mail*, March 8.

Graham, C. (1989), "Business Interest", *Canadian Press Newstex*, June 7 (QL).

_____ (1996), "Provinces to Get New Deal in National Unity -- Throne Speech", *Canadian Press Newstex*, February 27 (QL).

Hogg, P.W. (1992), *Constitutional Law of Canada*, 3d ed. (Scarborough: Carswell).

Janisch, H.N. (1989), "Reregulating the Regulator: Administrative Structure of Securities Commissions and Ministerial Responsibility", in *Law Society of Upper Canada: Special Lectures 1989: Securities Law in the Modern Financial Marketplace* (Toronto: De Boo).

Jordan, C. (1993), "Lessons from the Bennett Affair", *McGill Law Journal* 38, 1071-1094.

MacIntosh, J.G. (1994), "Legal and Institutional Barriers to Financing Innovative Enterprise in Canada", Government and Competitiveness Project Discussion Paper 94-10 (Kingston: School of Policy Studies, Queen's University).

_____ (1995), "International Securities Regulation: Of Competition, Co-operation, Convergence, and Cartelization", working paper (Toronto: Faculty of Law, University of Toronto).

MacIntosh, J.G. and D. Cumming (1995), "The Role of Interjurisdictional Competition in Shaping Canadian Corporate Law", presented at the Canadian Law and Economics Association Annual Meeting, September.

McFarland, J. (1994), "Provinces Cooling on SEC-type Body", *The Financial Post*, July 15.

McIntosh, G. (1987), "Weekly Business Focus", *Canadian Press Newstex* (QL), March 14.

_____ (1994a), "Business Interest", *Canadian Press Newstex*, May 11 (QL).

_____ (1994b), "Provinces Backing Away from National Securities Commission", *Canadian Press Newstex*, July 14 (QL).

_____ (1994c), "Ottawa Still Part of Federal Equation", *The Financial Post*, September 3.

_____ (1994d), "Ottawa and Provinces at Impasse on Securities Commission, Officials Say", *Canadian Press Newstex*, September 6 (QL).

McKenna, B. (1996), "National Securities Regulator Advocated in Report to Senate", *The Globe and Mail*, May 8.

McKenna, B. and A. Freeman (1996), "Eight Premiers Endorse National Securities Commission", *The Globe and Mail,* June 22.

McNish, J. (1996), "Securities-Crime Deal Close: RCMP, Ontario Police and Regulators Hope to Pool Resources for Major Investigations", *The Globe and Mail*, April 18.

Ontario Securities Commission Task Force on Small Business Financing (1996), *Final Report* (1994), *Ontario Securities Commission Bulletin* 17, 5753.

Ontario Task Force on Securities Regulation (1994), *Responsibility and Responsiveness: Final Report of the Ontario Task Force on Securities Regulation, Ontario Securities Commission Bulletin* 17, 3208.

Robinson, M.G. (1993), "Raising Start-Up Equity Capital: Alberta's Junior Capital Pool Program", Working Paper No. 9362 (Calgary: Faculty of Management, University of Calgary).

Romano, R. (1993), *The Genius of American Corporate Law* (New York: AEI Press).

Sawiak, G.V. *et al.* (1996), *Report to the Standing Senate Committee on Banking, Trade and Commerce on the Transaction Costs of a Decentralized System of Securities Regulation*, April.

Stromberg, G. (1995), "Regulatory Strategies for the Mid-1990s: Recommendations for Regulating Investment Funds in Canada", prepared for the Canadian Securities Administrators.

Waitzer, E.J. (1994), "Addressing Duplicative Regulation", Remarks of Edward J. Waitzer, Chairman, Ontario Securities Commission at Securities Superconference, Four Seasons Hotel, Toronto, March 3.

Welsh, L. (1989a), "Business Interest", *Canadian Press Newstex*, May 31 (QL).

_____ (1989b), "Business Interest", *Canadian Press Newstex*, June 6 (QL).

Westell, D. (1996), "New Push for National Regulator", *The Financial Post*, March 14.

Session Seven
WRAP UP

RAPPORTEUR'S REMARKS

Stephen S. Poloz, The Bank Credit Analyst Research Group

I would like to begin my remarks by posing a question. Let us consider all the examples of regulatory-induced inefficiency in Canada's financial system that were discussed in the conference and now appear earlier in this volume, quantify them, and add them up. How many here come up with a number that exceeds 0.1% of GDP? How many think it is above 0.5% of GDP?

Either way, the number is large when cumulated over 30 years.

We have heard during this conference about the total consensus on deposit insurance reform, and how that consensus has been ignored. Even John Chant's "regulate by function" idea, which several people spoke favourably about, is around ten years old. We heard yesterday that the main driver for reform in Ottawa is the sunset clause in the existing legislation — we can at least be thankful that there is a sunset clause. And, we also heard that all this pressure coming from the sunset clause has led us to decide — what? — to undertake a really big study this time.

I wonder if all this foot-dragging is a product of Canadian insecurity, of our typically consultative, indecisive nature, or of something more profound? I cannot say. But, as Chuck Freedman said during his presentation, we need to make some decisions soon, for the innovators are pounding on the door.

We have heard a great deal at this conference about the trade-offs the regulators face — prudential risk, systemic risk, the risk that competition will be insufficient — trade-offs that make the task of modifying the regulatory framework exceedingly difficult. But one cannot help but get the impression that regulators are trying to invent a rounder wheel, even as the wheel is threatening to fall off the wagon. We appear to be preoccupied with small, theoretically elegant trade-offs, while totally ignoring the opportunity cost associated with all this study, consultation and negotiations.

Jeff MacIntosh was the fist to mention this consideration. His view was that from the securities standpoint the opportunity cost of delaying reform might be fairly small. Some commentators questioned that judgement, but the point is that even small opportunity costs can cumulate to very large numbers over a period of 30 years, which is how long we have been waiting for a national securities commission.

I suspect that the financial institutions are quite in touch with the opportunity cost I am talking about. The public surely is not, and they are the biggest losers. Perhaps if the academics were busy making such calculations and publicizing them, the process of reform could get some additional momentum. One almost has the sense that if making profits is the only reason why someone is badgering the government for legislative change, then that is definitely something the regulators cannot be seen doing. The fact that those profit opportunities represent improved welfare for firm and consumer alike appears to be overlooked.

Randall Morck can surely not be accused of trying to make a wheel a bit rounder. His focus on the fundamentals of why intermediation happens and the inherent role of the notion of trust I found to be quite refreshing. I was particularly impressed with his finding that the voting share premium in Canada is significantly higher than that in the United States, and I am persuaded by his view that this symbolizes a significant lack of trust in our system. He makes a convincing case that regulators could accomplish a great deal with a few more disclosure rules.

The message I take from this is that we do not need another major study, but can move decisively ahead on a number of fronts. The key is to keep things simple.

John Chant has demonstrated once again why it is that, whenever the subject of financial market regulation comes up, his is the first name that is mentioned. His dominant theme is unabashed scepticism, possibly frustration, over the abilities of regulators to keep up with a dynamic and innovative financial system. I find myself completely convinced by this. John favours a functional approach to regulation as a consequence: one regulates activities, not institutions, then the institutions choose whether or not to engage in those activities.

Does anyone here believe that the system will look like it does today by the time the government produces another white paper? Tom Courchene described for us the sort of financial intermediary we might have ten years from now. We also heard from Doug Melville just a snapshot of the pace of change, including the development of virtual banks on the Internet. Maurice Levi has noted how easy it is to evade the 20% foreign content rule for pensions.

John Chant's solution to the regulatory issue is both elegant and simple. And it received endorsements from several participants at the conference, including Mark Daniels. Not so simple, say the regulators; in fact, practically impossible to do. Nick Le Pan outlined quite well for us the range of complex issues that regulators face. Looked at another way, however, Le Pan's presentation did little to refute Chant's claim that regulators will never catch up, let alone keep up, with a dynamic financial system.

So what to do? One possibility that perhaps should be considered is for the government to privatize deposit insurance while simultaneously creating some of Chant's "narrow banks". Indeed, these banks could simply be branches of the Bank of Canada. Then let the people choose between private financial institutions and those ultra-safe narrow banks. Regulation would be vastly simplified by this proposal. Right now, our banks represent a blend of private and public banking, given the moral hazard aspect of publicly-sponsored deposit insurance and monitoring. Separating the two and continuing to offer both would let the consumer evaluate his own risks and then decide. Competition would be the main regulator of the private financial institutions; on this I find myself in broad agreement with Roger Ware. But splitting the system in this way would also solve some difficult problems on the payments system side: Chuck Freedman would be able to sleep at night because all of the systemic risks he told us about would be internalized in the narrow bank system, which the Bank of Canada would control. Again, simplicity and consumer choice appear to me to be the best guides in developing financial regulation.

The key to reducing prudential risks to financial institutions is diversification. It is true for everyone else, after all. That is why regional banks are more prone to failure than national ones. And I ask myself why this diversification argument should not carry over into other dimensions as well. That is, diversification across types of financial intermediation businesses. Financial intermediaries, after all, amount to sausage factories: people eat sausages, but would never eat individually the things that go into sausages, any more than they would take their life savings and give it over to one individual entrepreneur with a wacky idea. Banks package up those individual risks into bite-size pieces for us, and it seems to me that conglomerate financial intermediaries should be better able to do so than narrow ones. Once again, I believe that we should allow both narrow and conglomerate financial intermediaries to exist, and let the consumer decide between them.

We see a similar message emerging from Maurice Levi's paper. Taken together, the evidence convinces him that global markets are not perfectly integrated; on my reading, the evidence is that they may not be perfectly integrated, but they are very highly so. Certainly, global financial markets are significantly more efficient than most other markets we operate in. Why should this be so? Well, an important reason is that governments have not yet discovered a means of inserting themselves into the global capital market, to throw some more sand into the wheels in the form of a transactions tax, so to speak.

I am inclined to agree with Maurice that this market is best left alone. I interpret his evidence that equity investors are not fully diversified globally as indicating revealed preference, not some market failure that requires remedying.

A major question that we encountered in the conference is how big should our banks be? I come at this issue first as a consumer, and my answer is "really big", for I get additional confidence from size. I think everybody does. And provided that there is at least one other to compete with that institution, I believe that competition will happen.

Harry Hassanwalia posed four questions concerning this issue, and he answered each one quite effectively, in my view. His conclusion is that there is no evident reason to control the size of banks. Now, when you go into a baker's shop and ask "How is the bread today?" the baker always says it is good. And, after all, Harry is a banker. Nevertheless, I was particularly impressed with his finding that bank market concentration is higher for smaller countries. That makes complete sense to me, and it means the usual size comparisons we make across countries are not all that informative on this issue.

This also makes me wonder why we should worry about economies of scale or scope at all. Again, that is up to the market and the institutions themselves to decide. If a bank goes above its optimal size, it will eventually lose market share and shrink. This mechanism sits all right with me.

John Evans clearly disagrees with this view, and I respect his reasons, especially the "too big to fail" problem. But banks are already too big to fail in this country, and it is not obvious to me that the problem is made more severe as they get bigger. Rather, it seems to me that the added diversification reduces the risk of failure. And I am concerned that we not make arbitrary regulatory decisions — 10% versus 20% or whatever — on the basis of such qualitative arguments.

So I propose that we provide the economists with some data to analyze. Economists, as you know, feel most comfortable analyzing behaviour in the neighbourhood of an equilibrium. So let us raise the ownership limit from 10% to 11% and let the economists analyze the data that emerge. Then, after due diligence through study and debate, we can go ahead and let the ownership limit be whatever people want it to be.

We also heard today a lot of muttering about linkages between commercial and financial interests. Although such linkages appear to work all right in some countries, perhaps such a notion is just too anti-Canadian for us. Randall Morck, in particular, has warned us of the dangers in such a model. We also heard from John Chant that making major philosophical changes like that would be very costly from a regulatory point of view. I accept that, but would rather see consumers choose.

How might this work? I see a working model right in my own firm. At BCA we are very proud of the fact that we are totally independent. We have no affiliation with any financial intermediaries. Since we have nothing to sell except investment advice, we can argue that our independence translates into unbiased analysis. Our clients appreciate this characteristic. It seems to me, then, that people might be willing to pay for such a characteristic in the case of banks. If people want banks to be independent of commercial interests, they will choose to deal with banks that declare themselves as such. Other banks, which see bigger advantages in commercial linkages, can pursue them, and the products they offer will appeal to a different sort of customer. Accordingly, I see little point in outlawing financial-commercial linkages, provided that we have a full disclosure framework.

To sum up, I take five broad conclusions from this conference: (i) the opportunity cost of foot-dragging in regulatory reform is going largely unrecognized and is not being accounted for; (ii) typical regulatory frameworks are not dynamic, but ought to be; (iii) diversification in financial intermediation is a good thing, and the regulatory framework should allow it to be carried out along all dimensions; (iv) Canadian banks probably are constrained to be smaller than their optimal size; (v) commercial linkages should be permitted within a system of full disclosure, so that consumers can choose among institutions.

There is no shortage of examples of financial regulatory failure in our recent history. We can point to the Latin American debt crisis, the Savings and Loan debacle in the United States, the Barings affair, Credit Lyonnais, Japan's jusen, the Daiwa Bank episode in New York, and the Sumitomo copper affair just last week. Each of these breakdowns can be explained in very narrow terms. But I cannot help wondering whether something much bigger is going on while we sit around and discuss whether banks should be allowed to sell insurance.

Indeed, it seems to me that financial institutions' ability to adapt to a changing world is being constrained by the existing regulatory framework, and we are all paying a price for that constraint. Change is the constant that we must shoulder, whether we are consumers, providers or regulators of financial services. And that suggests the following guiding principle in moving forward: If we are going to invest another four or five years in its development, let us make our next piece of financial services legislation sufficiently dynamic that we do not need a sunset clause.

ANNEX 1

1997 REVIEW OF FINANCIAL SECTOR LEGISLATION: PROPOSALS FOR CHANGES

CHAPTER 1

FRAMEWORK AND OBJECTIVES FOR THE 1997 REVIEW

Financial institutions are essential to our economic success as a nation. They fund the mortgages of Canadians, insure our homes and automobiles, attract and invest our savings, and provide loans to consumers and businesses across the country. Financial institutions employ over half-a-million Canadians. The strength of our institutions contributes to a world-class financial system in Canada.

This document sets out proposals to improve the legislation governing the operations of federally regulated financial institutions. These include banks, trust, loan and insurance companies as well as co-operative credit associations.

In June of 1992, new legislation came into effect governing the operations of federal financial institutions. The legislation resulted in amendments to the *Bank Act*, the *Trust and Loan Companies Act*, the *Insurance Companies Act*, and the *Cooperative Credit Associations Act*.

Canada, Department of Finance (1996), *1997 Review of Financial Sector Legislation: Proposals for Changes* (Ottawa: Department of Finance).

This package of legislation was the most comprehensive reform of financial sector legislation ever undertaken by the federal government. It removed many of the restrictions preventing financial institutions from fully competing with each other. Financial institutions were allowed to diversify into new lines of financial business through broader in-house powers and subsidiary operations. They were also permitted to market financial services offered by affiliates or independent financial institutions (with exceptions in the area of insurance).

Previous revisions to the *Bank Act* had included a 10-year sunset clause to ensure regular review of the legislation. At the time the 1992 legislation was implemented, it was decided that the breadth and scope of the changes warranted an early review of their effectiveness. Thus, sunset clauses were included in all four Acts and set for March 31, 1997.

Key Developments in the Financial Sector
Since the 1992 Reform

The financial services industry has changed significantly over the past few years, both in Canada and abroad. Domestically, the most pronounced development has been the significant restructuring in the deposit-taking sector, with banks acquiring a number of trust and loan companies, many of which were in financial difficulty. Consolidation has also taken place in the insurance sector.

The pace of consolidation has been spurred by several factors. One is slower growth of the demand for financial products. Another is the entry of financial institutions into new lines of business, either directly or through subsidiaries. As a result, different types of financial institutions now compete with each other for the market share on a wider range of products. In this environment, many financial institutions have restructured their operations to facilitate expansion into new markets, take advantage of complementary product lines, and build the size and strength which they believe is necessary to compete effectively.

The failure of a few financial institutions has focused attention on the federal supervisory system. In February 1995, the government released a discussion paper entitled *Enhancing the Safety and Soundness of the Canadian Financial System*. The paper proposed refinements to strengthen the supervisory and regulatory framework for federal financial institutions, the federal deposit insurance system, and federal oversight of clearing and settlement arrangements. Legislative proposals flowing from the 1995 discussion paper have been introduced under the recently passed *An Act to amend, enact, and repeal certain laws relating to financial institutions.*

The financial sector has also seen a continuing trend towards globalization of financial services markets. Major international trade agreements, such as the North American Free Trade Agreement and the General Agreement on Trade in Services under the World Trade Organization, have been signed since 1992. These agreements have enhanced the ability of Canadian financial institutions to compete abroad, by establishing principles for trade in financial services and by providing for dispute settlement mechanisms.

Scope and Objectives of the 1997 Review

The government began the 1997 legislative review process with two objectives. The first was to assess whether or not the legislation adopted in 1992 was functioning as intended. The second objective was to determine whether or not the legislative framework remained adequate in view of the significant developments occurring in the sector.

The government has consulted extensively on both of these questions. In September 1994, the Department of Finance provided a background report to the Standing Senate Committee on Banking, Trade and Commerce.[1] This report supported Committee hearings on the functioning of the 1992 legislation. An interim report was issued by the Committee in August 1995.

The Department of Finance has also held wide-ranging consultations with a variety of stakeholders. In March 1995, interested parties were invited to provide written comments on any aspects of the four financial institutions statutes. The department received over 30 written briefs. Discussions were held with most submitting parties, including consumer groups, industry and trade associations, professional societies, and individual firms.

---

[1] Developments in the Financial Services Industry Since Financial Sector Legislative Reform.

The primary conclusion of these consultations is that the legislative framework established in 1992 is generally working well. Most observers continue to support the broad objectives of the 1992 reform and believe that the legislative framework remains appropriate.

That being said, one of the important issues discussed in the course of these consultations is the state of competition in the Canadian financial sector, with some stakeholders suggesting that concentration in the hands of a few large institutions has reduced competitive forces. While the level of concentration may have increased over the past 10 years, there is no concrete evidence suggesting that this increase has had a negative impact on the state of competition.

Nonetheless, there have been representations raising this possibility. For example, a number of independent securities dealers have suggested that preferential treatment given to bank-owned dealers in the provision of standby and subordinated loans has reduced competition. Consideration will be given to the nature and the extent of these alleged problems and, if warranted, to their solutions. However, the government believes that a major overhaul to address concentration is not needed. The government is of the view that the legislative framework established in 1992 is generally working well and should be kept largely intact.

Another issue which has dominated the consultations is the marketing of insurance products by deposit-taking institutions through their branches. As announced in the *1996 Budget Speech*, the government has decided to maintain existing restrictions in that area. The government recognizes that the financial sector is still digesting many of the changes flowing from the extensive reform of the financial institutions legislation in 1992. The pressures of competition and rationalization are continuing today.

Stakeholders have pointed to several other areas where they would like to see changes. Consumer groups are asking the government to strengthen consumer protection provisions. Financial institutions have also noted a number of provisions in the legislation which do not function as well as intended or are not in keeping with industry trends. Stakeholders have also proposed changes to the *Canadian Payments Association Act* which is not expiring in 1997 but which has an impact on the operations of federal financial institutions.

The government recognizes that the issues raised are important and have significant implications for the smooth functioning of the financial sector. It also recognizes that the *Canadian Payments Association Act* has not been reviewed since 1980, and that the payments system landscape has changed dramatically since then.

After extensive consultation and detailed analysis, the government has decided that a number of important adjustments should be made. These adjustments would serve to:

- **strengthen consumer protection,**
- **ease the regulatory burden on financial institutions, and**
- **keep the legislation current with evolving trends.**

The government is also of the view that analysis of the regulatory framework of the payments system is warranted.

Specific proposals to strengthen consumer protection, and simplify and update legislation are outlined in the following chapters. Additional information about payments system issues is presented in Chapter 5.

At the same time, the government recognizes that there are broad trends at play, such as globalization of financial services markets, technological advances and a changing competitive landscape. In this environment of constant evolution, fundamental questions (brought forth by stakeholders on the structure of the industry and the role played by financial institutions) must all be addressed to ensure that we have the most efficient, secure and competitive financial sector for the next century. These fundamental questions are complex and must be addressed in a broad context.

Given the complexity of the task, the government will undertake a comprehensive review of the appropriate framework for the financial sector in the 21st century — one that will promote economic growth and job creation. A Task Force on the Future of the Canadian Financial Services Sector will be established to provide advice to the government on public policy issues related to the development of the framework. This study will shape the next round of amendments to the legislation which the government proposes take place no later than five years after the passage of the 1997 legislation.

CHAPTER 2

STRENGTHENING CONSUMER PROTECTION

The nature of the relationship between financial institutions and their clients is constantly evolving, due largely to the diversification of financial services and the ever-increasing use of technology in providing financial services.

In this context, consumers have expressed a desire for better protection in their dealings with financial institutions. This chapter describes proposals designed to provide that protection.

Privacy Safeguards

The protection of personal information is of utmost importance to this government. In today's environment, where technological advances permit easier access to and analysis of personal data, the government recognizes the importance to consumers of knowing why information is collected and how it will be used and stored. Consent is key if information is to be used for a new purpose or disclosed to outside parties. The government also understands that consumers want access to information held about them, and rights of recourse if information is misused.

Together with consumer and business groups, government representatives recently participated in the development of the Canadian Standards Association's (CSA) new Model Code for the Protection of Personal Information. The code represents considerable progress from previous practice.

In the financial sector, the collection and handling of personal information is a significant issue. Financial institutions rely on extensive amounts of often-sensitive information to market their services. The government acknowledges the efforts made by financial institutions to address privacy concerns over the past few years, including their participation in the development of the CSA code. The government intends to build on these successes with further improvements.

At the same time, any action in the financial services area should be consistent with the federal government's broader approach for privacy protection. The government recently announced that it is developing proposals for a legislative framework to protect personal data. At this time, the government wishes to take the opportunity of the review of the financial institutions legislation to take action on specific issues of concern to consumers of financial services.

The government proposes to introduce regulations governing the collection, use, retention, and disclosure of customer information by federal financial institutions.

More specifically, financial institutions would be required to:

- adopt a code of conduct governing the collection, use, retention and disclosure of information. The government encourages financial institutions to use the CSA code as a minimum standard in formulating their codes of conduct;

- designate a senior-level officer in each financial institution to implement procedures for dealing with consumer complaints;

- provide customers with written information on their privacy code and details of how customers can make complaints;

- report annually on the complaints received and the actions taken to respond to these complaints.

The Cost of Basic Financial Services

Consumers have raised concerns about the various service charges imposed by financial institutions and the difficulty of comparing charges across deposit-taking institutions. Banks and trust and loan companies currently offer a wide range of accounts to meet the different needs of consumers, including a variety of "no-frills" accounts with minimal charges. For example, most deposit-taking institutions offer accounts with unlimited free deposits and a number of free withdrawals monthly (varying from two to six). But many institutions also offer low-cost, monthly fixed fee packages with additional services.

It is the responsibility of consumers to determine the account that best meets their needs. But the government recognizes that comparing charges can be difficult.

The government will work with banks and trust and loan companies to simplify and improve the dissemination of information about fees.

The Availability of Basic Financial Services

At times, low-income individuals have difficulty accessing basic financial services, such as opening accounts and cashing cheques. Financial institutions' policies often mean that many individuals cannot qualify for basic financial services or find these services impractical. For example, identification requirements can exclude people who do not have a credit card or a driver's license. The financial services community is aware of these problems, and discussions are underway to address them.

The government will work with consumer and community groups as well as financial institutions to develop and implement a strategy to improve access to financial services for low-income Canadians.

Cost of Credit Disclosure

As part of the Internal Trade Initiative, federal and provincial governments are committed to harmonizing legislation dealing with the disclosure of the cost of credit for consumers. Federal and provincial governments are now finalizing proposals in this regard. The harmonization exercise is expected to benefit both consumers and lenders through enhanced and uniform disclosure practices across the country.

Following an agreement with the provinces, the federal government will amend the provisions on cost of credit disclosure in the financial institutions statutes.

Tied Selling

Choice, quality, and competitive prices are some of the benefits derived from a competitive, market-driven economy. However, market forces alone cannot always ensure competitive conduct. Effective competition laws are also needed.

The *Competition Act* provides a framework for business conduct in Canada. The Act provides for, among other things, remedies where firms engage in anti-competitive behaviour, which may involve tied selling. Tied selling occurs when a firm requires a customer to buy one product as a condition of purchasing another one. This could occur as a result of coercion. Alternatively, a firm might provide a lower price on one product if the customer buys another product and this could be beneficial to the consumer. If the Competition Tribunal finds that tied selling is lessening competition substantially, it may issue an appropriate order necessary to restore or stimulate competition.

The government believes that a balanced approach helps to achieve a competitive process in the marketplace. The approach recognizes that the offering of discounts and packages is beneficial to consumers who can acquire a series of products at cheaper prices than if they were purchasing them individually. It also recognizes that market forces generally prevent firms from forcing consumers to buy products that they do not want. However, the approach does not guarantee that firms will never attempt to coerce consumers into buying a product as a condition of purchasing another product, a behaviour that is obviously not to the advantage of consumers.

Concerns have been raised that the special nature of the relationship between financial institutions and their customers renders their customers especially vulnerable to coercion, and that market forces and the *Competition Act* may not provide sufficient safeguards for these consumers.

The government is prepared to explore with consumer groups, financial institutions, and other interested parties whether stronger measures are needed to protect consumers of financial products from coercion, and, if so, whether these measures could be implemented in a way that would not deny consumers the benefits of discounts and packaging of financial products.

Right to Prepay Mortgages

Current federal policy regarding loan prepayment differs according to the length of the mortgage term. Prepayment rights and penalties are legislated for mortgages with terms of more than five years, but not for those with terms of five years or less. This means that lenders do not have to offer prepayment of mortgages of five years or less, and can set penalties as they choose if they allow prepayment.

Concerns have been raised by consumers and other groups about this lack of legislation. Conversely, the maximum penalty in the *Interest Act* for mortgage terms of more than five years — three-months interest — is seen as inadequate by lenders to compensate for the risk of interest rate movements. It has been cited as a deterrent to the development of a longer-term mortgage market.

The government is prepared to consider amending the *Interest Act* to provide prepayment rights and a standardized approach to calculating maximum mortgage prepayment penalties for all new mortgages, regardless of the term. The government is also prepared to consider amending the financial institutions statutes to provide more explicit disclosure requirements for mortgage prepayment.

The government believes that these issues warrant further investigation and comment by consumer groups, mortgage providers and other interested parties to ensure that both borrowers and lenders are treated fairly.

Summary

As noted, consultations on the proposals listed above have and will take place. But the general direction of change is clear. The government will move forcefully to better protect the interests of consumers in their dealings with financial institutions. In particular, consumer privacy safeguards will be strengthened.

CHAPTER 3

EASING THE REGULATORY BURDEN ON FINANCIAL INSTITUTIONS

There is no question that regulations are required in the financial sector. Regulations not only protect the consumer, they set out the rules of the game so that the sector can operate smoothly. Having said this, there are a number of areas where regulations are not functioning as well as intended and should be simplified to ease the regulatory burden.

As stated in the February 27, 1996 Speech from the Throne, the government is committed to taking appropriate action to promote a proper climate for economic growth and jobs. In particular, the government wants to ensure that regulatory requirements are clearly defined, and that delays are minimized when regulatory approvals are required for businesses.

In this regard, there are five areas in the financial sector on which the government is focusing. These are: overlap and duplication between federal and provincial regulation; the self-dealing regime; the requirement to establish subsidiaries to carry on certain activities; the ability of opting out of the Canadian Deposit Insurance Corporation (CDIC) membership; and, the foreign bank entry regime.

In addition, the government is conducting a review of the approval process which will deal with the number of approvals required and who must provide them. This review will also lead to some technical changes designed to streamline administration of and compliance with the Acts.

Overlap and Duplication Between Federal and Provincial Regulation

The government continues to support reducing overlap and duplication in Canadian financial sector regulation, and is prepared to take action to meet this objective. Regarding the trust and loan sector, the government is committed to the ongoing harmonization discussions with the provinces. Some progress has been made over the past year in this area, and in order to encourage these discussions to a successful conclusion, the government proposes to amend the *Trust and Loan Companies Act* to reflect the work so far. For example, the government is prepared to refine the definition of a commercial loan to reflect agreement with the provinces on a harmonized definition. Discussions with the provinces will continue through 1996, and it is hoped that further progress can be made.

Another area of interest is Canadian securities regulation. At present, Canadian securities markets are subject to thirteen regulatory jurisdictions. The government is prepared to work with interested provinces towards the development of a Canadian Securities Commission. The establishment of such a Commission would promote efficient Canadian capital markets, reduce the cost of distributing securities and enhance the competitiveness of Canadian companies.

A third area relates to co-operative credit associations. The federal government regulates the Credit Union Central of Canada and some provincial credit union centrals. The provinces regulate local credit unions and their provincial centrals. At present, there are six provincial credit union centrals (in British Columbia, Alberta, Saskatchewan, Manitoba, Ontario and Nova Scotia) which are registered under the federal *Cooperative Credit Associations Act*, an obvious example of overlap and duplication between federal and provincial regulation.

The federal government is prepared to explore with the provincial governments the possibility of amending the *Cooperative Credit Associations Act* to end federal regulation of provincial credit union centrals.

Self-Dealing Regime

A key part of the 1992 reform was the implementation of comprehensive controls on transactions between a financial institution and persons who are in positions of influence over, or control of, the institution (commonly known as the "self-dealing" regime). While the government believes that the basic framework remains sound, it agrees with the financial services industry that certain provisions of the regime have proven impractical and have imposed unnecessary costs on many financial institutions.

The government proposes a number of changes to streamline the self-dealing regime. These changes involve streamlining the operations of the Conduct Review Committee that has to be established by the board of each financial institution, narrowing the range of related parties, and allowing subsidiaries of a federal financial institution to transact with each other. Details are provided in Annex A.

Subsidiary Requirements

Under the current legislation, financial institutions can engage in certain types of business only through subsidiaries. The requirement to establish subsidiaries reflects various considerations, including the government's policy of maintaining a separation between the core activities of the different types of financial institutions as well as risk containment.

Financial institutions have asked that the requirement to establish subsidiaries for certain activities be removed to reduce costs to their operations. The government has reviewed the types of business that can only be carried out through subsidiaries, and concluded that the existing requirement could be relaxed for certain activities.

The government proposes to permit financial institutions to carry on both information processing and specialized financing activities in-house.

Allowing in-house specialized financing activities would enable financial institutions to manage their venture capital support for small business more cost-effectively and should therefore generate increased funding for this important sector. Other prudential rules currently applying to specialized financing activities would be maintained, with one exception. The rule requiring investments to be sold within 10 years would be extended to 13 years to allow greater flexibility for financial institutions to provide ongoing support to emerging companies.

Deposit Insurance Opt-Out

Foreign banks which specialize in serving large corporate customers have asked the government to allow them to apply for exemption from the current

CDIC coverage. The rationale for allowing financial institutions serving the wholesale market to "opt out" of CDIC coverage is that the vast majority of their deposits are corporate accounts, with balances well in excess of the maximum for insurable deposits.

One of the key issues is how to define which institutions would qualify for the exemption. This could be done on the basis of the size of the deposit (e.g., over $200,000), the type of depositor (e.g., corporation, non-resident), or some combination of these two criteria. In designing the exemption regime, it would be important to ensure that consumers are informed of the uninsured status of deposits with exempt institutions, and that an appropriate transition framework is established for current CDIC member institutions which are granted an exemption.

The government proposes to allow financial institutions that do not take retail deposits to "opt out" of CDIC coverage, provided they are not affiliated with another CDIC member. The conditions under which financial institutions could make use of this provision will be discussed with affected parties.

Foreign Bank Entry Regime

Currently, the operations of foreign banks in Canada are governed by a series of rules which cover, among other things, the types of financial services they can offer and when regulatory approvals are required. Foreign entities have asked that some of these requirements be reviewed to reduce the regulatory burden they face and to ensure consistent treatment with domestic institutions.

The government proposes to modify its entry policy as follows:

For regulation foreign banks — entities which are regulated as banks in their home jurisdiction and for whom banking services constitute a large part of their operations — the key features would be:

- **They would be permitted to carry on financial services activities in Canada only through subsidiaries which are federally regulated financial institutions. The one exception to this would be securities activities carried out by an entity that is subject to the regulatory** regime applicable to these activities. Regulated foreign banks would have to seek the approval of the Minister of Finance prior to commencing operations in Canada.

- A regulated foreign bank which owns a Schedule II bank would no longer be required to hold other financial institution subsidiaries through the Schedule II bank. For example, a regulated foreign bank or bank holding company would be able to control its Canadian securities dealer affiliate as part of its foreign securities subsidiaries, separate from its banking subsidiaries in Canada and abroad. Appropriate undertakings would be required for access to information for supervisory purposes.

For "near banks" — entities which do not generally take deposits, are not regulated as banks in their home jurisdiction, but provide one or more banking-type services (e.g., consumer loans) — the key features would be:

- Once they have received approval under the *Bank Act* to enter the Canadian market, no further approvals would be required provided that their unregulated activities remain outside of retail funding.

- They would be allowed to hold any non-bank financial institution.

The existing Canadian operations of some foreign banks may be affected by these changes. The government understands the importance of having adequate transitional arrangements and will be discussing these arrangements with affected companies.

CHAPTER 4

FINE-TUNING THE LEGISLATION

There are a number of areas where changes were made in 1992, but where adjustments are required because the legislation is not working as well as it should. Changes are also necessary in other areas to keep the legislation current with evolving trends. This chapter describes key proposals to keep the financial sector legislation up-to-date.

Corporate Governance

1) General Provisions

The corporate governance provisions of the financial institutions statutes were updated in 1992, and are generally considered to be working well. Indeed, some of the rules introduced in the financial institutions statutes in 1992 have now become the norm for companies listed on the Toronto Stock Exchange.

The government proposes a number of changes in the area of corporate governance to encourage financial institutions to adopt appropriate corporate governance processes to manage risk, and to keep the legislation current with evolving standards.

The Office of the Superintendent of Financial Institutions (OSFI) will promote "best practices" for corporate governance and perform additional assessments of the effectiveness of corporate governance processes implemented by financial institutions. A best practices paper will be developed by OSFI addressing, among other things, the need for financial institutions to have appropriate structures and procedures in place to ensure that the board of directors can function independently from management. For example, at the option of the financial institution, the board of directors could appoint a chair of the board who is not a member of management. Alternatively, the board of directors could rely on a formal outside "lead director", or some other equivalent process.

It has been suggested that the statutory duty of the audit committee to "ensure that appropriate internal control procedures are in place" is vague, and that its effectiveness would be enhanced with better direction as to what is expected from the committee. The government proposes to clarify the statutory duty. The audit committee would require management to implement and maintain appropriate internal control procedures. In addition, the committee would review, evaluate and approve the internal controls of the financial institution.

It is also proposed that the circumstances under which a person is considered affiliated with a financial institution be expanded to include significant participants in share option schemes or pension plans, former Chief Executive Officers for a period of time, as well as directors of significant borrowers. This change would bring the concept of "unaffiliated director" flowing from the financial institutions legislation more in line with the definition of "independent director" recently developed for companies listed on the Toronto Stock Exchange.

In addition, the government proposes to allow the board of directors to conduct business by resolutions signed by all directors, in lieu of a board meeting. A minimum number of board meetings would have to take place.

Financial institutions increasingly have financial institution subsidiaries in different businesses. Transfers of assets between parent and subsidiary could benefit one group of creditors or one consumer protection plan at the expense of others. Yet, currently, the boards of directors of the parent and subsidiary institution which approve the transaction can be identical. Consideration is being given to limiting the use of these "mirror" boards where the financial institution's business is unlike the business of its parent.

There are a number of areas where changes are not proposed because they are currently under review in other fora. The government will follow these discussions closely. Upon conclusion of these discussions, the government will decide whether legislative amendments to the financial institutions statutes should be proposed. A short description of these areas is provided in Annex A.

2) Policyholders' Rights

In 1992, the rights of policyholders entitled to vote were substantially modernized. The new system recognizes that policyholders are not identical to shareholders. It also recognizes the costs of sending notices to a large number of policyholders, which may not even be of interest to many policyholders. In addition, the regime is designed so that a few policyholders cannot, by themselves, force fundamental changes in a mutual company. Overall, the system put in place in 1992 is working well and no major changes are proposed.

However, the government believes that it would be desirable to facilitate the disclosure of information and the participation of policyholders who are interested in the affairs of their companies. To this end, a number of proposals have been developed which will be the subject of further consultation with industry. These are contained in Annex B [not reproduced].

Joint Venture Arrangements

Joint venture arrangements can be extremely useful mechanisms for financial institutions wishing to expand into new areas of business. They are, however, currently subject to a number of rules which the financial services industry finds unduly restrictive. For example, there is a requirement that the eligible joint venture be controlled by a financial institution. Financial institutions claim that this requirement places them at a competitive disadvantage in foreign operations where their competitors have more flexibility for these types of arrangements. In its 1995 *Interim Report on the 1992 Financial Institutions Legislation*, the Standing Senate Committee on Banking, Trade, and Commerce identified the joint venture rules as an area where regulations inhibit competitiveness.

The government proposes to provide more flexibility to financial institutions seeking to enter into joint venture arrangements by removing the requirement that the eligible joint venture be controlled in fact by a financial institution. Details are provided in Annex B [not reproduced].

The proposed changes would enhance the ability of financial institutions to make alliances, enter new markets, and compete more effectively in Canada and abroad.

Access to Capital for Mutual Insurance Companies

Access to capital is key to the ability of mutual insurance companies to compete in Canada and abroad. In 1992, two measures were introduced in this regard. First, mutual companies were permitted to issue preferred shares. Second, small mutual life companies were allowed to "demutualize" or convert into stock companies.

Concerns have been expressed about the adequacy of these measures. Being restricted to preferred share financing is considered too inflexible to allow companies to respond to the changing needs and demands of the market. The process small mutual life insurance companies currently must follow to convert into stock companies is seen as complex and lengthy. Larger mutual life insurance companies have asked that a process for demutualization be introduced for them as well.

The government proposes a number of changes to enhance access to capital for mutual insurance companies. First, they will be permitted to issue participating shares. Second, the demutualization regime will be extended to apply to all mutual life companies, and added flexibility will be provided. Details are provided in Annex A.

Taking of Security Interest

Currently, there are inconsistencies between the *Bank Act* provisions and provincial security legislation relating to the taking of security interest. A working group has been established to examine whether legislative changes can be made to address these differences. The working group is expected to report shortly. The government will review the recommendations of the working group, and will consider legislative changes if a consensus is achieved.

Amendments to the *Bank of Canada Act*

The government proposes to use the opportunity of the legislative review to consider a limited number of technical amendments to the *Bank of Canada Act* to remove outdated impediments to certain activities of the Bank. For example, the changes include modernizing the range of instruments which the Bank may buy and sell; clarifying the ability of the Bank to carry on ancillary activities such as licensing anti-counterfeiting technology; and changing the threshold whereby unclaimed balances in deposit accounts that have been inactive for more than 20 years are sent to the Receiver General.

CHAPTER 5

REVIEWING THE PAYMENTS SYSTEM

A safe and sound payments system is a vital part of the operations of a modern sophisticated economy. Canada's payments system is administered by the Canadian Payments Association (CPA) which was established by legislation in 1980. Canada has one of the best paper-based payments systems in the world. However, the increasing use of technology is changing the payments system landscape, and it has been suggested that the framework developed twenty years ago should be reviewed.

For example, interested parties who have not traditionally played a significant role in the payments system would now like the opportunity to provide input into the future development of the system. Also, there have been recent concerns about whether or not Canada's payments system provides sufficient opportunity for competition and innovation.

The government recognizes that opening up the payments system to new players could introduce new risks to the system. Accordingly, it is critical that possible modifications to the payments system be examined carefully to ensure that the integrity of the system is not compromised.

Given the importance and the complexity of these issues, the Department of Finance will establish an advisory committee with a range of expertise in payments issues, including industry participants, academics, consumers, and other key users of the payments system. It is expected that the Department of Finance advisory committee will contribute significantly to the Task Force's work on the development of a suitable framework for the financial sector in the 21st century.

As part of its work on payments system issues, the Department of Finance will further explore its concern with unregulated entities issuing payment items permitting them to have indirect access to the payments system. These items, commonly known as payable-through drafts, are payment items that clear through the payments system via a CPA member. When issued by a non-CPA member, the decision to honour these items rests with the non-CPA member who may be an unregulated entity. Payable-through draft arrangements could have negative implications for the financial system. Accordingly, those who are contemplating entering into such arrangements should consider carefully the implications of doing so.

The government acknowledges that interested parties have a stake in rules made by the CPA, and recognizes the importance of the CPA's consultative processes. While a number of mechanisms have been put in place by the CPA to obtain the input of interested parties, more needs to be done. Accordingly, the government is calling upon the CPA to enhance its consultative mechanisms as soon as possible in order to ensure that the voices of all interested parties are heard.

CHAPTER 6

NEXT STEPS

The government has consulted extensively on most of the areas covered in this paper. The consultations helped shape the proposals.

The government is confident that the proposals for change are sound and will serve the best interests of the consumer and the financial sector. It welcomes comments on the details of the proposals to assist in the drafting of the required legislation.

Written comments regarding any element of this paper are invited and should be directed to the Financial Sector Division, Department of Finance, by August 30, 1996. All written comments received will be made available upon request to interested parties.

ANNEX A

SUPPLEMENTS TO CHAPTERS 3 AND 4

The following provides more detailed information on some of the proposals presented in Chapters 3 and 4 of the main document.

Self-Dealing Regime

The industry has indicated concerns with respect to the Conduct Review Committee that has to be established by the board of each financial institution. Currently, this Committee must approve in advance virtually all transactions with related parties. This is viewed as impractical. To address these concerns, the government proposes to refocus the role of the Conduct Review Committee. The Committee would have to establish appropriate internal procedures to comply with the self-dealing provisions, but would not have to review individual transactions. As is currently the case, the board of directors would continue to report annually to the Superintendent of Financial Institutions on the proceedings of the Conduct Review Committee.

It has been suggested that the definition of a related party (i.e. a person considered to be in a position of influence over the institution) is too broad. Under the current definition, many institutions have several thousand related parties. The requirement to maintain an up-to-date list of these related parties imposes a significant administrative burden for these institutions without, in many instances, conferring any real benefits — because transactions are unlikely to occur with many of the related parties, or be of any significance for the institution. Thus, the government proposes to narrow the definition of who is a related party as follows:

- Officers would only be considered related parties when they are the most senior officers of an entity. Currently all officers of a financial institution and of any entity which controls a financial institution are related parties.

- The business interests of natural persons who are related parties only because they are directors or officers would be related parties only when they are controlled by the natural person. Currently the business interests of these natural persons are related parties even if the natural person has only a substantial investment in the business rather than a controlling interest. The business interests of persons related because they are principal owners would remain as related parties down to the level of a substantial investment.

- The rule that deems a person to be a related party for one year after the person has ceased to be a related party would be eliminated.

The government proposes that transactions between subsidiaries of a federally regulated financial institution no longer be subject to the self-dealing regime. This means that subsidiaries of a given institution would not be considered related parties. The self-dealing regime would continue to apply to transactions between a financial institution or any of its subsidiaries with related parties of the financial institution such as owners, officers and directors and their business interests.

Corporate Governance

As noted in Chapter 4, there are areas where changes are not proposed because they are currently under review in other fora. The government will follow these discussions closely. Upon conclusion of these discussions, the government will decide whether or not legislative amendments should be proposed.

The first area relates to civil liability for continuous disclosure. The Interim Report of the Toronto Stock Exchange Committee recommends that issuers and others who are responsible for continuous disclosure that is misleading be liable in civil actions.

There have also been representations to change the liability of auditors and actuaries from joint and several liability to a regime of liability proportionate to the defendant fault in causing damage. Although these may have merit, any changes to the requirements for financial institutions should be postponed until the preferred approach for business corporations generally is developed.

Finally, directors and officers have a duty to act in the best interests of the company. There is a view that this duty could be extended to other stake-holders, such as depositors and policyholders. In light of emerging trends in corporate law, it would be premature to expend directors' and officers' statutory duties. The government will be conducting further consultations on this issue.

Access to Capital for Mutual Insurance Companies

1) Share Financing

The government proposes to permit mutual insurance companies to issue participating shares with the following terms:

- Shareholders would be allowed to participate in the ongoing earnings of a mutual company on a basis proportional to their capital investment. Shareholders would also be entitled, on dissolution of a company, to the portion of the remaining property of the company attributable to the shares.

- These shares could confer on the holder the right to vote at meetings of the company in the event that a specified event has occurred or a specified condition has been fulfilled. In addition, shareholders would have the right to vote on certain "fundamental changes" affecting the company, such as amalgamation proposals.

- Companies would be required to establish a method for allocating earnings and expenses between policyholders and shareholders and the appointed actuary of the company would be required to opine on the fairness and equity of the allocation method. The method and the opinion would be filed with OSFI.

2) Demutualization

The demutualization regulations embody a number of key principles which are important to guiding the demutualization process, and which would be retained. These include a requirement to place a fair value on the company and to allocate that value to policyholders, along with a requirement that an independent expert provide an opinion on the fairness and equity of the value placed on the company and on the method and assumptions used to calculate that value. An independent actuary's opinion on the fairness and equity of the nature, amount and value of benefits to be provided to policyholders is also required. At the same time, it is recognized that more flexibility could be added to the regulations, for example, to remove the three-year restriction on issuing shares with conversion privileges to directors, officers and employees of the converted company. As well, the wording of the regulations would be altered to clarify that the value to be placed on the company should reflect prevailing market conditions.

As is contemplated in the current legislation, the larger mutual life insurance companies would be required to remain widely held after a conversion. Regulations to define the meaning of "widely held" would be promulgated to clarify that no person may have a significant interest in the converted company.

It is proposed that more flexibility be added to the demutualization regime in two other ways. First, the Superintendent would have the authority to exempt companies from specific aspects of the regulations on a case-by-case basis (e.g., documentation to be provided to policyholders). Second, the Minister of Finance would have the authority to exempt companies in financial distress from any aspect of the demutualization process. This authority could improve the chances of a company in financial distress finding a strategic partner and remaining a going concern, where appropriate. The government will consult with mutual life insurance companies on these proposed changes and on whether additional flexibility in the regulations is needed to accommodate other types of capital raising transactions.

ANNEX 2

CANADIAN FINANCIAL REGULATION:
A System in Transition

by Edwin H. Neave

Since the mid-1970s, financial industry changes have stimulated legislative revision in most of the world's principal regulatory jurisdictions. In Canada as in other countries, the financial services industry has changed dramatically during the past quarter-century as developments in computing and communications, increasing trade, and increased exchange rate volatility have contributed to a global explosion of financial innovation. There is now interindustry competition, both domestic and international, for the same clientele. Organizational changes within the financial system have attenuated the former distinctiveness of the banking, insurance, trust, and brokerage industries, as for some time now each of these industries has been making incursions into what were formerly others' principal territories. The system continues to change rapidly; indeed, the pace of structural change may even be increasing.

In this context of sweeping change, regulatory revision matters for several reasons. Changes to legislation affect the composition of the financial services industry, its profitability, the wealth positions of shareholders, and the

This article originally appeared as *Canadian Financial Regulation: A System in Transition*, C.D. Howe Institute Commentary 78 (Toronto: C.D. Howe Institute, March 1996), and is reprinted by permission of the C.D. Howe Institute.

well-being of other stakeholders. Well-framed regulation can also help guide the system's continuing evolution, chiefly by attempting to enhance competition while preserving system safety and soundness. The task is a delicate one because the freedom of both entry and exit implied by vigorous competition are not always compatible with safety and soundness.

This *Commentary* analyzes economic issues pertinent to the proposed 1997 revisions of the *Bank Act* and related legislation. In particular, since Canada has witnessed a spate of costly financial failures over the past decade, it is useful to ask whether the proposed revisions might lessen the possibility of future failures. I will not argue that regulation either can or should try to prevent failure, but legislative revision can influence both the likelihood of failure and the costs of those failures which do occur. Legislative revision can encourage good governance by ensuring that unusually risky management policies receive full publicity as early as possible. It can also aim to ensure that the consequences of unwise decisions will be borne by the decisionmakers and investors responsible for them.

As to the stakes involved, the efficiency and safety of Canada's financial services industry are of key importance to Canadian households and businesses. The industry employs several hundred thousand persons and generates profits on the order of $10 billion annually. Canadian financial services are highly regarded throughout the world, as are the professional educational services provided by organizations like the Institute of Canadian Bankers. Greater efforts to sell Canada's operating and educational expertise abroad offer a potential means of increasing the nation's export earnings.

This *Commentary's* principal tasks are to identify the issues most likely to inform debate regarding the proposed revisions[1] and to analyze the economics of different policies for dealing with the issues. It begins by discussing the principal economic forces shaping today's financial services industry. This is followed by an outline of how strategic issues are likely to be viewed from the differing perspectives of management, supervisory authorities, monetary authorities, system clients, and shareholders. Then come a sketch of the paper's theoretical underpinnings, a statement of the principles used to apply the theory, and a discussion of the economic arguments relevant to each of the major issues. The final section lists policy conclusions based on the economic arguments. Since the factors involved differ from one issue to the next, not all conclusions are reached with the same degree of finality.

Today's Financial Services Industry

Today's financial services industry is best analyzed in terms of functions and the economic environment in which they are performed. This section first outlines financial system functions, then shows that financial markets are becoming more integrated on a worldwide basis. However, the integration is not universal — fragmentation of smaller, particularly local, markets persists. Finally, to shed some light on the forces driving financial system restructuring, the section examines financial firms' revenue and cost structures.

Functions

The financial services industry performs four basic functions, each of which can be further subdivided. First, financial intermediaries[2] (FIs) gather up savings, both from unsophisticated consumers and from sophisticated corporate clients. The proportions of retail and wholesale business vary according to the kind of intermediary involved, but for both types of client the financial system acts to store funds safely and to provide a reasonable return on savers' balances.

Second, most FIs act as lenders or investors at retail or wholesale levels, again in varying proportions according to the specialized nature of the intermediary involved. Some FIs provide consumer credit and retail mortgage loans, others lend to firms and governments at the corporate and wholesale levels, some combine both functions. Both FIs and the securities markets provide longer-term funds for financing business activity, but in most western countries (including the United States), the amount of new capital formation financed by intermediaries still exceeds that financed by securities market issues.

Third, the financial industry provides a variety of retail and corporate services. An example of a retail service is helping consumers with risk management through selling them insurance and investment advice, the latter often being accompanied by securities trading services. Examples of corporate services include selling information to corporations, assisting corporate risk management through financial engineering and derivatives trading, and providing advice and assistance with mergers and acquisitions. The contribution of service fees to intermediaries' revenue is increasing, and in some countries services income now roughly equals net interest revenue.

Fourth, banks and other depository intermediaries play a special role, issuing readily transferable deposit liabilities that are used as means of payment. Both the soundness of the institutions holding the balances serving as means of payment and the media through which payments are actually effected are of concern to the policy analyst.

It is useful to list basic financial functions because the intermediaries performing the functions and the traditional forms by which they are delivered are both changing. The former four pillars of the financial services industry — the banking, insurance, securities, and trustee businesses — have been substantially replaced by multipurpose institutions. In some regulatory jurisdictions, banks now perform the traditional trading functions of securities brokers, some of the traditional risk management functions of insurers, and some of the financial activities formerly associated with international investment banking, and insurance companies or their affiliates actively solicit deposit business. Trustee and banking activities are also coming closer together, although regulatory firewalls continue, and appropriately so, to separate potential conflicts between these latter businesses. Whether or not they are organized as individual companies is less important. In related developments, traditionally nonfinancial corporations increasingly offer such financial products as loans and credit cards.

In addition to shifting boundaries between traditional sectors, the financial system is witnessing a rapid shift toward greater use of communications media, particularly electronic forms. Financial products are now sometimes marketed by telephone, sometimes (principally on a test basis so far) through electronic networks. In addition, the convenience of using transferable deposits as means of payment continues to grow as both cash and paper cheques are increasingly replaced by electronic funds transfers.

In Canada, an increasing proportion of retail funds transfers uses the Interac network. These transfers currently take the forms of cash withdrawals and debit card payments to merchants. In the future, computer-driven transfers using either Interac or the Internet seem likely to become of increasing competitive importance. These changes increase the importance of access to transactions media and re-emphasize the importance of underlying settlement mechanisms. Whatever the medium of the original transfer — paper cheques, Interac, or Internet transactions — net interinstitutional balances are still settled through the Canadian Payments System.

Integration and Segmentation

The influence of technological change is worldwide, and financial institutions increasingly are crossing national boundaries to offer both retail and corporate financial products.[3] However, change is restricted neither to merging nor to crossing traditional boundaries, industrial or national. Formerly segmented markets are becoming more closely integrated as arbitraging and intermediation continue to increase. As an example of the former, international currency arbitraging has subjected the foreign exchange and associated derivatives markets to intense competition. As an example of the latter, investment banks such as Goldman Sachs or Morgan Stanley (the so-called bulge bracket firms) compete fiercely for various forms of international merchant banking and securities business. Some larger banks' affiliates, such as Deutsche Morgan, now compete with the investment banks for the same forms of international business.

While the linkages between markets are increasing, the changes are by no means uniform — the world's financial system exhibits widely varying degrees of integration between its different markets. Competition in domestic or local markets served by one or a few financial services firms differs in degree from competition in the international markets, and some domestic markets may have less effective competition. On the other hand, the trend toward further integration may expand to presently fragmented markets as access to the financial system through telephone, television, and other electronic media becomes increasingly popular. The new forms of delivery mean that transaction costs no longer increase with distance between the transacting parties, making it possible for small as well as large firms to reach the same consumers, almost regardless of where they are located, at relatively low cost.

Organizational Change

Economics drives financial system change as technological and mangerial developments provide new ways of meeting clients' demands for better and less costly services. Management restructures firms to try to secure new sources of revenue, new forms of cost reduction, or both.[4] The formation of financial supermarkets, the growth of large international investment banks, and recent merger activity in several countries all represent attempts to exploit combinations of these possibilities.

Recent reorganization has usually meant increased institutional size and sometimes new combinations of functions. For example, over the past decade, Canada's banking industry has absorbed many failing trust companies, and has maintained domestic ownership of securities firms. Insurance companies are also combining as evidenced by the recent acquisition of North American Life by Manulife. The effects are not peculiar to Canada: bank mergers are commonplace in both the United States and the United Kingdom. In the United States, the long-awaited removal of Glass-Steagall prohibitions against combining banking and the securities business once again appears likely; while the United Kingdom has just witnessed the merging of Lloyds Bank and the Trustee Savings Bank, creating a financial firm with assets of just under US$240 billion. A recent press report (*Globe and Mail*, November 7, 1995) suggests that bank mergers are being actively discussed in Japan as well.

It is relatively easy to explain mergers based on attempts to enhance market access, to cut costs, or to restructure failing firms. In other cases, however, the driving forces are more difficult to identify. Sometimes, mergers are driven by attempts to increase the resulting firm's access to long-term funds or even to new capital, usually on the grounds that greater financial resources will enhance competitive ability. Other mergers represent attempts to effect geographical diversification and thus reduce lending risk.

Restructuring is not limited to acquiring other firms. Throughout the world, the financial services industry is shedding excess capacity that has resulted from technological change. Increasing productivity of computing and communications equipment has changed the industry's optimal labor-capital ratios, and worldwide the industry is showing sharply declining total employment. Excess physical capacity for serving retail and corporate clients is also emerging as the role of the branch office is diminished by increasingly popular forms of electronic delivery. In the future, those branches which remain open will have to market broader ranges of products if they are to remain economically viable units.

Technological change is driving back office as well as front office reorganization, as new forms of transacting and data processing create either reduced demands for capacity expansion or excess installed capacity. For example, recent growth in Interac electronic transactions has replaced previous continuing growth in paper transactions. Since some data-processing facilities were built to meet forecasts of further growth in paper clearings, Canada probably now has more centralized data-processing capacity than is economic. In addition to simply shedding excess capacity, it seems likely that financial firms will experiment with merging data-processing services, renting out facilities, and using them for such other purposes as providing information to clients. Until restructuring occurs, the cost of excess capacity is being borne by the industry.

Increasing use of smart cards may reduce demands for centralized data processing still further, both by eliminating some accounting for individual transaction, and by reducing the need for clearing small items. Once an intermediary has "charged" a smart card, subsequent withdrawals need only be recorded on it rather than in a client's account statement. No cheque-clearing activity will be needed to record smart card withdrawals, since settlements will be for the total amounts drawn from a given machine or from the network to which it is connected. Whatever data processing the transactions do require will occur at the terminal where the card is presented, and the only need to communicate with the intermediary's central computers will be to settle the net transactions balances.

Changes in the financial industry's organization are driven by demand as well as by supply changes. For example, financial institutions continue to adapt to such demand changes as increasing disintermediation at both the wholesale and retail levels. In this process, clients have been replacing deposits with investments, usually in securities, that promise higher expected rates of return (albeit with commensurate increased risk). Partly in response, the financial industry is increasing its emphasis on providing new investment vehicles and investment advice. Competition in both retail and corporate financial services increasingly takes these latter forms.

Stakeholder Perspectives

The financial system's changing nature presents strategic issues whose importance depends on the perspectives of the stakeholders involved, whether they be clients, management, supervisors, monetary authorities, or shareholders.

Clients

Consumer interests are best served by encouraging financial market competition. But to ensure that safety and soundness are not impaired, all financial institutions holding consumers' assets should be supervised by the regulatory authorities, at least to the extent of assuring that the institutions act as prudent stewards of their clients' funds.

Since clients can be affected negatively if their privacy is infringed, suitable restrictions on database usage are needed to limit this possibility. The potential for difficulty arises principally because databases represent valuable economic assets, and it is entirely natural to expect the firms assembling the data to expect to profit from so doing. Moreover, so long as there is no obvious problem of infringing on privacy or of creating conflict of interest, these profit expectations are altogether appropriate. Nevertheless, institutions should not sell information assembled in their normal course of business to nonaffiliated firms without first obtaining the explicit consent of the client. With a couple of exceptions to be discussed later in this *Commentary*, explicit rather than implied consent should be obtained before data are used for the purposes of marketing new products.

Nor should institutions gather information from their document-processing activity (except to secure an existing position). For example, a financial intermediary may monitor a borrowing client's cheques to determine whether the client also makes payments to other lending institutions, because this is helpful information for assessing client creditworthiness. The intermediary should not, however, use the same information to solicit additional business, such as insurance or credit card business, from that client. In situations where conflicts of interest are likely, such as between banking and trustee activity, traditional "Chinese Wall" prohibitions are well justified, and should not be changed.

Management

From management's perspective, one of the principal strategic issues involves dealing with the erosion of a formerly profitable franchise. One analyst notes that

As financial services become more technologically based, they are increasingly competing with nontraditional financial service suppliers such as AT&T. For example, in addition to offering its own enhanced credit card in competition with bank-supplied credit cards, AT&T owns a finance company. Also, once established, financial services technology can easily be purchased by non-financial firms. Thus in 1992 General Motors also established a credit-card operation linked to the purchase of its vehicles at a discount. Currently, banks issue less than half of all new credit cards; much of the new business is going to nontraditional firms such as AT&T and General Motors. As a result, technology exposes existing FIs to the increased risk of erosion of their franchises as costs of entry fall and the competitive landscape changes.[5]

In Canada GE Credit, a lending intermediary, figures prominently as a non-traditional form of competition, principally for the banks. GE Credit is, however, at a disadvantage relative to a bank which can obtain a substantial proportion of its funds from deposits, and it is perhaps worth recalling that, in the past, Canadian finance companies eventually proved unable to compete with banks because of the cost differences arising from the ways they raised their funds. On the other hand, GE Credit can raise funds relatively cheaply on the strength of a parent company guarantee, and it does not use an expensive branch network to conduct its lending operations. In response, banks can securitize their loans, and can also earn fees by securitizing other lending inter-mediaries' assets. Banks, however, face some inescapable cost disadvantages by operating lending subsidiaries (at least unless they own no more than 10 percent of the subsidiary's shares). They both pay deposit insurance premiums and are taxed as financial institutions. In addition, under requirements of the Bank for International Settlements, banks face capital standards that do not apply to such firms as GE Credit. Accurately assessing the net effect of all these cost differences is beyond the scope of this paper, but the competition of firms like GE Credit does represent one way in which the value of a banking franchise is being eroded, and the banking industry continues to work at finding appropriate strategic responses.

Supervisors

When the system is viewed from a supervisory perspective, one of the principal strategic issues is whether regulators' capability to influence the system might be weakening:

> The improvement in FIs telecommunications networks also enhances the power of FIs vis-à-vis regulators, effectively aiding regulatory avoidance....The growth of telecommunications networks and improvements in technology have changed, perhaps irreversibly, the balance of power between large multinational FIs and governments — both local and national — in favor of the former. This shift in power also creates incentives for countries to lower their regulations to attract entrants; that is, it increases the incentives for competitive deregulation. This trend may be potentially destabilizing to the market in financial services with the weakest regulators attracting the most entrants.[6]

Since the failure of the Bank of Credit and Commerce International, national regulators are highly aware of these possibilities and are working to ensure that weakly regulated foreign financial institutions are subject to adequate oversight. Even so, new problems are likely to arise in the future. In particular, there is the possibility that weakly regulated foreign institutions will attempt to sell products or services on the Internet.

Regulators will have to consider the possibility of controlling or monitoring Internet data transmission. For example, if a client makes a deposit by transmitting a credit card number over the Internet, will it be possible to determine what regulatory jurisdictions are involved? If the jurisdiction is not the client's home jurisdiction, how can regulation insure that the client knows this? And even with such information, how can the client judge the safety of another jurisdiction? Naturally, the client has a responsibility to safeguard his or her own funds, but regulation can help to make it more difficult to be misled by unethical service providers.

Second, existing regulatory frameworks principally cover single forms of traditional activities, such as insurance *or* banking. Without some amendment, the existing frameworks may have difficulty in regulating such new business combinations as, say, insurance *and* banking. The risks of such a combination depend in part on the relations between the two businesses, and thus cannot always be adequately supervised as independent risks.[7] Regulators must explicitly coordinate their investigations of separate business units to ensure that such overall risks are adequately supervised.[8]

Third, regulators need to examine how the operations of new communications and electronic transfer media affect opportunities for competition. In particular, as Interac becomes an increasingly important means of conducting interinstitutional transactions and possibly an increasingly important means of marketing financial products, the Interac Association's founding members will gain a potentially important competitive advantage relative to other financial institutions. To encourage competition for the provision of financial services, it is important to find ways of protecting the original Interac developers' investment while attempting to ensure that new firms' attempts to gain access are not frustrated by excessively high charges. The mid-December consent order by which Interac will allow new forms of access to its facilities is a move toward increasing competition, and one which will be analyzed further below.

Fourth, supervision needs to provide incentives for good governance. It is now widely recognized that the former level of premium deposit insurance both subsidized riskier institutions and provided them with perverse incentives to increase their portfolio risks. To allay the perverse incentives problem, regulators should continue to ensure that the cost of any form of asset insurance rises as intermediary risk increases.[9]

Another way of providing incentives for good governance is to improve the public information base. For example, if supervisors were regularly to release more financial information about the firms they inspect, changes in management policy would be communicated more readily and more quickly to the marketplace. If such information indicated that an intermediary was becoming increasingly risky, its costs of uninsured funds would likely increase in response. In these circumstances, the riskier intermediary would pay more for funds than a safer competitor, and it might well conclude that profits could be improved by behaving more like its safer competitors.

The very nature of intermediation means that information releases would provide estimated rather than exact statements of financial condition. It would therefore be helpful to have joint committees of regulators and industry representatives work out appropriate bases for information release.

Nevertheless, the provisions of more reliable information on a continuing basis may lead to better financial decisions,[10] and may also allow sound institutions to bear fewer of the costs of cross-subsidizing their riskier competitors.

A fifth strategic issue for the regulatory authorities is to consider insuring such forms of asset holdings as the liabilities of pension funds. The Canadian public does not usually have reliable information regarding the safety and soundness of the pension funds in which very large proportions of their assets are concentrated. This situation seems likely to become all the more urgent as governments increasingly rely on Canadians to provide for their own retirement rather than draw from public pension funds. Serious consideration should be given to providing liability insurance for private pension funds, with the insurance coverage being based on risk-related premiums.

Finally, a public that is being asked to provide increasingly larger proportions of retirement income from its own resources should not be hampered in its efforts to do so. The present restriction on the maximum percentages of foreign assets in registered retirement savings plans (RRSPs) and other forms of investment that can be held without affecting their tax status hampers the public's ability to choose the risk-return tradeoffs and investment opportunities it finds most nearly appropriate. In addition, by limiting opportunities for worldwide diversification, such restrictions may actually increase the volatility of investment returns.

The Monetary Authorities

One of the most important strategic issues faced by the monetary authorities is how to prevent inflation from creating unanticipated redistributions of wealth, thereby playing havoc with the value of private investments. Either short-term bursts of rapid inflation or continued rates of high inflation can present real dangers from deliberate policy choice, from the unintended effects of policy combinations, or accidentally as a result of missing an intended target. Consider each in turn.

Policy choices. An absence of firm monetary control makes it easier for governments to resort to the printing press when mounting deficits can no longer be covered at reasonable costs by international borrowing. Borrowing can postpone the day when it becomes necessary to reduce deficits, and has done so for Canada. But governments that increasingly borrow from abroad eventually lose control over their long-term interest rates. It is crucial that, as international borrowing continues to become more expensive, real and continued restrictions on spending can and will be imposed.

Unintended effects of policy combinations. Consider an international example. Japan's property and stockmarket boom and bust in the late 1980s was caused by a combination of distortions in the land market and a highly expansionary monetary policy, the latter being motivated primarily by attempts to prop up the dollar.[11] The costs of these policies are still being suffered, as bad loans continue to surface and more reports of troubled institutions are released. At least some of the currently proposed merger activity in Japan represents adjustments driven by the consequences of this earlier inflationary episode.

Accidents. While a stimulative monetary policy may be able to increase economic growth over the short run, over the longer run continuing money supply increases will clearly lead to accelerating inflation. Accordingly, many believe that price stability provides the best environment for investment and growth. The problem with attempting to assure price stability is that current financial system change may be increasing the possibility of accidents. As financial liberalization continues to shift the demand for money function and to change the practical definition of the money supply, new means of payment seem likely to alter velocity, and if velocity increases it may also become more volatile, increasing the difficulty of monetary control. The same new means of payment eventually may affect practical definitions of what constitutes the money stock.

Yet even in a world of mobile international capital, monetary policy can still influence interest rates, and through them output and inflation, so long as the exchange rate is not held fixed.[12] For all these reasons, financial reform should attempt to ensure that the difficulties facing the monetary authorities are not increased.

Shareholders

Much of Canada's financial industry is owned by its shareholders — investors who expect to earn an investment return commensurate with its risks.[13] Regulations or restrictions on financial firms' activity can impair institutional profitability and negatively affect shareholder's wealth. Reducing firms' profitability also reduces their ability to raise new investment capital and thus to fund future financial system growth. To obviate these possibilities, revisions to financial legislation must recognize the needs of financiers to generate competitive profits.

Theoretical Perspectives

The principal theme of the reform issues considered below is a tradeoff between competitiveness, on the one hand, and safety and soundness, on the other. This section outlines theoretical concepts useful in analyzing particular variations on this theme. The relevance of each concept is indicated in its particular subsection.

Types of Financial Deals

The economic theory of financial transacting (in short, the theory of making deals) holds that any financial deal involves providing funds, managing risks, or a combination of the two.[14] Whether the deal principally involves funding, risk management, or a combination of the two, it is useful to categorize each deal, albeit roughly, as either standardized or nonstandardized.

Standardized deals are consummated under conditions of risk. They arise in such circumstances as financing acquisitions of relatively liquid assets, require relatively little continued monitoring, and normally take the form of market transactions. Nonstandardized deals are likely to be struck under the less easily quantified condition known as uncertainty, and arise in such circumstances as financing acquisitions of relatively illiquid assets. Normally, nonstandardized deals require more monitoring than their standardized counterparts, and the original terms of such nonstandard deals may need to be amended as difficulties are uncovered by the monitoring. Nonstandardized deals typically are arranged through intermediaries, or even within financial conglomerates, to obtain the greater monitoring and adjustment capabilities needed for their profitable conclusion.

Standardized deals have readily established market values, but non-standardized deals do not. It is relatively easy to evaluate the portfolios of financial firms holding mainly such standardized assets as traded bonds or stocks, because the individual assets have readily established market values.

It is equally easy to value such standardized liabilities as negotiable certificates of deposit. It is more difficult to evaluate nonstandardized asset portfolios, such as those created by intermediary lending.[15] Rather than trading them, financial intermediaries typically hold their assets to maturity. It can be equally difficult to value such nonstandardized liabilities as pension fund obligations when plan benefits are adjusted by a cost of living index.[16]

Trading produces public information about the values of standardized instruments, but there is much less public information about the values of portolios consisting mainly of nonstandardized instruments. FIs produce information for themselves when they acquire nonstandardized assets, but since the assets are not usually traded, information about them remains private. Yet the financial system performs its resource allocation role most effectively when information is widely and publicly available,[17] so it is important that supervisory information be disseminated whenever it proves cost effective to do so. Situations in which more public information would be desirable are identified below.

Size, Cost, and Profit Functions

To frame legislation appropriately, it is useful to understand the economic forces driving organizational change within the financial services industry. It is particularly useful to summarize what is known about relations between FI size and profitability. Three functions — screening, monitoring, and information processing — are performed in providing financial services to different market segments. Theoretically, each of the three functions is characterized by scale economies whenever it involves a fixed setup cost and reasonably constant incremental costs. Moreover, the functions all use similar physical and human resources, irrespective of the particular financial product for which they are performed. When the same inputs can provide a variety of products, the functions performed are likely to be characterized by scope as well as by scale economies.

Scale and scope economies are frequently cited as explaining the large and growing size of FIs, but there is actually little evidence that bigger, multiproduct FIs enjoy cost advantages over their smaller and more specialized competitors. A recent summary of cost-function research in the United States and other countries suggests that "economies of scale may exist for banks in the $100 million to $5 billion range," but there is no evidence of scale economies for larger institutions. Evidence for the existence of cost complementarities (economies of scope) is similarly weak. In addition, "studies of nonbank financial service firms such as thrifts, insurance companies, and securities firms almost always report neither economies of scale nor of economies of scope."[18]

Economies of scope and scale certainly cannot explain observable cost differences among FIs having the same size and performing the same functions. Rather, research on this topic points to the importance of managerial capability as an explanatory factor. Studies of cost dispersion suggest that "cost inefficiencies related to managerial ability and other hard-to-quantify factors may better explain cost differences and operating cost efficiencies among financial firms than technology related investments per se."[19]

To the extent that benefits do stem from increasing size, they may arise on the revenue generation side rather than on the cost side as a result of greater opportunities to meet client needs. For example, large institutions may be able to introduce existing products in new areas or new products in existing market areas, and thereby improve their revenue prospects relative to those of smaller competing firms.[20] One study of banks' profit functions concludes that mergers are at least as strongly motivated by attempts to remove managerial inefficiencies or to find sources of increased revenue as they are by attempts to gaining new forms of scale or scope economies.[21]

But even profit-function studies have not yet included all the harder-to-quantify factors that might explain FI size. For example, large institutions can probably diversify more fully than their smaller counterparts, and thus obtain better risk-return tradeoffs than smaller institutions. In addition,

> the real benefits to technological innovation may be long term and dynamic, related to the evolution of the US payments system away from cash and checks and toward electronic means of payment. Such benefits are difficult to pick up in traditional economy of scale and scope studies which are largely static and ignore the more dynamic aspects of efficiency gains.[22]

The foregoing review suggests that, on balance, economic factors are driving financial intermediaries toward still greater size increases. However, there may also be at least one opposing force. The increasing use of electronic networks implies that the financial firm of the future may find it economic to use more decentralized information processing. This, coupled with distance marketing using novel forms of financial services delivery, may give small institutions both marketing and operating advantages they do not now possess. The currently weakening linkage between communication distance and cost may give such developments further impetus. The significance of these factors for policy analysis is that decentralized information processing may enhance entry to what are now fragmented markets. To the extent that entry is enhanced, markets that are presently segmented may become more competitive in the future.

Asset Concentration and Competition

Asset concentration is a part of the current scene and, despite the introduction of more decentralized information processing, it appears likely that financial firms' average size will continue to increase. This trend, however, raises a frequently voiced concern regarding a possible connection between asset concentration and market power.

To begin, however, it is important to note that Canadian financial firms are relatively small players in the international markets. For example, most of the international institutions prominent in foreign exchange and derivatives trading, as well as in combinations of the banking and securities businesses, are much larger than their Canadian counterparts. From the point of view of competing for international business, Canadian financial firms would likely be more successful, and be able to generate more export earnings for Canada, if they were considerably larger.

In domestic markets, on the other hand, the principal Canadian banks are by far the largest players, even though, in relation to the size of the economy, they are about the same size as the principal banks of many other western countries (other than the United States). Moreover, despite their relatively large domestic role, Canadian banks do not appear to have any substantive degree of oligopoly power. Studies at the industry level in the United States, Canada, and other countries suggest that banking industry revenue is generated in contestable markets.[23] Since contestability reduces the possibility that firms with large market shares can exercise oligopolistic pricing practices, empirical studies suggest a degree of effective competition between large financial institutions. Such findings are consistent with the observations that Canadian bank's return on assets, and Canadian banks' return to equity, are generally somewhat less than the comparable figures for their US competitors.[23A]

Industry studies examine relations between changes in factor costs and overall profitability, and thus do not address the possibility that some individual domestic markets might still be uncompetitive. Market studies, however, suggest this possibility cannot altogether be ruled out. Using time series data for individual Canadian markets over the 1982–93 period, Barry Scholnik finds evidence of increasing differentials between consumer and prime loans, as well as between a mortgage rate and a guaranteed investment certificate rate of comparable term.[24]

Scholnik's findings are perhaps best regarded as suggestive rather than definitive. Increases in interest rate differentials might be due to oligopolistic pricing, but they could also be due to improved estimates of the costs of doing individual types of business. In recent years, large financial intermediaries have renewed their attempts to estimate these costs, and the changes in pricing might thus be based on improved methods of accounting for the costs of information processing or from improved methods of assessing asset risk in relation to the intermediary's overall portfolio.

Moreover, even if Scholnik's or similar results are confirmed by further study, increasingly cheaper access to geographically dispersed financial markets suggests that individual spreads may become narrower in the future, as smaller depository intermediaries and specialized lending intermediaries learn to exploit any monopoly rents that might be found in niche markets.[25] The possibility for comparison shopping by electronic means should enhance the likelihood of new competition.

There is also a body of work that, while often cited in examining the behavior of asset concentration, is actually irrelevant to understanding the meaning of oligopolistic practices and pricing policies. This work includes studies suggesting that larger banks may not fully meet the financing needs of small business.[26] Given the nature of bank credit provision activities (short-term, low-risk lending frequently secured by relatively liquid assets) and the nature of small business' financing demands (high-risk equity funding the most difficult and costly to obtain), such findings, are not surprising.

The banking system has attempted to respond to such criticisms, although it is by no means clear that it should. Canada's largest source of short-term finance will not necessarily find it profitable to do every type of deal. Indeed, low-risk, short-term lenders are quite unlikely to profit from supplying high-risk equity financing to small business.[27] To urge banks to provide the financing anyway is to argue for distorting the workings of the financial system. The problems of small business finance are real, but the banks are not the intermediaries best suited to address them. For this reason, an appendix to this paper presents another way to meet small business demands for long-term, high-risk finance. Commentary on asset concentration also sometimes fails to recognize the cyclical nature of profits. Bank profits usually increase when monetary policy is expansionary, and decrease when policy is restrictive, but the declines do not always receive the intense scrutiny that the increases do.

Quite apart from questions of cyclicality, temporary increases in profits do not necessarily indicate that the system has reached, or even that it is proceeding toward, an uncompetitive equilibrium. No matter how competitive markets might be in equilibrium, successful financial firms can be expected to earn monopoly rents in certain disequilibrium situations. Indeed, it can be argued that the prospect of earning rents over some period of time is a principal driver of financial system change. Change occurs as firms innovate, taking on new risks as they search for new sources of revenue or new methods of cost reduction. For example, firms may seek to enter new, uncompetitive markets or to offer new products which, at least for a time, have no ready substitutes.[28] Without the prospect of rents, incentives for innovation might well be lessened. Moreover, so long as competing institutions are free to enter the business generating the rents (although they will first have to learn how to emulate the innovative firm), the rents themselves should be attenuated with the passage of time. Thus, temporary profitability may reflect system adaptability rather than market power.

Influencing the Transition

The purpose of financial reform is to secure social benefits, whether they derive from enhancing competition, from fostering safety and soundness, from fostering transaction integrity, from disseminating information, or from recognizing politico-economic imperatives. The best available ways of enhancing the competition-safety tradeoff are by encouraging competitiveness and by removing any obstacles to equality of competitive opportunity. However, recognizing the financial system's special role of storing up accumulated wealth means that, in certain circumstances, competitiveness may need to be traded off against attempts to ensure safety and soundness.

For example, the advocate of unalloyed competition regards financial firms' failure with equanimity, almost irrespective of the incidence of the costs of failure. The policy analyst seeking to balance tradeoffs will consider both the incidence of costs and whether unmanaged failure might affect confidence in the system. There might be benefits to be realized from managing failure, but any such benefits will almost surely be obtained at the costs of reduced competitiveness and limited opportunity. Thus, the policy question for regulators and legislative reformers is how to achieve the best net balance of benefits and costs, acknowledging both that judgment will be required to strike the balance and that the costs and benefits will be difficult to identify, let alone quantify.

The International Context

Canadian financial regulation must be framed in a world context. If Canada's regulation is at considerable variance with that of other countries, Canada can lose profitable business. For example, if Canada taxes the international business of its financial institutions more heavily than do other countries, that business is placed at a competitive disadvantage. Similarly, if Canada's accounting standards differ from those of comparable jurisdictions — say, in the way they recognize intangible assets acquired as a result of a merger — Canadian institutions may face higher effective rates of taxation than the institutions of other countries.

Both political and economic imperatives argue for retaining Canadian ownership of some forms of financial activity. Rightly or wrongly, many developed nations believe they can best fulfill their economic, development, prudential, and monetary policy goals by retaining domestic control of at least the banking portion of their financial systems. While the extent to which Canada should pursue these imperatives is beyond the scope of this paper, the danger in permitting political purposes to dictate the system's industrial organization should not be overlooked. Politically motivated restrictions on competition often lead to support of uncompetitive institutions, which can weaken the entire system. In such cases, the economic costs of the limitations should at least be estimated so that the tradeoff can be debated.

Encouraging Competitiveness

Canada can encourage financial system competition by removing obstacles to entry as well as to the development of an integrated national capital market. As has been argued above, the economic pressures for change are great, and the burden of proof for restrictive regulation should rest with those who argue for the status quo, rather than with those who propose innovation. In a period of rapid — indeed, radical — change, it is difficult to do more than guide evolution in the direction of greater competition while attempting to ensure that safety and soundness are maintained.

As far as possible, the opportunities to compete should be equal, irrespective of the potential competitor's original industry. Even so, it is still helpful to ensure that the incentives facing management encourage responsible governance of risk-reward tradeoffs. In addition to making every effort to enhance competitiveness, regulators should work to ensure that the costs of bankruptcies will be borne by the providers of risk capital (shareholders). It is, of course, also important to ensure that shareholder returns will be commensurate with the risks they bear.

Removing obstacles to potential competition — working to provide a level playing field — should not be confused with attempts to ensure equality of outcome. Some parts of the financial industry will face difficulties, and some firms will fail, when regulation encourages a competitive struggle. If they are unable to adapt, the least efficient players will be driven out by competition — a desirable outcome from an efficiency standpoint. To shelter weak firms from their own inadequacies, whether by protection or by subsidy, is to impose unnecessary costs on consumers and to delay necessary system adaptation. The players that survive a competitive struggle may be large, but the public will benefit from the efficiency increases that restructuring brings so long as competition is maintained.

Competition and innovation are more likely to be stimulated if firms from different parts of the financial industry can exercise the same business powers at roughly similar costs. For example, if legislation permits different institutions to perform the same functions, the level playing field principle argues that the effective costs of performing the same functions, including the amount of invested capital needed to conduct the business, should be roughly similar.

The same principle argues that the regulations governing the performance of a given function should, as far as possible, be the same for all players.

Supervisors' principal means of influencing financial firms are through changing management incentives, either positively or negatively. Efforts to publicize portfolio quality, especially where nonstandardized assets are involved, can be highly effective mechanisms for addressing problems of poor or ineffective corporate governance. The legislative framework should be drawn up to ensure that, as far as is possible, supervisors' estimates of portfolio quality are communicated promptly to the public. So long as the information release is on a regular basis, market perceptions can adjust gradually rather than suddenly, as is now the case with episodic announcements about changes in financial condition.[29]

The Current Framework

Recent *Bank Act* revisions and related legislation have mainly granted the financial services industry additional freedoms. Not only have the protections afforded the four pillars been dismantled, but provisions restricting foreign bank activities have also been relaxed. The changing competitive environment may have reduced the value of some franchises, and some fees for services have been unbundled. At the same time, Canada's banking system has largely absorbed most of the trust and securities businesses, resulting in a smaller overall number of players and greater asset concentration than formerly existed.

The competing players in today's financial services industry face different kinds of regulation. Bank and insurance company operations are governed by their respective acts, while savings intermediaries (such as mutual funds), lending intermediaries (such as GE Credit), credit card issuers (such as AT&T), and financial planners are not regulated by specific financial legislation. The idea of a level playing field argues for regulating all players that perform the same function in the same way. On the other hand, since different players perform different combinations of functions, it may still be necessary to regulate them differently. The essential policy question is to distinguish those firms whose combinations of functions are similar enough to merit the same forms of treatment from those which differ enough to merit different treatment.

Since the functions of banks and insurance companies are increasingly over-lapping, one of the most pressing issues is to harmonize their regulatory treatment. Banks now provide some insurance-like activity through the design and trade of derivative securities.[30] Banks are also permitted to operate insurance subsidiaries, but not to sell insurance in their branches. Insurance companies can hold balances arising from the ordinary course of their business, but cannot, under the current *Insurance Companies Act*, offer chequing accounts or other readily transferable forms of deposit balances. Moreover, insurance companies cannot now become members of the payments system.

Another issue involves ensuring that the clients of depository intermediaries understand which of their funds are insured and which are not. While they may not be certain of what it covers, most consumers are at least aware that coverage exists under the Canada Deposit Insurance Corporation (CDIC). However, a bank client can place some funds in an insured account or investment, while purchasing uninsured term instruments from one of the bank's affiliated corporations, and be unaware of the difference. As a second example, consumers may not always understand that the different forms of investments which can be classed as RRSPs do not necessarily qualify as insured funds simply because they constitute part of an RRSP.

In the same vein, many consumers are probably unaware that CompCorp guarantees insurance industry liabilities or that the Securities Investor Protection Corporation offers asset protection for clients of securities firms. They may also be unaware that not all private sector pension funds are covered by liability insurance.

Brian Smith notes that the "financial sectors of most countries have been moving toward a system of universal banking" and "subject to a few restrictions, the recent reforms allow Canadian financial institutions to operate effectively as universal banks."[31] Yet academic knowledge regarding the economic importance of Canada's financial-industrial combinations is limited — more analysis is needed, for example, about the financial system performance tradeoffs they present. For policy, the principal policy question is this: If financial-industrial combinations present greater advantages than is commonly believed, are there regulatory impediments to the benefits' being realized?

Implementation

The foregoing review suggests that the principal issues for attention in the current round of revisions to Canadian financial regulation involve business powers, access to payments mechanisms, consumer asset insurance, and disclosure. This section discusses each of those issues in turn. Because they are so frequently raised in popular commentary, the issues of derivatives trading, ownership concentration, and self-dealing are also considered briefly.

Changes in Traditional Forms of Business

The main questions regarding changes in traditional forms of business are whether insurance companies should be able to provide consumers with access to the balances the companies now hold and whether banks should be to sell insurance products in their branches.

Insurance Companies and Their Balances

Currently, insurance companies cannot accept deposits as a stand-alone line of business nor can they make the balances they now hold readily transferable. Insurance companies can, however, hold deposits that are generated in the course of their ordinary business activities, such as those arising from the proceeds of an insurance policy or the stream of payments from an annuity. For distribution, these balances must currently be transferred to depository intermediaries, which are often direct competitors. This disadvantage could be mitigated if insurance companies were able to offer transferable balances within their own business groups. There are at least two alternatives for achieving this possibility.

Alternative 1: Balances arising from ordinary business. If the balances arising from insurance companies' ordinary business were as readily accessible to their clients as are bank or trust company funds, clients would be less likely to move their deposits to other financial institutions. Changes to the *Insurance Companies Act* would be required to make the insurance company balances themselves transferable (whether using cheques or electronic means). According to a recent insurance industry brief, however, some insurance companies want to permit their customers access to a line of credit rather than to transferable balances.

Whether it were to offer transferable deposits or access to a line of credit, for clearing purposes the insurance company would need access to the Canadian Payments System (CPS), either by arrangement with a current member of the Canadian Payments Association (CPA) or through obtaining CPA membership directly. Since CDIC protection is presently a prerequisite to CPA membership, an insurance company cannot now become a member of the CPA unless it operates a CDIC-insured depository intermediary (see Alternative 2). If CPA legislation were amended to allow membership in CompCorp to serve as a prerequisite[32] for membership in the CPA, insurance companies obtaining such membership would be able to clear cheques drawn against the balances they can now hold.

The principal advantage of Alternative 1 is that insurance companies would become more effective competitors for transferable balances and, by obtaining readier access to the payments system, they would be in a better position to market new products. A second advantage might be that the financial services industry would evolve in a natural manner determined mainly by perceived profit opportunities. The principal disadvantage is that insurance companies' transferable deposits would be administered under a different body of law than would the transferable deposits of other financial intermediaries. Moreover, such transferable deposits would form part of the money supply, but would not necessarily come under the same potential for monetary control.[33] While federal insurance companies are supervised by the Office of the Superintendent of Financial Institutions (OSFI), their liabilities are insured by CompCorp rather than by the CDIC. As a result, insurance companies that offer transferable deposits would not necessarily be subject to the same forms of inspection, the same standards of solvency, or the same insurance protection as traditional depository intermediaries such as banks or credit unions. Moreover, insurance companies would probably not qualify, at least on the same basis, for the kinds of liquidity support available to ordinary depository institutions. Finally, to permit one group of nondepository intermediaries to offer means of payment that are outside the usual legislative framework for governing those means is to set a precedent that might be exploited by other institutions whose financial standings are less sound than those of the insurance companies.

Alternative 2: Transferable deposits. An insurance company which acquired or formed a depository intermediary could accept deposits as a stand-alone line of business and could also qualify for CDIC protection. If the capital requirements were unduly onerous for a single insurance company, the intermediary could be owned jointly by several insurance companies.

If the intermediary were a trust company, individual insurance companies' shareholdings could exceed 10 percent. The principal obstacle[34] to using a trust company is that provincial laws (especially in Ontario) restrict the possibility of setting up even a nationally chartered trust company for the purpose of administering transferable deposits. If the intermediary were a bank, individual companies' shareholdings could not exceed 10 percent unless it were a Schedule II bank. On the positive side, eligible financial institutions, including mutual insurance companies and widely held joint stock insurance companies, could be shareholders of such a bank, and the bank's operations would not be restricted by provincial law.

Alternative 2 seems to me to offer several advantages over Alternative 1. First, it treats the transferable deposits retained by an insurance industry intermediary in the same manner as any other transferable deposits.[35] Second, by obtaining CDIC protection of the subsidiary's deposits, the intermediary could qualify for CPA membership. Third, CPA membership would, in turn, permit the intermediary to apply for membership in Interac.[36] Fourth, the institution offering transferable deposits would be entitled to the same liquidity support as other solvent depository institutions. Finally, Alternative 2 uses a similar mechanism to that used by banks, which must also form subsidiary corporations to carry out insurance activity. The principal disadvantages to Alternative 2 are possible customer inconvenience and the ownership and operating restrictions mentioned in the previous paragraph.

To implement Alternative 2 would require insurance companies to release certain client data (related to the existence of the deposit) to the affiliated depository intermediary. So long as the insurance company did not sell the data to nonaffiliated businesses without the explicit written consent of the client, no serious infringement of client privacy would likely result.

With regard to differences in organizational form, it does not appear that the minimum amount of capital resources required of a combined enterprise differs according to whether the principal firm is a bank or an insurance company. Insofar as policy is concerned, there does not seem to be any strong economic case for arguing that the parent company should be a holding company (the US model) or an insurance company (a variant of the UK model in which the bank is the parent company.[37]

Banks in the Insurance Business

While banks can own insurance subsidiaries and offer such products as group insurance policies, they cannot sell insurance in their branches nor can they use bank-gathered data to identify insurance prospects. The banks claim, and the industry studies they cite support, the conclusion that current insurance distribution techniques are relatively costly. At least one insurance industry executive has acknowledged the same point.[38] As a result, experiments with new methods of distribution such as — selling policies over the Internet, over the telephone, and in bank branches — seem warranted.

If the *Bank Act* were amended to permit banks to sell insurance in their branches, the banks would still have to satisfy provincial licensing requirements before sales could commence. They would then probably use their existing databases to contact clients, just as the insurance companies using Alternative 2 would communicate their client data to a subsidiary bank or trust company. Banks should not, however, be able to sell client information to other, unrelated institutions without obtaining the explicit consent of the client. Nor should banks be empowered to generate client lists from information recorded on the cheques or preauthorized payment instruments they clear. Finally, if banks are permitted to sell such products as life insurance, the terms of the permission should preclude cross-selling or other anticompetitive practices.

On the positive side, allowing banks greater powers to sell insurance would provide a competitive stimulus to reduce distribution costs. New distribution methods might also reduce the cross subsidization of the distribution of complex products by that of simple products. Finally, any resulting improvements to the distribution system should enhance Canada's competitiveness *vis-à-vis* the rest of the world.

On the negative side, the possibility that the banks represent asset concentrations which would eventually permit them to dominate the business contrasts with similar experience in both the United Kingdom and Australia, which have permitted banks to sell insurance in their branches for the past several years.[39] A more likely outcome is that banks would become the "discount agents" of the insurance business, while the more traditional distribution channels would perform like "full service" agents. Europe has long allowed both banks and insurance companies to compete on a roughly equal footing, and both types of institution continue to flourish.[40] Quebec also permits insurance sales in *caisses populaires*. A second possible negative result, that the timing of such a change is currently inappropriate, is more difficult to evaluate. A number of other countries, including the United Kingdom and Australia, have taken this route over the past few years.

Access to Payments Mechanisms

Access to the payments system is an important determinant of competitive ability. The CPA controls and operates the CPS, the country's principal facility[41] for clearing cheques and effecting money transfers between institutions. Even though it is still needed to effect final settlement of inter-institutional transactions, the CPA is no longer the only effective mechanism for transferring funds. The Interac Association operates an electronic payments facility that is currently used mainly for interinstitutional cash dispensing and for debit card payments.[42] Access to the Interac network is through automated banking machines (ABMs) and through direct debit terminals in vendor premises. ABMs and vendor terminals are the property of individual financial institutions[43], while the communications network and software linking ABMs and terminals are the property of the Interac Association. Interac is becoming important for interinstitutional cash dispensing (30.6 percent of the total number of cash dispenses in 1994), and for making direct payments to retailers (185 million transactions amounting to $9.45 billion in 1994). According to the Interac Association, "since the late 1980s, the volume of paper-based instruments has stagnated while electronic payment methods have recorded steady growth."[44]

Access to the CPS is important both to compete for transferable deposits, as discussed above, and to clear transactions. If insurance companies were to use Alternative 2, there would be little need to consider further changes to the conditions for membership in the CPA, apart from two possibilities. First, if direct clearers (clearing members)[45] currently pay lower fees than indirect clearers (nonclearing members), the equal competitive opportunity principle indicates the same fee schedule should apply to both. That is, if a direct clearer performs a service for an indirect clearer, the fact of performing that service should not be used to create a competitive disadvantage for the indirect clearer.

Second, whichever alternative the insurance industry ultimately adopts, the CPA is a public facility and its administration should treat different members even-handedly. For example, insurance companies might well have representatives on the CPA board, and would be able to do so if they operated the gateway institution discussed under Alternative 2 above.

While Canada's payments system probably works more efficiently than that of most countries, questions about the effects of its operations merit further study. For example, a recent study shows that, in Canada in 1992, cheques accounted for nearly 99 percent of cashless transactions, as opposed to 12 percent in the United Kingdom and 13 percent in the United States.[46] On the other hand, the Canadian Bankers' Association notes that in 1995, using BIS methodology, paper-based items constituted only about 38% of transactions between members. The importance of the differences in the numbers, and the possibilities of their having more than one interpretation, both point to the need for a more thorough comparison of practices in different countries.

At its present level of operation, Interac is an important part of the electronic funds transfer landscape. The increasing use of debit cards and the future introduction of smart cards suggest that Interac's importance will continue to grow. If, as also seems likely, scale economies mitigate against the emergence of competing networks, Interac's prominence could imply that competition will be lessened unless all potential users obtain equal rights to use the network. On the other hand, the original Interac members are entrepreneurs who have created an economically valuable entity and who are entitled to obtain a fair return on their investment. Thus, two competing interests must be addressed in assessing the desirability of changes to Interac's present arrangements.[47]

One way of ensuring that Interac's original owners receive a fair return on their investment would be to set up a corporation whose shares would be owned by the original members. The corporation would generate its revenues from the access fees it charged to network users, and its shareholders would receive a return to their invested capital that derived from its net profits.[48] Equal access to the network would be implemented by imposing the same access fee schedule on all users, original developers or new entrants. As far as possible, such a fee schedule should be independent of institutional size so that small institutions would not face serious competitive disadvantages.

Before the December consent order, only members of the CPA could join the Interac Association. Now, other parties (for example, retail stores) are to be permitted access to Interac facilities through such means as linking their own terminals to the network. The changes provided for in the consent order require further analysis, both for their potential impact on competition and for their potential impact on risk.[49] But it seems clear that easier access to transferable deposits will increase competition. In particular, the linking of retailer-owned machines to Interac will likely reduce the cost of providing connections, and the accessibility of the payments system will increase. With respect to ensuring equal competitive opportunity, it will be important to determine whether the order effectively provides that all users pay fees according to the same schedule.[50]

The consent order may affect both transfer risks — that is, the risk of loss through individual transfers (especially retail transfers) — and the status of balances used as means of payment. Transfer risks can be dealt with principally by insuring financial responsibility of the network operators and subscribers, and do not appear to present issues of major import. On the other hand, the deposit balances underlying transfers should continue to be held by regulated depository institutions. For continued smooth working of the payments system, the consent order should not be viewed as implying that transferable balances could be offered by any firm, regardless of its financial position or the financial regulation to which it is subject.

The issue is not whether the client making the transfer has the funds, as Interac permits ready verification of balances. Rather, the institutions holding the transferable deposits must be widely seen to be sound institutions with equally sound management. If a depository institution were to fail suddenly, numerous payments losses might be suffered. More important, confidence, either in the payments system or in the financial system's ability to ensure safe storage of wealth, could be impaired. To offset these possibilities, depository intermediaries should continue to qualify for CPA membership. On the other hand, the consent order appears to allow the issuer of a credit card to use Interac for cash withdrawals and other forms of payment.

A restriction on transferable deposits would limit some firms' ability to compete for depository intermediary business, but the potential for enhanced safety and soundness seems to me to exceed the cost. To illustrate, if the insurance companies were to adopt Alternative 2, they could offer transferable deposits just like other depository intermediaries now do. But a small and closely held investment fund that did not qualify for CPA membership might be able to use Interac for some purposes, such as receiving funds, but still not be able to offer the same transferable deposit facilities as depository intermediaries. Such a fund would have to sell its liabilities on the basis of their appeal as investment products, rather than on the basis of convenient ready access to the funds.

The Internet constitutes a third possible means of effecting payments. This worldwide computer communications network currently serves principally as an electronic bulletin board,[51] and as such facilitates comparison shopping. In the future, the Internet is likely to be used to order goods and to make payments by credit or possibly by debit card. Internet transactions involving credit cards would normally be settled by vendor transmission to a financial intermediary. Although users pay differing access fees to different service providers, there are currently no fees for using the Internet itself.

Internet transactions will involve issues of determining the jurisdiction in which business is being done, as well as issues of how to regulate any accumulated deposits. There is also a possibility that some form of "Internet money" using deposit balances will evolve.[52] Should "Internet money" become widely acceptable, at least two questions arise: who will act to guarantee its safety as a store of wealth, and who will receive the seigniorage benefits[53] from its issue? Although a standards group is now working toward effective means of monitoring transaction integrity; questions of possible seigniorage benefits do not yet appear to have been thoroughly addressed.

Consumer Asset Insurance

Even though they are comparatively unable to evaluate nonstandardized assets, consumers should still be offered incentives to place their funds carefully. At present, however, there are limited possibilities for encouraging consumers to make discriminating choices among the institutions in which they place their funds. For example, since some insured financial insitutions now sell both CDIC-insured and uninsured products, consumers should be able to determine immediately whether a given financial product is insured.

Another way to aid the consumer would be to place a total insurance cap of $60,000 on all funds, whether deposits or investments, that a given client places with an institutional group, whether in single or in joint accounts. (At present, the CDIC insures both deposits and investments to $60,000, which effectively doubles the cap.)[54] This capping would provide consumers with a marginally greater incentive to diversify, although it would not give them an incentive to screen financial institutions' different risks.

To the extent that consumers can discriminate between institutions at all, their choices are likely to be made on the basis of publicly available summary ratings. But to require consumers to co-insure deposits is to assume too much about their ability to value financial institutions' nonstandardized assets.[55] Greater disclosure will help sophisticated traders make better choices about financial institutions' asset values, but consumers are likely to be helped mainly by the simple measures discussed earlier in this subsection.

Regulatory authorities, however, have greater resources and expertise to discriminate between different institutions' risks. Thus, so long as deposit insurance continues to be offered, it will remain up to organizations like the CDIC and OSFI to discourage institutions from taking what the regulators deem to be undue risk. Disincentives could extend beyond charging risk-based insurance premiums. For example, regulators could require weaker institutions to raise more capital in, say, the debentures market. A weak institution faced with such a requirement would pay a premium for raising the additional funds, and that premium should provide at least some of the requisite disincentives.

Since substantial proportions of Canadian consumers' assets are held in private sector pension funds, it is well worth considering whether, as a matter of public policy, these funds should have to purchase liability insurance. For consumers' financial well-being, pension fund insurance is probably at least as significant as deposit insurance, and the need for pension fund insurance will likely increase as consumers come to rely more heavily on private than on public pension resources. Ontario now provides pension fund insurance, and the coverage becomes increasingly costly as the risk of the pension fund increases. These provisions offer a starting point for considering how to extend the same kind of insurance to pension funds in other provinces.[56]

If their risk composition is the same, different insurance funds, public or private, should be able to raise funds at the same market rates. Since the CDIC is viewed as backed by a government guarantee while funds like CompCorp are not, some inequity of treatment arises. Some members of the insurance industry argue that CompCorp should have a government guarantee to make it similar to the CDIC, while others favor making CompCorp a government institution like the CDIC. Given the practical difficulty of dissociating the CDIC from any government guarantee, the latter suggestion seems fairer. Were CompCorp to obtain such status, however, further restrictions on its financing and operations might have to be imposed, and the insurance industry would need to balance the expected benefits against these possible additional costs.

Enhanced Disclosure

As mentioned, above, I personally favor the public dissemination of whatever financial information is found to be cost effective in improving resource allocation. However, it is difficult to make nonstandardized asset portfolio valuations less opaque without publishing more supervisory information. In particular, insurance funds and OSFI should publicize the information they have regarding an institution's financial condition. Procedures for releasing this information should be worked out in consultation with industry representatives to ensure that it is as reliable as possible and to avoid arbitrary impositions of regulatory judgments.[57] The ratings of private financial agencies are useful, but private agencies do not necessarily have access to the same information base as do regulators. In addition, regulators' incentives to release information can differ from those facing rating agencies.

Regular information releases would mitigate what is now a dynamic problem created by sudden changes in expectations. Typically, regular information releases would show how an institution's financial condition is changing over time, which would therefore pose less risk of creating a liquidity crisis than does the present practice of making announcements only when an institution is nearly or wholly insolvent. Moreover, the announcement effects attendant on regular information releases would present an increasingly risky inter-mediary with a powerful incentive to change its policies before solvency problems arose. As a result, publicly reported information should also lessen the problems of safe institutions' cross-subsidizing unsafe ones.

The only disadvantage of regular information releases would seem to be that moving suddenly to such a new system could create dynamic instabilities during an adjustment period. For this reason, new forms of information release are probably best implemented gradually.

Derivatives Trading

The lesson from the collapse of Barings Bank and from other losses in derivatives trading is not that financial innovation should be restricted nor that supervisory powers should be increased substantially. Supervisors should, however, require that financial firms ensure the adequacy of internal risk-management controls. The increases in accurate disclosure now being worked out by regulatory and industry committees will help improve market transparency, as will increased exchange of information between central banks and supervisory bodies in different countries. There should be penalties for failing to act responsibly, whether the failure arises from taking direct action or from not ensuring proper oversight. Such penalties might well apply to both management and regulatory authorities found to be insufficiently diligent in the discharge of their duties.

Ownership Concentration

The 10 percent restriction on share ownership positions in banks and larger trust companies is intended to ensure that large institutions will be widely held. As a practical matter, the restriction does not prevent sale of particular functions performed by a given institution, — for example, a bank could sell its data-processing activity to a foreign buyer — but OSFI approval would be required if the actual servicing were to be moved outside of Canada.

The 10–50 percent rule restricts banks and other Canadian financial institutions from owning certain firms, and hence can hamper them in forming joint ventures in other countries. It can also restrict the operations of certain types of domestic financial services affiliates. For example, it is not always possible for a Canadian financial firm to take, say, a 30 percent equity stake in a joint venture in another country. If such restrictions were to be removed, Canadian financial institutions would be able to compete on a more nearly equal footing with institutions from other countries. The possible cost — that, say, a 40 percent stake could create a liability for Canadian financial institutions and their regulators in a situation where they did not have legal control of the risks to which they were subject — must be weighed against the possible benefits from expanded opportunities to compete.

At present, non-NAFTA Schedule II banks are restricted in the number of branches they can operate and in the percentage of total Canadian deposits for which they can account. Although these restrictions do not appear to be causing any difficulty, they are inconsistent with the principle of providing equal opportunity to compete. Thus, their removal seems desirable.

Self-Dealing

Problems from self-dealing can be expected to arise mainly where the incentives for self-dealing are at their greatest. In the financial system, these circumstances seem to occur most frequently with small, closely held depository intermediaries. While it may be desirable to have such intermediaries in certain markets, the increased risks associated with these institutions mean that they merit much closer supervision than larger, widely held intermediaries. While no special additional legislation may be needed for this purpose, supervisors should pay attention to situations where problems are most likely to arise. At the same time, rules that impede large institutions from making small transactions should be reviewed and, where appropriate, relaxed. For example, an institution with $1 billion in regulatory capital is presently required to obtain regulatory approval for any sale of illiquid assets in excess of $400,000 — an apparently unnecessary impediment when it is recognized that such transactions are also subject to the approval of an independent committee of outside directors.

Policy Options

This *Commentary* has attempted to provide background analyses pertinent to the proposed changes in the *Bank Act* and related legislation. Its conclusions regarding the principal issues are summarized briefly below.

Business powers for insurance companies. The insurance industry is seeking to enhance its existing business powers. Some of these enhancements may be implied by the recent consent order, which appears to open the way for credit card issuers to use Interac for cash withdrawals and other payments. Most of the remaining policy issues seem to concern powers to offer transferable deposits, which, since such deposits form a part of the money supply, should be conveyed through intermediaries subject to the same monetary control and prudential standards as are existing depository intermediaries.

There do not appear to be important federal limitations on the ability of eligible insurance companies to operate banks; indeed, if any legal obstacles to widely held insurance companies' capability to operate depository intermediaries can be identified, they should be removed. (There are identifiable provincial obstacles to insurance companies' operating trust companies, but these might take some time to remove.) Similarly, any differences in the effective costs of an insurance company's carrying out the same businesses as a financial grouping headed by a bank should be removed.

If insurance companies gain powers to operate depository intermediaries at the same costs as banks, access to both the CPS and Interac will be crucial for their success in competing for transferable balances. There seems little problem with a depository institution's qualifying for CPA membership. With regard to Interac, the interests both of Interac's original developers and those of other potential users need to be addressed. If the consent decree does not already provide for it, the members of the Interac Association should be strongly encouraged to consider the pricing policies outlined in this paper.

Business powers for banks. Competition is likely to be increased by permitting banks to sell insurance products in their branches, and the *Bank Act* should be changed to grant them this power. However, such anticompetitive practices as tied selling should be prohibited.

Consumer asset insurance. Consumers should be offered realistic incentives to diversify, but not unrealistic demands to assess the credit ratings of the institutions in which they place their funds. The CDIC should take administrative action to limit the cap to an effective $60,000. There is a case for extending asset insurance (using risk-adjusted premiums) to cover the liabilities of pension funds, and an appropriate legislative framework should be designed to achieve this.

Enhanced disclosure. Disclosure of additional regulatory information would create the dynamic instabilities so often raised as a potential problem. Administrative action by OSFI and the CDIC, taken in consultation with industry representatives, could accomplish these goals.

Derivatives trading. Although derivatives trading features prominently in public discussions, recent actions of regulatory authorities to improve reporting standards and to supervise intermediaries' risk management systems appear to address the principal issues. Management and regulatory responsibilities to supervise effectively should be clarified by revising the appropriate legal frameworks.

Ownership concentration. Canadian banks' ability to compete internationally is currently restricted by the 10–50 percent rule. The application of these limitations to international operations should be removed by changes to the *Bank Act.*

Self-dealing. While there appear to be no problems of self-dealing that require additional legislation, continued close attention by the regulatory authorities is needed.

Appendix: Small Business Financing

Small business financing, particularly startup equity, requires specialized skills not normally possessed by such traditional short-term lenders as banks, even though they are usually regarded as an appropriate source of funds. Moreover, even though some banks are attempting to extend their funding activity beyond the short-term, highly liquid arrangements they usually favor, the problems of small business finance are truly difficult ones. As a result, the difficulty small business faces in raising long-term capital is unlikely to be mitigated either by changes in legislation or by the well-intentioned efforts of some banks. This appendix outlines the essential nature of the problem and offers a way to deal with this difficult financing issue.

The principal factors contributing to the high cost of equity (or long-term debt) finance for small business are, first, the difficulty of valuing uncertain future cash flows and, second, the difficulty of providing incentives for sound management of the firm. To obtain funds, small business must bear financiers' fixed costs of investigating and governing small deals. This can mean that the cost of equity or long-term debt is relatively larger, per dollar raised, for small business than it is for large business.[58] An over-the-counter stock market will not solve this problem, because the fixed costs of floating even an over-the-counter issue make that kind of financing prohibitively expensive for businesses seeking, say, less than $1 million in funds. Recently formed special financing vehicles might be able to alter these costs, but at present have little incentive to do so. Moreover even if those incentives were to change, the problems of valuing uncertain cash flows and of providing both appropriate governance and appropriate management incentives still need to be addressed.

One way of proceeding toward a more effective solution is to encourage those with the best available information base to provide both the financing and its governance. The Canadian Federation of Independent Business (CFIB) might be the place to start developing such an information base, and certainly the CFIB should have a good understanding of performance incentives in small business. On these grounds, it might prove possible for the CFIB to form a lending/investment intermediary supported by the guarantees of its members. Such an institution would principally raise its funds in the capital markets and make them available to small businesses. Since it would be member operated, the scheme would provide strong incentives for repayment, and it would use the best available expertise to ensure the funds were soundly placed. The aggregate guarantees of economically successful members should make it possible to raise initial funds for the scheme. If a lending/investment intermediary of this type were able to operate successfully, securitization of some of its assets could be used to enhance its capacity to expand.

Notes

This paper has benefited greatly from the comments of Jim Baillie, Tom Courchene, Tom Kierans, David Laidler, Frank Milne, and Bill Robson. However, none of the foregoing can be held responsible for the author's interpretations, nor do the paper's conclusion necessarily reflect the views of either Tory, Tory, Deslauriers and Binnington or the C.D. Howe Institute.

1   While they are pertinent to the operations of the financial system, issues arising from taxation policy or from accounting practice are for the most part not examined here. Nor are such essentially technical issues as those involved in the process of demutualizing some insurance companies.

2   In this paper, "financial intermediaries" refers to any financial firms which assume liabilities and issue their own obligations in exchange. Thus, lending intermediaries, mutual funds, trust companies, insurance companies, and banks are all regarded as differently specialized forms of FIs. When distinctions are needed to emphasize a particular function such as deposit taking, a more specific term such as "depository intermediary" will be used.

3   Insurance companies have long been active in crossborder selling of retail products.

4   Of course, not all mergers or acquisitions, or all ventures into new products, have succeeded. But the counterexamples principally reflect the difficulty of making plans under uncertainty rather than indicating that the trends toward new business combinations and new products are diminishing.

5   Anthony M. Saunders, *Financial Institutions Management: A Modern Perspective*, (Burr Ridge, Ill.: Irwin, 1994), p. 238. Although Saunders writes as if the credit cards were issued by General Motors, they are actually issued and administered by the Toronto-Dominion Bank.

6   Ibid., p. 237

7   Ian Plenderleigh, Bank of England, London, personal communication, November 1995.

8   To the extent that most of its investigations focus on individual business units within a given group, even the Office of the Superintendent of Financial Institutions may face some of these issues.

9   Risk-related premiums do not provide perfect solutions to the incentive problem. In particular, both moral hazard and adverse selection problems may still be present (see, for example, J.L. Carr, G.F. Mathewson, and N.C. Quigley, *Ensuring Failure: Financial System Stability and Deposit Insurance in Canada*, Observation 36 [Toronto: C.D. Howe Institute, 1994]). Nevertheless, since risk-related premiums offer a good and a practical way of ensuring that incentives work in the right direction, on balance their use is desirable when deposit or other forms of asset insurance are provided. Finally, risk-related

premiums on their own might not provide a sufficient incentive, unless the charges were prohibitively high.

10   This is not to argue that information should be gathered without regard to its cost. Rather, the problem is to determine how much, if any, additional information release would prove cost effective. The presumption of the paragraph is that some additional reporting would be cost effective. In particular, it would probably benefit stronger institutions by identifying situations in which weaker institutions were being cross-subsidized.

11   See, for example, "Survey of the World Economy," *The Economist,* October 7, 1995.

12   The Bank of Canada and the federal government have agreed on targets for price level increases that will be maintained until 1997.

13   While not identical to those of shareholders, the interests of policyholders in mutual life insurance companies are similar.

14   Using this categorization, any form of savings is regarded as the client's lending to or investing in a financial intermediary.

15   The instruments used in securitization are traded, standardized instruments normally secured by an underlying portfolio of nonstandardized assets.

16   Life insurance liabilities, on the other hand, may be relatively easy to value on an actuarial basis.

17   See, for example, Stephen A. Ross, "Institutional Markets, Financial Marketing, and Financial Innovation", *Journal of Finance* 44 (1989): 541–556; and Sanford A. Grossman, "Dynamic Asset Allocation and the Efficiency of Markets," *Journal of Finance* 50 (1995): 773–787.

18   Saunders, *Financial Institutions Management,* p. 228.

19   Ibid.

20   In some parts of the financial industry, however, the smaller institutions have proven to be the more innovative. Very probably, larger firms are better at the types of innovation based on expensive infrastructures, while the smaller firms are better at the types of innovation which do not depend heavily on infrastructural investment.

21   See A. Berger, D. Hancock, and D.B. Humphrey, "Bank Efficiency Derived from the Profit Function," *Journal of Banking and Finance* 17 (1993): 317–348.

22   Saunders, *Financial Institutions Management,* pp. 229–231.

23   See, for example, Alli Nathan and Edwin H. Neave, "Competitiveness and Contestability in Canadian Financial Industries," *Canadian Journal of Economics* 22 (1989): 576–594; and Sherill Shaffer, "A Test of Competition in Canadian Banking," *Journal of Money, Credit and Banking* 25 (1993): 49–61.

23A See, for example, "The Three C's of Canadian Banking," Speech by John C. Cleghorn, Royal Bank of Canada, January 25, 1996.

24 Barry Scholnik, "Bank Spreads and Financial Deregulation in Canada," working paper (Edmonton, University of Alberta, Faculty of Business, 1995).

25 Recent developments include Internet access to loans (Bayshore Trust) and higher percentages of lending against accounts receivable (Bank of America).

26 See, for example, Brian F. Smith, "Financial Reforms in Canada" (Waterloo, Ont., Wilfrid Laurier University, The Mutual Group Financial Services Research Centre, 1995), pp. 23–29.

27 When banks do form venture capital affiliates, they operate as separate profit units, and the personnel staffing them follow career paths different from those of most bankers.

28 Some innovative firms seem more concerned with the reputation effects of developing a spectrum of new products than with extracting monopoly rents on individual innovations.

29 There is a danger that either regulatory disclosure itself or valuation based on regulatory guidelines can distort decisionmaking. To avoid at least some of this danger, industry advice in developing any new standards should be obtained.

30 The liabilities represented by derivatives instruments can be shorter term than those created by writing property and casualty policies, and are usually of much shorter term than those created by writing life or health insurance policies.

31 Smith, "Financial Reforms in Canada," p. 79.

32 CompCorp has recently been restructured to fulfill an insurance industry role similar to that played by the CDIC.

33 When brokerage firms offer money management accounts with chequing privileges, the cheques are cleared through a bank. From the point of view of the insurance industry, this route could mean paying competitors heavy charges for arranging the clearings and revealing to competitors some aspects of the insurance companies' marketing strategies.

34 Apart from possible customer objections to dealing with both an insurance company and its affiliated depository intermediary. However, banks have long carried out transactions using affiliates without much apparent customer objection.

35 In this connection, it might be noted that UK insurance companies are now permitted to solicit deposits over the telephone.

36 The December consent order seems to permit insurance companies to join Interact whether or not they operate a depository intermediary. It remains to be established, however, whether the order permits insurance companies to offer transferable deposits or only, say, to issue credit cards.

37 See, for example, Smith, "Financial Reforms in Canada."

38 See Dominic D'Allesandro, Speech to the Life Insurers' Market Research Association, October 23, 1995; partially reported in the *Globe and Mail*, (Toronto), October 24, 1995.

39 Plenderleigh, personal communication, November 1995; and Ric Battellino, Reserve Bank of Australia, Sydney, personal communication, November 1995.

40 Smith, "Financial Reforms in Canada."

41 The CPS is the successor to the clearing system developed by the chartered banks. When the CPS was set up, the banks were not compensated for having developed the clearing system that formed its basis.

42 Credit cards are often used as a means of giving clients access to Interac facilities. Whether the charge is to the credit card or to a debit card is sometimes determined by the vendor, sometimes left to the discretion of the client. For example, some foreign cash-dispensing machines will only make charges to a credit card account, while others will make charges to either a credit card account or a chequing account.

43 Under the December consent order, retailers and others who join Interac can now own the terminals they install.

44 Interac Association, *Interac Source Book* (Toronto, 1994), p. 4.

45 An institution can qualify as a clearer if it accounts for at least 0.5 percent of CPA transactions.

46 Canadian Life and Health Insurance Association, "The Need for Payments System Reform" (Toronto, 1995).

47 Since the Interac Association is a private entity, any changes to its methods of operation may be beyond the scope of revisions to the *Bank Act* and related legislation.

48 Although there is no theoretical standard for determining it, the return should include monopoly rents for some period of time. Afterward, the appropriate rate of return to the developers would be the market rate of return on investments of comparable risk.

49 The changes are so recent that the required analysis can only be sketched here.

50 To some extent, this issue is less important than before, because new users will be able to provide their own cash machines. Nevertheless, the access fees paid by different users should be determined according to the same schedule.

51 More nearly precisely, the Internet evolved from the US Department of Defense network known as ARPANET. After some years, ARPANET became available to public users at zero marginal cost, and the Internet grew accordingly.

52 Presumably "Internet money" will be in the unit of account of the firms that hold the balances. There are suggestions that experimental use of Internet money is already occurring.

53 Consider a bank which issues its own notes. It might pay interest on deposits or offer services to its depositors that would not be available to noteholders. There is thus a seigniorage benefit which differs from that of issuing deposits. "Internet money" would probably correspond more closely to bank-issued notes than to either interest-paying deposits or deposits accompanied by other services, such as chequing accounts.

54 There are also issues about the extent to which, in a workout, the CDIC might incur costs so that all depositors are wholly covered. These issues relate to

CDIC operations and as such are beyond the scope of this paper. See Carr, Mathewson, and Quigley, *Ensuring Failure*.

55 Carr, Mathewson, and Quigley (ibid.) argue that, while consumers will not have all necessary information, they will have enough to discriminate between safe and risky institutions. But in practice, consumers do not even seem to know which products are covered by deposit insurance and which are not. The same authors also argue that regulators are not always able to identify troubled institutions sufficiently early.

56 Ontario insures funds through the Pensions Benefits Guaranty Corporation. In a sense, the premiums charged are risk based, since they differ according to both a pension plan's percentage of unfunded liabilities and to the solvency standards it satisfies.

57 While sophisticated financial market players likely would be helped by such information, the typical consumer probably will not be.

58 After taking due allowance of differences in risk. Financing small business, particularly over the longer term, is likely to be substantially riskier than financing larger businesses.

CONTRIBUTORS

John F. Chant	Department of Economics, Simon Fraser University
Mark R. Daniels	Canadian Life and Health Insurance Association, Inc., Toronto
Martine Doyon	Department of Finance, Ottawa
John L. Evans	Evans Strategic Policy, Ottawa
C. Freedman	Bank of Canada, Ottawa
C. Goodlet	Bank of Canada, Ottawa
Harry Hassanwalia	Royal Bank of Canada, Toronto
Nick Le Pan	Office of the Superintendent of Financial Institutions, Ottawa
Maurice D. Levi	Faculty of Commerce and Business Administration, University of British Columbia
Jeffrey G. MacIntosh	Faculty of Law, University of Toronto
Douglas W. Melville	Canadian Bankers Association, Toronto
Randall Morck	Faculty of Business, University of Alberta
Stephen S. Poloz	The Bank Credit Analyst Research Group, Montreal
Roger Ware	Department of Economics, Queen's University
Bernard Yeung	Graduate School of Business, University of Michigan and Milken Institute for Job and Capital Formation

PUBLICATIONS OF THE JOHN DEUTSCH INSTITUTE

Policy Forum Series

F1.   *Industrial Strategy*, Richard G. Harris, 1983.

F2.   *The Federal Budget of 1983*, Neil Bruce, 1983.

F3.   *Medicare in an Age of Restraint*, William G. Watson, 1984.

F4.   *Special Import Measures Legislation*, Klaus Stegemann, 1985.

F5.   *Tax Reform and the Consumption Tax*, Jack M. Mintz, 1985.

F6.   *The International Debt Problem*, Gordon R. Sparks, 1985.

F7.   *Reform of the Bankruptcy Act*, Frank Lewis, 1986.

F8.   *Universality and Social Policies in the '80s*, Alan Green and Nancy Olewiler, 1985.

F9.   *The May 1985 Federal Budget*, Douglas D. Purvis, 1985.

F10.   *The February 1986 Federal Budget*, Martin F.J. Prachowny, 1986.

F11.   *Reform of the Corporate Income Tax System*, Jack M. Mintz and Douglas D. Purvis, 1987.

F12.   *Business Transfer Tax*, Robin W. Boadway and Jack M. Mintz, 1987.

F13.   *Rent Controls in Ontario*, Richard J. Arnott and Jack M. Mintz, 1987.

F14.   *Macropolicy Issues in the Medium Term*, Jack M. Mintz and Douglas D. Purvis, 1989.

F15.   *The Role of Immigration in Canada's Future*, Charles M. Beach and Alan G. Green, 1988.

F16.   *Public Sector Management*, R. Gordon Cassidy and Jack M. Mintz, 1989.

F17.   *The February 1990 Federal Budget*, Martin F.J. Prachowny, 1990.

F18.   *Canadian Transportation Policy*, David W. Gillen, 1990.

F19.   *Takeovers and Tax Policy*, Jack M. Mintz, 1990.

F20.   *Pay Equity: Means and Ends*, Michael G. Abbott, 1990.

F21.   *Europe 1992 and the Implications for Canada*, Douglas D. Purvis, 1991.

F22.   *Economic Developments in the Soviet Union and Eastern Europe: Implications for Canada*, Douglas D. Purvis, 1991.

F23.   *The February 1991 Federal Budget*, Martin F.J. Prachowny and Douglas D. Purvis, 1991.

F24.   *North American Free Trade Area*, William G. Watson, 1991.

F25.   *Economic Aspects of the Federal Government's Constitutional Proposals*, Robin W. Boadway and Douglas D. Purvis, 1991.

F26.   *The February 1992 Federal Budget*, Thomas J. Courchene and Martin F.J. Prachowny, 1992.

F27.   *Tax Effects on the Financing of Medium and Small Public Corporations*, Roy D. Hogg and Jack M. Mintz, 1992.

F28.   *Tax Policy for Turbulent Times*, Roy D. Hogg and Jack M. Mintz (eds.), 1993.

F29.   *Deficits and Debt in the Canadian Economy*, Richard G. Harris (ed.), 1993.

F30.   *Capital Budgeting in the Public Sector*, Jack M. Mintz and Ross S. Preston (eds.), 1993.

F31.   *Financial Derivatives: Managing and Regulating Off-Balance Sheet Risks*, Thomas J. Courchene and Edwin H. Neave (eds.), 1994.

F32.   *Who Pays the Piper?: Canada's Social Policy*, Roy D. Hogg and Jack M. Mintz (eds.), 1995.

F33.   *The 1995 Federal Budget: Retrospect and Prospect*, Thomas J. Courchene and Thomas A. Wilson (eds.), 1995.

F34.   *Reforming the Canadian Financial Sector: Canada in Global Perspective*, Thomas J. Courchene and Edwin H. Neave (eds.), 1997.

Roundtable Series

R1. *Canadian Balance of Payments, Perspectives and Policy Issues*, Douglas D. Purvis (ed.), 1983.
R2. *Economic Adjustment and Public Policy in Canada*, Douglas D. Purvis (ed.), 1984.
R3. *Declining Productivity and Growth*, Douglas D. Purvis (ed.), 1985.
R4. *The Impact of Taxation on Business Activity*, Jack M. Mintz and Douglas D. Purvis (eds.), 1987.
R5. *Rent Control: The International Experience*, Richard J. Arnott and Jack M. Mintz (eds.), 1987.
R6. *Economic Impacts of Tax Reform*, Jack M. Mintz and John Whalley (eds.), published by the Canadian Tax Foundation, 1989.
R7. *Tax Expenditures and Government Policy*, Neil Bruce (ed.), 1988 (French version also available).
R8. *Economic Dimensions of Constitutional Change*, Robin W. Boadway, Thomas J. Courchene and Douglas D. Purvis (eds.), 2 Volumes, 1991.
R9. *The Future of Fiscal Federalism*, Keith G. Banting, Douglas M. Brown and Thomas J. Courchene (eds.), published jointly with School of Policy Studies and Institute of Intergovernmental Relations, 1994.
R10. *Infrastructure and Competitiveness*, Jack M. Mintz and Ross S. Preston (eds.), 1994.

Bell Canada Papers Series

B1. *Productivity, Growth and Canada's International Competitiveness*, Thomas J. Courchene and Douglas D. Purvis (eds.), 1993.
B2. *Stabilization, Growth and Distribution: Linkages in the Knowledge Era*, Thomas J. Courchene (ed.), 1994.
B3. *Technology, Information and Public Policy*, Thomas J. Courchene (ed.), 1995.
B4. *Policy Frameworks for a Knowledge Economy*, Thomas J. Courchene (ed.), 1996.

Walwyn Lecture Series

W1. *Regulatory Reform and the Search for Solvency*, Henry N.R. Jackman, 1987.
W2. *Capital Management vs Operations Management*, Marshall A. (Mickey) Cohen, 1987.
W3. *Free Trade: What's in it for You?*, Hon. Gerald A. Regan, 1989.
W4. *Economic Growth in the Coming Years: What it Means for a Community*, Marcel Côté, 1992.